Secretarial Procedures

THEORY AND APPLICATIONS

Second edition

Helen Harding

PITMAN PUBLISHING
128 Long Acre, London, WC2E 9AN
A Division of Longman Group UK Limited

© Helen Harding 1990

First published in Great Britain 1990
Reprinted 1991, 1992

British Library Cataloguing in Publication Data
Harding, Helen
  Secretarial procedures. – 2nd ed
  1. Secretaries. Duties
  I. Title
  651.3′741

ISBN 0 273 03086 8

Printed and bound in Great Britain

Contents

Preface

In preparing this second edition of Secretarial Procedures I have attempted to achieve several objectives, given that over five years have elapsed since the preparation of the original text and in the knowledge that things have been moving on during that time, both in terms of technological developments and methods of assessment.

Nonetheless my original intentions, when first putting a book together still remain, *viz* to try to incorporate into one volume the sort of material that I consider essential for students intending to take up secretarial positions and in doing so to concentrate on adopting a secretarial rather than an office practice perspective. Obviously this is no mean task and there will inevitably be omissions, but hopefully few!

As teachers we are all faced with the pressures exerted upon us to do seemingly so much more with our students (there are so many innovative areas to cover and the boundaries between job and subject areas are less well defined these days). However, there is much less time in which to do it all, so it is vital that we can call on suitable support materials. We need to encourage our students to think for themselves, to read, to research, to question, to analyse, to solve problems, to take decisions and to build upon their existing skills and knowledge. Judicious use of text books is part of this learning process.

I have endeavoured to impose a certain structure by following a pre-determined format. Topics are introduced with a list of objectives which outline the sorts of skills and competences which should be aimed at in working through the unit. Units are dealt with in sufficient detail to support the theory and practical workshops provided via taught sessions, yet minising the need to provide or dictate additional material. The format adopted is also useful for revision purposes as it includes many key words and lists.

The units conclude with self-test questions which enable weaknesses to be quickly and easily identified. These are followed by personal activities which students may wish to undertake to provide an added dimension to the learning experience. There are also group activities to encourage team building and co-operation. Finally, there is a selection of situation-based activities which incorporate a variety of tasks, the foundations for which have been outlined in the unit.

Users of the first edition will notice that more text has been included but there are fewer units. The main reasons for this are that while very few things have disappeared altogether, several new topics have appeared and there has been a marked shift in emphasis with regard to the treatment of technology. No longer is it viewed as 'new technology'. It is very much part of our daily lives and as such is treated in an integrated way throughout the text rather than as a 'bolt on' at the end.

A few years ago it seemed relatively straightforward to state precisely which examinations a textbook catered for. Now things are less clear cut. NVQ is upon us and the ground rules are somewhat different with the emphasis very much on assessing competence in the performance of a range of clearly defined activities. In order to assess competence, performance criteria need to be drawn up and it is essential that students acquire the necessary skills and knowledge in the different areas if they are to satisfy the criteria and reach the required levels of competence.

A lot will depend on the ways in which students are encouraged to learn. This will largely be based on learning by doing which in turn can only be successful if it is underpinned by understanding and this is where textbooks come in. This text has been designed very much with students in mind and concentrates on providing essential syllabus coverage for the range of secretarial-type programmes (even where some are termed 'Business Administration' within the NVQ schemes) as well as the standard single subject syllabuses. While pitched particularly at Intermediate or NVQ Level III the text contains much material that is relevant to both the lower levels and as foundation reading for the higher level.

Rather than include specific questions from past examination papers (examination boards will supply these in any event), I have chosen to include a selection of my own tried and tested activities. These may be scaled up or down according to time availability and levels of competence sought in the students concerned.

Any learning should be about much more than passing examinations. It should be a process of gathering experience from which to draw as one's career pattern unfolds. It should provide information but it should also pose questions. It should draw certain conclusions but also whet the appetite for more. Education is a journey and 'getting there' should be an enjoyable experience, especially where the terrain is constantly changing as is the case with Secretarial Procedures. I therefore hope that this text proves to be a useful guide.

HBH

Throughout the book I have referred to a secretary as 'she' and a manager as 'he'. This is simply for fluency and is in no way meant to infer that the roles may not be reversed.

Acknowledgements

The author and publishers wish to acknowledge the following permissions to reproduce material:
ACCO Europe Limited
Aldus Page Maker
British Telecom
Herman Miller Ltd
Kroy (Europe) Limited
Pitman, a division of Longman Cheshire Pty Ltd, Australia
Rexel Business Machines
Toshiba Information Systems UK Limited
Vickers Furniture

I should like express my special thanks to my good friend and former colleague, Janet Willcock, who has used Secretarial Procedures since it was first published, for her interest, support and constructive advice in the preparation and proofreading of this second edition.

I should also like to express my gratitude to Kern Roberts for his general support and guidance with the project.
HBH

June 1989

1

Understanding organisations

Aim of the unit

The unit provides insight into business organisations, the way they are structured, the relationships
which exist, the duties and responsibilities of executive personnel and the functions undertaken by
departments.

Specific objectives

At the end of this unit you should be able to:

1 Define what is meant by 'an organisation'.
2 Differentiate between the public and private
sectors.
3 Draw up and complete organisation charts.
4 Represent aspects of organisational structure
in the form of a diagram.
5 Explain different types of organisational structure.
6 Identify the main advantages and disadvantages
of the committee structure.
7 Explain what is meant by 'span of control'.
8 Compare and contrast the patterns of relationship which exist in large and small organisations.
9 Outline the objectives and roles of different
departments.
10 Describe the duties and responsibilities of
executive personnel within departments in an
organisation.
11 Identify the role and function of a Secretary/
Personal Assistant within the context of a large
organisation.
12 Highlight the types of technological support
available to organisations.

Introduction

Before you can begin to appreciate the role of a
secretary within any organisation you need to develop some understanding of the way in which
organisations are formed, managed and controlled
and where the office fits into this structure.

Types of business organisation

Basically business organisations may be split into
profit-making and non-profit making organisations.
The former include both manufacturing/trading
concerns and service industries like banking,
insurance and the legal profession, whereas the
latter function to provide a service, like hospitals,
educational establishments and local government.
In the United Kingdom these organisations fall into
either the public or the private sector.

The **public sector** can be divided into two
sections – state-owned or nationalised undertakings
like the Bank of England, British Rail and British
Steel and municipal undertakings in which the
services are operated by the local authority for the
benefit of the community.

The **private sector** comprises several types of
organisation, which are determined by the size and
ownership of the enterprise. The **sole trader**, as the
name implies, is essentially a business operated and
typically owned by an individual (eg a corner shop).
A **partnership** is formed by two or more individuals
who have joint ownership and share in the financing
and operational activities of the business in predetermined proportions. Many professionals like
accountants and solicitors, or contractors like elec-
tricians, plumbers or decorators, operate on a partnership basis.

Secretarial work in the case of the sole trader will be undertaken informally, often by the owner or by a member of his or her family. The same may be true of a small partnership; however, the volume of work may warrant the appointment of part-time or even full-time secretarial support.

Larger organisations in the private sector form **limited liability companies**, whereby the legal responsibility is no longer with the individual or the partners but with the newly formed company. This is then treated as a corporate entity in law. The advantages of limited liability are obvious, but company formation is a complex and somewhat costly operation. Limited companies may be either private, where shares are not offered for sale on the open market, or public, where shares are quoted on the Stock Exchange. Examples of **public limited companies** (plcs) are major national companies like banks, department stores and product manufacturers.

What is meant by 'organisation'?

Considerable confusion exists in the use of words like 'organisation', 'management' and 'administration'. Such words mean different things to different people and receive different treatment in different circumstances.

Basically, organisations are established with the intention of achieving specific goals or objectives. Problems arise as a result of the need for all organisations to reappraise and modify their aims and objectives continually in the light of economic and social change. These changes are usually expressed in terms of supply and demand.

It is important to note that the main goal of an organisation is to ensure survival, and generally speaking, the larger the organisation the more likely it is to survive – hence 'Big is beautiful'! It must not be forgotten, however, that in times of severe recession even the larger companies may experience trading difficulties resulting in cutbacks and rationalisation (eg closure of certain branches and mergers of others – both inevitably leading to redundancies). You need only read the financial pages of a daily newspaper to obtain some idea of these activities.

In management terms, 'organisation' usually refers to the structural elements and the relationships between individuals. The structure is the framework within which decision-making takes

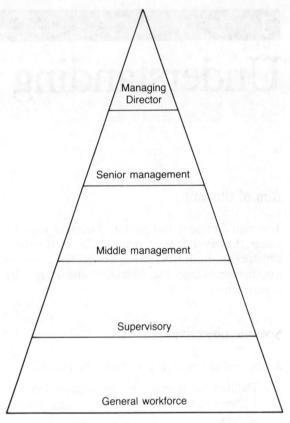

Fig 1 Organisational pyramid

place and this will vary according to the size and nature of the organisation. In a sole trader's business the organisation will be totally dependent upon the individual, but in a complex company there will be many organisational levels with their own degrees of responsibility, authority and status. Typically known as a 'hierarchy', this can best be expressed in the form of a pyramid with the 'boss' at the top and the workforce at the bottom, with numerous levels of management in between (see Fig 1).

Types of organisational structure

As we have seen, organisational structure refers to the distribution of tasks and responsibilities within the organisation. All organisations need a system by which authority and control may be exercised with the intention of achieving certain objectives. Typically, authority lies with top management who determine overall policy and decide how it may best be put into practice. Clearly a few individuals at senior management level cannot undertake all managerial functions and therefore a system of delegation will emerge in the form of middle management and supervisory levels (*see* Fig 1).

At its simplest, then, organisational structure serves to indicate who in the organisation has authority, who is responsible to whom, and for what – at any level. This is exemplified in four types of organisational structure:

- line organisation
- functional organisation
- line and staff organisation
- committee organisation

Line organisation

In a line organisation structure overall authority starts with the person at the top and operates in a vertical line downwards towards the lowest person within the organisation. This is very much a 'military' formation and has the advantage of being simple in that individuals know who their immediate superior is and understand where they figure in the 'line'. Thus there is a clear chain of command based on rank. Chains of command exist, although they are less apparent, in organisations such as the Civil Service and major national department stores. There are also very clear lines of communication, and responsibility is greatest at the top and least at the bottom.

Functional organisation

In functional organisation specialists are allocated to specific work areas or functions – hence the term. Different experts are placed in charge of different functions, eg buying, selling, engineering, accounts and personnel, irrespective of where the work falls in the overall picture (*see* Fig 7, p 9). An individual's skills are used 'across the board' regardless of departmental divisions. The main advantage for the organisation lies in making optimum use of specialists, while a main disadvantage can be confusion on the part of general staff resulting from 'too many bosses'.

Line and staff organisation

A combination of line and functional structure operates under this system and should, in theory at least, possess the advantages of each. It fixes responsibility and should ensure better discipline and the best use of expert staff. However, confusion can arise where duties are not clearly defined. Line officers may, for example, resent any executive authority awarded to functional or staff officers.

Committee organisation

Under the committee organisation system, responsibility and authority are allocated not to an individual but to a group of individuals. Some committees undertake management functions like decision-making (*see* Unit 8); others do not. They function at the operational level, receiving information, perhaps making recommendations and dealing with specific topics. Committee structures have the advantages of enabling good communications, utilising specialists, pooling talent, sharing responsibility and providing a good medium for education and training. The disadvantages are that they can be wasteful in terms of time and resources and the general dereliction of responsibility. Committees function well when they adhere to clearly stated terms of reference; these give a real sense of purpose to meetings so long as aggressive individuals are not allowed to dominate.

Note: It is important to recognise that these four types of organisational structure may coexist within any one organisation, eg in any large company there will be grades of staff (line), specialists (function) and group decision-making (committee).

Patterns of organisational relationship

Organisations function according to patterns of relationships between all members of the enterprise. Relationships are usually based upon positions within the organisational framework and are designed to exercise and maintain control while achieving the aims of the organisation. These patterns necessarily vary according to the size of the organisation and the nature of its work. For example, the relationships to be found in a firm of accountants or solicitors differ from those found in a large manufacturing organisation (ie between management and shop floor). In the case of a small firm staff relationships tend to be close and operate at a personal level, whereas in a large organisation relationships tend to be impersonal and remote.

There are typically four main types of staff relationship found in organisations:

- line relationship
- lateral relationship
- staff relationship
- functional relationship

Line relationship

Direct line relationships exist between immediate superiors and immediate subordinates (*see* Fig 2). A superior will give instructions to his or her immediate subordinate and will be responsible for seeing that the work delegated in this way is satisfactorily carried out by the subordinate. Conversely, subordinates take instructions from immediate superiors and are responsible to them for satisfactorily carrying out instructions and delegated duties.

In Fig 2 the Secretarial Support Services Supervisor is directly responsible to the Office Manager for efficiency in this area. The Supervisor in turn will instruct the WP, Typing and Clerical Section Heads directly, but not the operators, typists and clerks who will be instructed by their immediate superiors.

Lateral relationship

Where two or more members of staff come within the control of the same immediate superior there is a lateral relationship (*see* Fig 2, where all supervisors have a lateral relationship). All are immediately responsible to the same superior, namely the Office Manager, but they need not have similar qualifications and experience or receive the same salaries, nor be accorded the same status. They may not instruct one another or instruct a subordinate

member of staff who does not come under their control, eg the Reprographics Supervisor cannot instruct a typist.

Staff relationship

It is common practice within any organisation for managers to seek expert advice from other managers in order to be effective in their jobs. For example, in Fig 3 the Chief Accountant may contact the Chief Training Officer for advice about a course for an accounts clerk in this team. This would be a staff relationship, as represented by the dotted line. The Chief Training Officer will offer advice only when requested to give it. If, however, the request for training of accounts clerks were to come from the General Manager via the Personnel Manager, this would be a functional relationship (*see* below).

Functional relationship

A functional relationship is similar to a staff relationship in that it too is an advisory one. The difference lies in the fact that the person called in to provide the advice has the authority of his or her specialist knowledge and can therefore carry out duties in another manager's domain. For example, the Personnel Manager has the authority to recommend staff training and anything else connected with staff across the board, irrespective of which department the member of staff is in. The broken line in Fig 3 represents the functional responsibility of the Personnel Manager for personnel work in all departments.

Note: It is important to recognise that these four types of staff relationship often coexist within the same organisation dependent upon its size, eg

- superiors and subordinates (line)

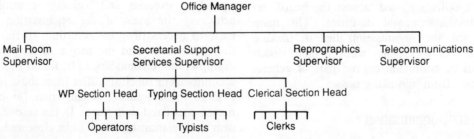

Fig 2 Line relationship

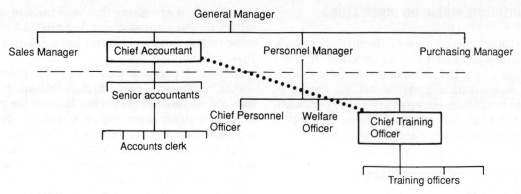

Fig 3 Staff relationship

- supervisory or middle management personnel (lateral)
- experts and professionals (staff/functional)

Management structure

Both the structural and staff relationship aspects of organisations have been discussed. It is now appropriate to focus attention on the principal participants at managerial level within public and private companies.

Directors: responsibilities and duties

All organisations, even relatively small ones, have at their head a team of leaders in the form of directors. It is their responsibility to determine company policy consistent with the product or service undertaken. They are also responsible for the legal and financial obligations of the organisation, especially in the case of a public company where directors are ultimately accountable to the shareholders. Shareholders are members of the public who have invested in company shares, thereby subscribing to its finances.

Board of Directors

A company organisation chart will have at the top a Board of Directors which has many responsibilities reflecting its representation of shareholders' interests (if it is a public company) and its authority to manage a company's affairs. The following is a list of typical duties:

- determining policy and formulating objectives
- ensuring the provision of sufficient capital
- controlling the distribution of dividends
- sanctioning capital expenditure
- ensuring that the company operates in accordance with its Memorandum and Articles of Association (*see* Unit 8) as laid down in the Companies Acts
- complying with all other statutory requirements like Factory Acts, the Health and Safety at Work Act and employment legislation
- analysing trading results and reporting to shareholders and other interested parties
- appointing a Managing Director
- ensuring effective management and the maintenance of sound morale throughout the organisation.

Chairman of the Board of Directors

The Chairman may be named in the Articles of Association or elected by the directors. The duties of a Chairman are outlined in Unit 8. The roles of Chairman and Managing Director are not the same, and in some organisations it may be considered unsatisfactory for the same person to hold both positions, eg there can be conflicts of interest.

The Managing Director

Appointed by the Board of Directors, the Managing Director is responsible to them for the effective management of the company within the specified framework. The Managing Director may be known as the General Manager or the Chief Executive.

Departments within an organisation

Different organisations have different departments, whose titles and functions vary considerably. Fig 4 provides a brief indication of the sort of classifications found within a typical trading company, together with their objectives, their key personnel, their functions and responsibilities and the sort of secretarial support they are likely to need.

Diagrammatical presentation of organisations

Organisation charts are intended to display patterns of interrelationship which exist between divisions, departments, sections and individuals within an organisation (*see* Figs 5 and 6). They are useful in that they show at a glance the distribution of authority in an organisation and indicate individual responsibility, spans of control and delegation (*see* Figs 7, 8 and 9).

Individual personal names will not generally appear, as it is the post which is relevant rather than the identity of the person holding the post. Charts are often given to new employees during induction courses (*see* Unit 3) or may be included in staff handbooks. In these circumstances names and even locations may be included on the chart in order to help familiarisation.

In the example of a functional organisation (Fig 7) the Managing Director's span of control is shown. It extends across five areas/functions, each of which is controlled by an 'expert' manager who in turn delegates authority for the performance of the function to the departmental or section heads.

Fig 4 Classification of departments

Department	Objectives	Key executive	Functions and responsibilities	Secretarial support
Marketing/ Sales	Sales promotion Development of new markets	Marketing Manager/ Sales Manager	Market research Advertising Publicity Management of sales team – representatives and agents Home and export sales, promotion and distribution Public relations Customer follow-up	Sending out quotations Compiling price lists Processing orders Figure work Export documentation Display typing Organising travel Arranging sales promotions Preparing product releases for the press General secretarial duties
Purchasing	Ensuring the supply and delivery of the best goods at the best terms	Purchasing Manager	Researching markets and suppliers Negotiating terms Placing contracts Maintaining supply records Matching deliveries to production schedules	Record-keeping Sending out enquiries Arranging meetings Organising travel Forward planning Calculations and figure work General secretarial duties
Accounts	Financial control of company's assets Calculation of profit and loss Forecasting and budgetary control	Chief/Company Accountant	Credit control Maintaining financial records Reporting financial matters to management Computation (of buying and costing) Wages and stock control Internal audit Budgetary control Tax matters	General secretarial duties Emphasis on figure work

Department	Objectives	Key executive	Functions and responsibilities	Secretarial support
Production	Factory planning and control to produce finished goods	Production/Works Manager	Management of plant and equipment Stock control Production planning Work study Quality control Stores administration Despatch operations	General secretarial duties Delivery scheduling Production scheduling Stock control
Research and Development	Improvement of products Development of new techniques to improve efficiency Standardisation of procedures	Management Services Manager	Technological innovation Organisation and methods Developing product or service to meet consumer needs in order to secure or improve levels of demand	General secretarial duties Knowledge of technical side of company's products or services
Company Secretary	Coordination of all administrative functions	Company Secretary	Strong link with Managing Director All legal affairs, insurance matters, financial matters, share registration, shareholders' interests Office planning and organisation Office systems and services	General secretarial duties Attendence at meetings Access to confidential information Collation and dissemination of legal and financial information and documentation
Personnel (see Unit 3)	The maintenance of good working relations between management and workers	Personnel Manager	Recruitment and selection of employees Training and welfare Dismissal and redundancy Job grading Merit rating Performance appraisals Staff records Industrial relations Negotiations with trade unions Employment legislation	General secretarial duties Handling of confidential personnel records/data Organising induction and training programmes Administering interview tests

In the example of a departmental organisation (Fig 8) the position of the Secretary/Personal Assistant is highlighted. Very often secretarial positions are not indicated in organisation charts as the nature of the roles can be difficult to define. In this example the Managing Director has a wide span of control, and the burden is lessened a little by a Secretary/Personal Assistant; the importance of this role is acknowledged by showing it on the chart. It should be noted that the secretary is responsible to the Managing Director and has no authority over the departments.

In Fig 9 direct management is delegated to three general managers, each of whom has a Secretary/Personal Assistant. This effectively reduces the span of control by bringing in an extra management level or tier, but the chain of communication to top level management is very much longer.

Alternative layouts

The specimen organisation charts of Figs 5–9 are prepared in the traditional vertical styles, which is still the most commonly used. However, it is possible to use other layouts, examples of which are given in Figs 10a and b.

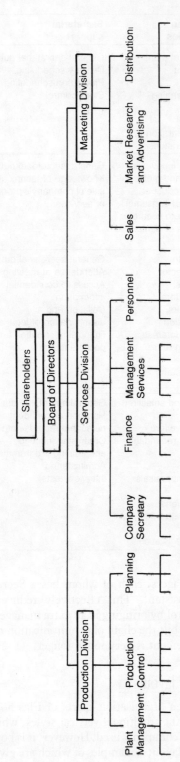

Fig 5 Organisation chart of a national company indicating divisional responsibilities at senior management level

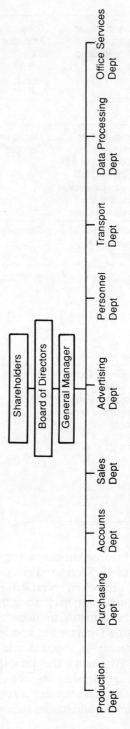

Fig 6 Organisation chart indicating a typical department structure

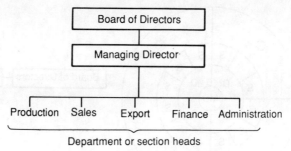

Fig 7 The span of control within a functional organisation

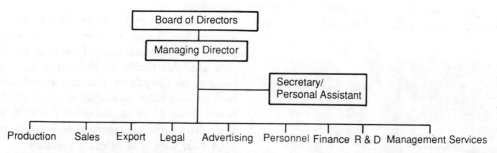

Fig 8 The position of the Secretary/Personal Assistant

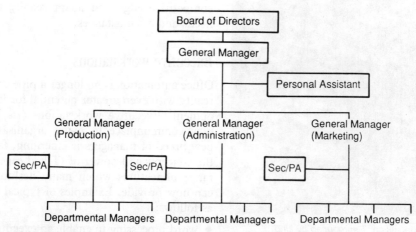

Fig 9 Delegation

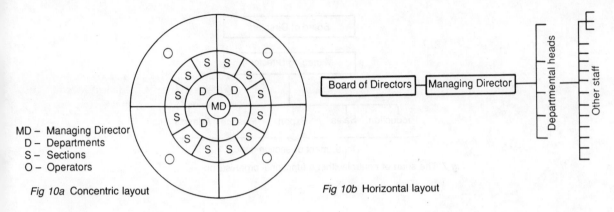

MD – Managing Director
D – Departments
S – Sections
O – Operators

Fig 10a Concentric layout

Fig 10b Horizontal layout

Technological Support

It is not only individual aspects of business activity which now benefit from developments in technology. Organisations themselves and their senior

Fig 11 Executive workstation; *Reproduced by kind permission of Vickers Furniture*

management personnel are now in a position to take full advantage of the many decision-support systems which are being developed and continually improved.

These Management Information Systems (MIS), as they are frequently termed, are designed to harness the vast quantities of information which are now available thanks to the capacities of modern computers. They form an enormous company database to hold information gathered by all the functional areas of an organisation's activities. They may also enable managers to access data provided by a wide variety of external agencies.

Effective corporate planning depends on the availability of up-to-date, high quality information, both from within an organisation and from external sources. Thanks to sophisticated information technology (IT) this range of information is now readily available to decision-makers (often from desktop terminals), so enabling them to retain their competitive edge and adapt readily to changing needs and circumstances.

Executive workstations

Office automation is no longer a pipe dream. It is a reality with even greater potential for future development. Executive workstations (*see* Fig 11) are now commonplace in many organisations and a new breed of managers is emerging, familiar with the concepts and power of IT and eager to use the range of features which many desktop terminals can now provide. Examples of typical features are as follows:

● word processing to enable an executive to create material or edit that prepared by someone else

- electronic mail to transmit and receive messages (*see* Unit 4)
- a personal database to store useful and frequently consulted information such as addresses and telephone numbers
- an electronic diary and forward planner (*see* Unit 5)
- specialist applications software (see Unit 7) to meet individual requirements, eg spreadsheet, advanced financial modelling, CAD (Computer Aided Design)
- access to electronic filing facilities (*see* Unit 6)
- access to centralised databases (*see* Unit 9)
- access to the organisation's own MIS;
- some form of voice annotation facility to enable verbal corrections or amendments to be made to previously generated text
- access to an integral telephone system, so enabling verbal messages to be stored and relayed later.

A final comment

Some of the content of this unit will undoubtedly be new to you, and you may at first find it difficult to absorb. None the less you should try to grasp the ideas in order to more readily appreciate the role of a secretary within an organisation. The purpose of this unit is to provide you with the essential back-cloth for everything else which follows. Without the existence of organisations in pursuit of certain goals there would be little need or demand for offices, business communications networks, systems and procedures, records, meetings and office technology. Take this a step further, and clearly there would be no need or demand for secretarial support staff! Hence the need to study the background to organisations.

Miller and Dobson plc

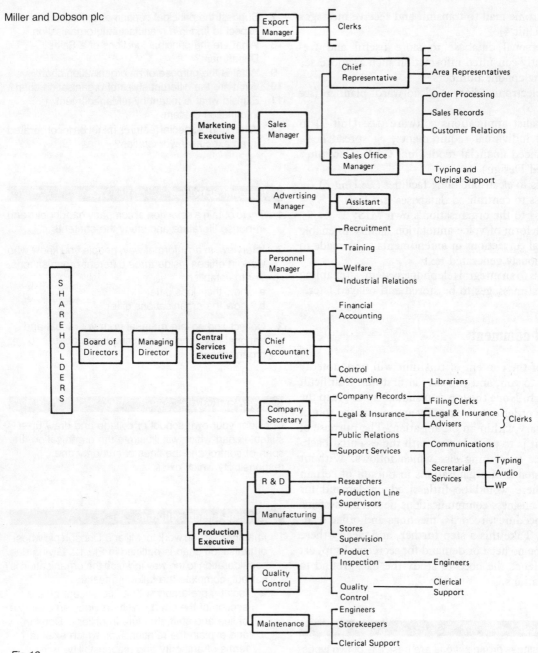

Fig 12

d Outline the duties of the Company Secretary in an organisation like Miller & Dobson.

e Identify and label on the organisation chart those functions which would necessarily be controlled by experts.

f Assume that on the preparation of a new chart the position of Secretary/PA to the Managing Director would be included. On Fig 12 show how this role would be represented.

2 Assume that you work in the Public Relations Section of the Marketing Department of Miller & Dobson and that you are often asked to organise conducted tours for parties of visitors. These tours normally begin with a short introductory talk by someone from the Public Relations Section, continue with visits to the production lines, the Advertising Department and the Packing Section, and finish with tea in the company canteen.

Your task is to draw up a 2½ hour programme for a party of twelve students from a local technical college and prepare a suitable handout on the work of these departments. This handout will be given to the visitors at the end of the afternoon, together with a small selection of sample products.

3 Imagine that you work in the main reception area of a medium-sized manufacturing division (concentrating on the production of three products) of a large public company. It is company policy to have a large chart illustrating the organisation of each division in the foyer of each location. During recent redecoration, the chart, which consisted of magnetic labels on a backing board, was dismantled by the cleaners and the pieces put away in a box. The Managing Director has commented on its absence and wants it restored.

a Once the blank chart is redrawn on the magnetic board it will be a matter of simply placing the appropriate labels in the correct places. The actual task will be delegated to a junior. Prepare a trial chart for the junior using the following labels (which are in random order):

Sales • Product C • Distribution • Finance • General Supplies • Personal Assistant Records • Wages • Transport • Product A General Manager • Administration Purchasing • Managing Director • O & M Accounts • Raw Materials • Warehousing Product Development • Product B Personnel • Support Services • Training Welfare • Research and Development • Overseas

b On completion of the chart suggest the 'span of control' problems which the product managers are likely to experience.

2

Understanding the office environment

Aim of the unit

The unit defines the office in the context of large and small organisations by detailing its role and function and analysing the services it provides, the members who make up its staff and the environment within which it operates.

Specific objectives

At the end of this unit you should be able to:

1 Explain the functions of the office within an organisation.
2 Describe the different office services which are likely to be performed within an organisation.
3 Explain what is meant by centralisation of services.
4 Suggest services which tend to lend themselves to centralisation.
5 Outline the advantages and disadvantages of centralisation.
6 Compare and contrast the office work of large and small organisations.
7 Suggest and describe alternative layouts for offices.
8 Comment on the importance of environment in relation to office work.
9 Draw up a detailed list of the environment aspects which affect office working conditions.
10 Identify staff who work within the framework of an office.
11 Describe the duties and reponsibilities of different office staff.
12 Outline the skills, competences, qualities and attitudes looked for in office staff.

Definition

The Offices, Shops and Railways Premises Act 1963 defines an office as 'a building or part of a building, the sole and principal use of which is as an office or for office purposes'. An office can simply be described as any place where office work is performed, whether in ultra-modern, landscaped buildings belonging to a multinational corporation, in a government department (central or local), in a firm of accountants, in the office attached to a retail outlet or in the spare room of a self-employed tradesperson. Where the offices are and what facilities they have is unimportant. What we are concerned with is the work which goes on, its purpose, the functions performed, the systems used, the services provided and the departments, sections and personnel required to perform these functions satisfactorily.

Placing the office in context

Prior to looking at the specific functions of an office and the services which are performed in relation to office work, it is useful to attempt, very briefly, to place the office within the context of the organisation as a whole. It must not be overlooked that offices do not function in isolation; their very existence is dependent upon other aspects of business organisation. Whether they are part of a manufacturing company or concerned with the provision of services, offices perform three major functions:

- a **secondary** function in that they are secondary to the primary concern of the organisation, whether the manufacture of goods or the provision of services. Without these there would be no need for office support!

- a **complementary** function in that all services they provide must necessarily complement the other activities of the organisation. In other words an organisation could not survive without the ordering of supplies, the payment of wages and the channelling of communications, to quote a few examples.
- a **controlling** function in that they exercise control over things like budgets, stock, finance and staff.

Basically an office performs a support service of communication and record, and in doing so operates at the hub of an organisation. Its functions are largely concerned with the handling and processing of all forms of information, including that concerned with finance, and its role is that of an intermediary between the outside world and the different departments within the organisation.

Specific functions in the role of the office

1 Receiving and collecting information:
   - at a personal level—by word of mouth
   - by telephone
   - by written communication—both internally and externally.
2 Sorting and classifying information:
   - analysing content
   - systematically arranging for further processing and distribution.
3 Processing and interpreting information:
   - gathering statistics
   - feeding information into a computer
   - interpreting computer printouts
   - costing and budgeting.
4 Recording information for future reference:
   - by setting up all forms of record system
   - by maintaining all such systems.
5 Communicating information presented in the most effective way:
   - verbally on a person-to-person basis
   - by telephone
   - on paper
   - by graphic or visual presentation
   - by datacoms
6 Protecting the business and safeguarding its assets:

- by care of finances
- by care of stock and fixtures and fittings
- by insurances
- by statutory obligations.

These functions will involve the performance of the following office services:

- receiving mail
- distributing mail
- despatching mail
- receiving visitors
- receiving and routing telephone calls
- placing telephone calls
- arranging meetings
- arranging and controlling transport
- typing
- transcribing from dictation
- duplication and copying
- filing
- keeping records
- controlling stock
- processing documentation of all kinds
- receiving cash
- paying out cash
- calculations of all kinds
- bookkeeping and accounting
- preparing visual displays
- record processing
- word processing
- data processing
- ensuring inter-office communications

Changing roles

It is important to bear in mind that virtually all aspects of office work are now greatly assisted by technology. Information handling and dissemination is made easier and faster thanks to computer power and more effective systems of networking. The volume of data which can be stored is practically limitless with vast savings in space over conventional paper-based systems and file maintenance is greatly improved. With modern systems access time is faster than ever and information can be quickly and easily updated as and when necessary.

Data held at remote locations can also be interrogated quickly and effectively and there is the added bonus of being able to merge data collected from a variety of sources as a result of the sophistication of integrated applications packages.

Together with improvements in telephone systems and the movement towards digitisation, such developments have considerably altered the nature of much office work. No longer is it a dream of the future for documentation to be ready *before* a deadline: search tasks, previously taking weeks to locate relevant information from large quantities of paper-based files, can now be completed in a matter of hours from information held on disk.

These are just a few examples of the many facilities which now exist to support the office in processing information. More detailed consideration is given in later units.

Centralisation of office services

In many large organisations a number of the services listed would be centralised. This means that the service would be organised and controlled from a central point. This point may be central in terms of location within a building or perhaps central in that instructions would come from head office in respect of what should be done, how, when and by whom, with regular reports on progress.

In terms of office services the centralised approach will often mean the location of personnel in one area, eg a word processing pool or reprographic centre.

Advantages of centralisation

- better administrative control
- improved supervision
- standardisation of systems
- better handling of peaks of work
- economies of space
- better utilisation of equipment and staff resources
- utilisation of specialist staff
- economies in terms of expenditure on heat and light

Disadvantages of centralisation

- increased paperwork
- inflexibility of systems
- delays through location and bureaucracy
- rigid control of staff
- impersonal working relationships and environments

- lack of variety in work
- restriction of experience and promotion opportunities

Note: Centralisation is a two-edged sword, and advantages and disadvantages will necessarily be viewed differently by management and employees. What may be looked upon as an advantage by management may well be considered a disadvantage by an employee.

Centralisation of computing facilities

In modern offices one of the areas in which decisions need to be made with regard to centralisation is that concerned with the provision of computerised resources. While the pros and cons will still be very much those referred to previously, certain other issues will need to be addressed and these will include:

- equipment compatibility
- the advantages/disadvantages of being 'locked in' to one supplier, eg the company who supplied the mainframe computer
- potential for networking and improved communications
- availability of programs/applications packages
- security
- maintenance of the system
- training
- terminal access
- departmental and individual user needs
- upgrading
- cost factors
- staff motivation
- job enrichment resulting from task variation
- the implications of devolving responsibility to departmental level while attempting to retain corporate identity
- the possibilities of departmental empire building

The differences between large and small organisations

An important point to note is that the work performed in any office, irrespective of its size, will basically be the same. It will be the scale of operations which will differ; the larger the scale, the greater will be the degree of specialisation which it is possible to introduce and the greater the need for individual design and certain specialist facilities. Therefore, whereas in a small company a secretary may in addition to secretarial duties act as telephonist/receptionist and perhaps even do some bookkeeping as well as make the tea, in a large organisation there would be distinct lines of demarcation and also special facilities to cope with the different tasks.

Obviously there are advantages and disadvantages to both operations. If you start in a small firm you may feel that you are a Jack (or Jill) of all trades, but variety, as well as being the spice of life, provides invaluable experience which you may not find so readily in a large organisation. Where there is a high degree of task specialisation and centralisation of services, it is unlikely that you will be given the opportunity to turn your hand to as many different things as in a smaller office, where you may have a better chance to show your initiative and versatility. However, in a large firm you may see a more obvious career structure and you may even work through an extensive induction programme designed to give you the opportunity to experience different areas of work. Also, the working conditions may be superior and there may be more 'perks'. Likewise there may be more staff of about your own age in a large organisation.

These are factors which all prospective office workers will have to try to reconcile before they apply for jobs in the first instance. Some people prefer a small set-up where everyone knows everyone else and where the tasks are varied and provide flexibility, while others prefer a more impersonal working environment where duties are clearly defined and there is a very definite promotional structure.

Office environment

No textbook on this subject would be complete without reference to what may best be described as the 'office environment'. This comprises the working conditions, the design and layout of the offices, and the effect which these have on the overall efficiency of the organisation. This is an area which is receiving considerable attention now, as evidence suggests that factors like morale and productivity have a close relationship with working conditions.

Facilities management

A new management discipline is gradually emerging to cater for the demands of environmental change. Facilities management is concerned with the effective management of the working environment and the influence which these environments have on organisational productivity.

Facilities Managers, who may come from a variety of backgrounds including administration, telecommunications, finance, surveying and data processing, undertake activities ranging from advising on the acquisition or relocation of premises, making the best use of space available, to the day-to-day management of the building and all its facilities. This requires an individual who is capable of adopting a broad overview and necessitates liaising with people inside the organisation from top management to the cleaning staff, as well as with outside contractors, suppliers, consultants, landlords and many others. The need for Facilities Managers has grown in recent years, particularly as a result of the desire to automate offices within buildings which have not been custom designed to cater for the new technology associated with Office Automation (OA).

Facilities management is broadly concerned with the following aspects:

• premises	• heating
• layout	• lighting
• furniture	• ventilation
• fittings	• maintenance
• equipment	• health and safety
• decor	• security

Premises

The premises may be custom designed or modified from existing buildings. They may be purchased, leased or rented, and they may be located in a city centre, in the suburbs or on an industrial estate. They may be ultra modern or old fashioned. All these factors will have a bearing, given the circumstances and the nature of the organisation, on how successful they are in their contributions to the working environment. The office building needs to be viewed as part of the business since it represents the business's infrastructure and as such forms the basis for carrying information around.

Layout

Office accommodation needs differ but basically organisations are likely to opt for the variations of individual cellular offices to some form of open plan layout, dependent on the type of organisation, its size, the accommodation at its disposal, the extent of its office work, the level of office automation, the number of personnel and the nature of their work.

Broadly speaking alternative layouts offer different advantages and disadvantages and consequently what is seen as an advantage of one layout will tend to be viewed as a disadvantage of the other. The following is a simple breakdown of the advantages and disadvantages of the open plan design.

Advantages

- economical in terms of resources, which will include space, equipment, furniture and fittings, lighting, heating and staff
- facilitates close supervision
- improves work flow
- enhances the potential for teamwork
- encourages a friendly atmosphere

Disadvantages

- can be noisy and cause distractions
- lack of privacy
- difficulty of finding acceptable levels of heating, lighting and ventilation to suit all tastes
- more liable to breaches in security of information
- the danger of spreading disease

It is impossible to please everyone with regard to layout and there is no 'best solution'. Each situation must be considered on its own merits with a view to how the layout selected can best cater for the work done, thereby ensuring maximum efficiency and a high level of productivity. Some work will necessitate privacy while other types will only flourish in the sort of atmosphere where teamwork and the stimulus provided by easy contact with others is made possible.

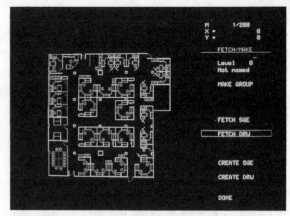

Fig 13 Computer Aided Design; *Reproduced by kind permission of Herman Miller Ltd*

Computer Aided Design (CAD)

Gone are the days of 'guestimates' with the Office Manager left to rough out a plan for placing office staff, and layouts being changed at virtually a moment's notice with the Maintenance Section brought in to move a few desks over a weekend. Now the process is much more systematic and relies on securing accurate answers to a number of fundamental questions including the following:

- what are the department's future space needs likely to be?
- what does each member of the department actually do?
- do any members of staff require cellular offices?
- which members of staff need contact with which others?
- what are each member's furniture and equipment requirements?
- what centralised facilities does the department use?

Once there are answers to such questions it is possible to make use of computer aided design techniques to suggest alternative layouts from the variables supplied. Many CAD services are also linked to computer controlled production techniques so once the layout has been determined, the furniture requirements can also be supplied to meet every need. Some furniture manufacturers may even see the project from the design stage, through manufacture, to door-to-door delivery in their own container lorries followed by a complete installation service.

Flexibility is the key

One point to be remembered in respect of office planning is that the only certainty is change. Flexibility should therefore be the key to success. Even the much talked about German style Bürolandschaft landscaped design of the 1970s which provided a considerable degree of flexibility then, presented problems in the 1980s.

The arrival of so much desktop computer technology with all its associated electrical 'spaghetti' left little option but to channel cabling across carpeted areas under rubberised floor surface trunking. However, with developments in wire or cable-management in modern systems furniture and the possibilities provided by investing in raised flooring to channel all wiring, cost effective solutions can be found to deal with such problems.

Furniture and fittings

Developments in office furniture and fittings were substantial during the 1980s, with great attention being paid to ergonomic design. **Ergonomics** is defined as the study of how to fit the job to the person, and is concerned with the efficiency of workers and working arrangements.

There is a strong move towards providing office furniture and fittings which improve the quality of office life, in that they tend to reflect the standards which are now expected and considered acceptable in carefully planned and well equipped homes. The ranges of furniture and fittings are vast and should be capable of satisfying all tastes and all budgets.

Modern office furniture is much more than desks, chairs and filing cabinets. It is geared to people and the work they do. It is stylish as well as functional (*see* Fig 14) and is designed to be part of an integrated working area. For example, the desk may be split level to be used in comfort with a desk top computer or a word processor. Desks are also well equipped with an advanced wire management system to accommodate and hide away all the necessary computer cabling. This not only helps to ensure

Fig 14 A modern office

safety but allows easy access for maintenance purposes. They may be free standing or arranged in different cluster formations where users can easily access shared materials and facilities.

Systems furniture

Systems furniture, as it is called, is especially suitable for open plan offices. Curved and straight upholstered screens may be used to partition working areas as necessary. It is totally flexible and very mobile, so enabling task groups to be set up and disbanded as required. When wall space, so highly desired by offices which had ranks of filing cabinets, is in short supply, alternative storage facilities are essential. Systems furniture incorporates both ample overhead and undersurface mobile storage which is vital where a company operates what is termed a 'clear desk' policy in which all materials must be removed from desk tops at nights for security purposes.

Equipment

Equipment will also contribute substantially to the office environment, and will have a considerable bearing on the selection of furniture and fittings. For example, where equipment has to be shared it needs to be located in the most appropriate position to enable access by all users and where noisy equipment is part of an open plan area it is essential to provide acoustic hoods and screens to help eliminate the noise. Equipment will be dealt with in more detail in Unit 10.

Decor

Office decor is 'big business', and many design consultancies have been set up to help organisations in this respect. As with domestic decor, it is very much a question of personal taste and indicative of the impression which it is desired to create. For open plan offices it is important to have the sort of decor which will meet with general approval and provide a comfortable yet unobtrusive atmosphere in which to work. Decor will include items like wall and floor coverings, curtains and blinds. It is always important to remember that people spend something like half their waking lives at work, so their working conditions should be favourable and conducive to a high level of productivity.

Heating

Legislation in the form of the Offices, Shops and Railway Premises Act 1963 sets down a minimum heating requirement of 16°C (60.8°F) after the first hour. It is important to note that this is a **minimum** requirement, and possibly considerably lower than the sort of temperatures that many office staff will be accustomed to in modern, centrally heated homes. It is also perhaps interesting to note that the law does not specify a maximum temperature!

Heating can come in various forms from radiators to air ducting and underfloor systems, and may be supplied from oil, solid fuel, electricity or even solar means. These are, of course matters for consideration and decision by management.

Lighting

Lighting too must be adequate for the purpose and certain office jobs will of necessity require better quality lighting than others. It will also be desirable to attempt to provide certain workers, eg those working at drawing boards, with as much natural light as possible. In many modern offices lighting may be electronically controlled to dim and brighten automatically according to the needs of the environment. However, where a layout is made up of individual work areas, some of whom are screened off from others, it is important that they do not end up as dark 'cubby holes', so each workstation will have its own overhead task light. Ambient/task lighting is particularly important where there is what is known as 'deep space', ie the amount of office space out of direct natural light.

Ventilation

Just as heating and lighting are important for personal comfort and operational efficiency, so too is adequate ventilation. Inefficient and wasteful ventilation can be one of the major contributory factors towards energy loss in buildings. In commercial offices heating alone accounts for about 60 per cent of total energy costs. Haphazard opening of windows can waste much costly heat and yet it is important that workers feel they have sufficient ventilation as stuffy, stale atmospheres will only serve to decrease productivity.

Nowadays we hear growing reference to 'building sickness' or 'sick building syndrome' and with more, highly publicised outbreaks of Legionnaire's Disease, companies are becoming increasingly aware of the importance of a healthy working environment and of the need to consider ways of achieving it. Part of it will be concerned with improving air quality and this may result, for larger organisations, in installing air conditioning. In most modern offices air conditioning will be the norm, particularly where offices are located in city centres where noise and traffic pollution render it virtually impossible to rely on opening windows for fresh air. However, installing air conditioning, which in itself can be the cause of many employee complaints, is not the only option available to smaller companies or those located in older buildings which do not adapt so readily. Air quality can be improved by introducing simple extractor fans and ventilator units, while even simple table top fans can provide comfort on a particularly warm day.

Maintenance

Given the level of investment that goes into the design, decoration, furnishing and equipping of office buildings, it is reasonable to expect attention to be given to introducing a tight schedule of maintenance. Maintenance will range from regular cleaning, to the servicing requirements of the heating, lighting and ventilation systems (including liaising with outside contractors and consultants to carry out essential control checks on safety and health grounds), to the day-to-day support required to repair and service faulty equipment.

Much of this will be done on a contract basis and will come within the remit of a Facilities Manager, where there is one, to be party to contract negotiations, to monitor the delivery of the contractual obligations once the contracts are in operation and to ensure quality service and strict adherance to the terms and conditions agreed.

Good maintenance also helps to reduce the likelihood of accidents and the resultant heavy insurance claims. It can also reduce the need for constant 'troubleshooting' in response to events which might have been avoided had due care been given to maintenance in the first place.

Health and safety

Safety factors play a vital part in contributing to a good working environment and the legislative re-

quirements are dealt with below. However, it is important to note the need for companies to treat any staff complaints seriously. These may include a variety of physical symptoms such as eye irritation, dry skin, headaches and general lethargy, which are common in many modern air-conditioned environments.

Other environmentally-associated conditions include those connected with working with new technology, eg an increase in headaches, back and neck complaints and the emergence of tenosynovitis which is a disorder caused by repetitive muscle movement such as that which can be demanded by operating modern office keyboards. Electric shocks brought about by build-ups of static electricity in offices is another complaint of the technology age and one which needs to be treated seriously.

Organisations have an obligation to their staff to monitor health and safety at work and most will introduce some form of regular control checks which will be duly recorded. These might include:

- examining air conditioning
- monitoring fresh air supplies
- checking lighting levels
- measuring noise emission
- checking temperatures and humidity levels
- checking fire fighting apparatus
- inspecting kitchens, staff restaurants and restrooms
- checking for the presence of specific substances or bacteria

Many organisations will bring in independent companies and consultants to carry out separate tests and so guarantee unbiased reports.

Health and safety legislation

Historically many workers, including those working in offices, were inadequately protected by health and safety legislation. Prior to the **Health and Safety at Work etc, Act** (HASAWACT) **1974**, many workers were not covered in any way. Admittedly there was the **Offices, Shops and Railway Premises Act 1963**, but this is more concerned with the adequacy of facilities than with actual matters of health and safety (a brief breakdown of the main points of this Act is given on p 22).

The HASAWACT 1974, which came into force in April 1975, provided a new integrated and comprehensive system of law to deal with the problems of health and safety in the working environment. It dealt with people and organisations and covered virtually everyone in or connected with work. The Act is an 'enabling' one, ie it is fairly general in terms of the legislation laid down but provides for regulations and codes of safe working practice to be drawn up as considered necessary and desirable in the interests of health, safety and welfare within the broad general framework of the Act.

For the first time it places a duty on employees as well as employers. Both parties now have a legal obligation to take an active part in efforts to maintain health and safety in the place of work.

Why do accidents happen?

Accidents arise from different combinations of circumstances and events, for example:

- carelessness
- thoughtlessness
- untidiness
- negligence
- rushing
- failure to observe and follow instructions
- lack of supervision
- lack of training
- faulty or poorly maintained equipment
- fatigue
- emotional/mental disturbance
- excessive noise
- distractions
- the influence of drugs or alcohol
- adverse conditions of some kind, eg darkness, cold, ice
- horseplay
- acts of God

It is probably reasonably easy to think of examples of accidents which would fall into one or more of the above areas. Almost half of all office accidents are

---

Offices, Shops and Railway Premises Act 1963

1 Defines what is an office (rather lengthy).

2 Exemptions are granted
   a where business is staffed by close relatives and
   b where weekly hours normally worked do not exceed 21

3 The Act requires minimal standards (although they are loosely defined in many cases, such as 'sufficient and suitable') in the following aspects:

cleanliness • prevention of overcrowding • temperature • ventilation • lighting • sanitary conveniences • first aid • washing facilities • drinking water • accommodation for clothing • seats for sedentary workers • eating facilities • fencing for machinery • fire precautions

4 More precise standards are laid down for the following:

   a Temperature of 60.8°F (16°C) by one hour after the office opens.
   b Minimum 400 cu ft of space per worker – ignoring ceiling height above 10 ft.
   c Every employer with more than twenty employees must obtain a fire certificate from the fire authority (that reasonable precautions have been taken).
   d Once a week sweeping or cleaning of floors.
   e Every office must have a first aid box, and where there are more than 150 employees, at least one person must be trained in first aid.
   f Sanitary conveniences must be provided; if more than five employees, there must be separate ones for each sex, and then 5 for the first 100, and 4 for each 100 employees subsequently.
   g Wash basins must be provided in the same ratios to staff as sanitary conveniences.
   h A supply of drinking water must also be made available.

5 The Act is enforceable by inspectors appointed by local authorities.
Such physical conditions as enforced by this Act are important because:

1 Health of workers is affected (note the effect of bad lighting on sight; excessive noise on nerves; overcrowding on morale; and draughts on physical health).
2 Effect on efficiency of the office (bad light causes errors; noise, bad heating and ventilation can cause distraction).

---

due to falls, either on the flat or on stairs. Next comes lifting and handling materials and equipment – responsible for much back strain, which is a common reason for absence from work. Other typical accidents in offices are caused by stepping on, striking against and dropping things, by machinery and by electric shocks. Typical examples are:

a falling over obstacles on the floor
b tripping over trailing flexes or wires
c lifting heavy items unaided and in the incorrect manner
d leaving drawers open and subsequently bumping into them
e falling from chairs and desks, instead of using steps or ladders
f tampering with electrical equipment
g failing to report faults, eg loose connections, damaged cables, loose floor tiles, frayed carpets
h not watching where you are going
i overloading old style filing cabinets and causing them to overbalance
j failing to mop up spills
k failing to extinguish cigarettes

What are the duties of employers?

In accordance with the HASAWACT 1974, every employer must ensure 'as far as is reasonably practicable' (a phrase used frequently throughout the legislation) the health, safety and welfare at work of all his employees. This means that employers must carefully weigh up any risks which might conceivably be involved for his employees against the costs he would incur in attempting to minimise the risk by installing and implementing such safety measures as are considered necessary. Such measures would be likely to include aspects like:

• exit routes in the event of an emergency, eg fire
• safe working environment
• safe and well-maintained equipment
• necessary protective clothing provision
• necessary safe storage facilities
• adequate safety information
• appropriate training and supervision

Employers also have two other important duties towards employees:

1 To issue a written statement of general policy with respect to health and safety matters and their organisation, and arrangements for implementation and revision within the organisation (employees have the right to demand such a policy statement from employers)
Note: The requirements of every employer will vary in this area. However, a specimen of a very basic safety policy is shown on page 25.
2 To provide for the appointment of safety representatives from employees by trade unions 'recognised' by employers in any negotiation procedures

What are the duties of a safety representative?

No specific qualification is required, although an elected representative must have been in the employer's service for two years or in similar employment. However, it will be desirable that representatives receive some sort of training for the functions they are expected to perform, which will include:

• investigating any potential hazards reported by colleagues in the workplace
• investigating any reports of unsafe working practices or conditions likely to be injurious to health
• regular inspections of the workplace
• any necessary consultation with health and safety inspectors

Safety committees

In most larger organisations there will be a safety committee where elected members will meet at regular intervals to consider safety matters. Where there is no committee as such, but where two safety representatives make a request in writing, the employer is under a legal obligation to set up a committee.

What are an employee's duties and responsibilities?

According to the Act, one of the duties of every employee (including those working part time) is:

'to take reasonable care for his own health and safety and that of other persons who may be affected by what he does or what he omits to do at work.'

Also an employee has a duty:

'to cooperate with an employer or any other person

who has duties to carry out under the Act or related legislation.'

This would apply to such duties as wearing appropriate protective clothing and following any specified regulations.

What happens when there is a contravention of the law?

Failure to comply with the duties outlined in the HASAWACT is a criminal offence and both employers and employees could be liable to prosecution. It is important to appreciate that ignorance of the law is in itself no defence. Both parties need to know the extent of their responsibilities and to ensure that they perform them to the letter.

Accident prevention in the office

Management should always take every opportunity to impress upon staff the need to be safety conscious and aware of their obligations according to the Act. Consideration should be given to the main causes of accidents and particular attention should be paid to typical ones with a view to reducing their likely recurrence. Certain obvious precautionary steps are taken in many offices. Where a Safety Officer has been appointed they will normally speak to all new staff on safety matters during an induction programme (*see* Unit 3). Many organisations use regular safety campaigns launched by their safety committees and include such items as refresher courses, first aid, films on safety, warning posters and pamphlets. Another procedure which can be easily and regularly implemented is the setting up of a safety checklist by the Office Manager or Supervisor. A specimen list is given below.

Specimen safety checklist

1   Keep all gangways and corridors clear.
2   Examine all floors and stairways regularly for possible hazards.
3   Avoid leaving boxes, parcels or other items lying around.
4   Place warning notices on/near any temporary or permanent hazard.
5   Encourage office staff to be tidy at all times.
6   Pay attention to work flow and rearrange furniture to avoid possible collisions.

7   Fit prominent warning notices on all clear-glass doors.
8   Avoid placing items at heights which are difficult to reach.
9   Check all machines and equipment regularly and maintain a Faults Book.
10 Check all electrical flexes, cables and plugs regularly.
11 Have power points professionally checked for safety.
12 Always use step stools or ladders to reach things positioned high up.
13 Take care in loading filing cabinets.
14 Store all flammable liquids and other substances in fireproof cupboards.
15 Keep a well-stocked, regularly checked first aid box handy.
16 Ensure that all fire evacuation procedure notices are clearly situated and easy to follow.
17 Specify any particular company rules in respect of smoking.
18 Have fire extinguishers checked and serviced regularly.
19 Ensure that all staff are familiar with all safety procedures.
20 Promote the interests of health and safety at all times.

Office supervisors should also encourage safety awareness among all office staff and each individual should be made aware of certain basic safety procedures. It is usual to issue a code of practice to all employees, appertaining to the particular work area in which they are engaged.

Accident Books

In all organisations it is a statutory requirement that an Accident Book be kept. There will also be a standard procedure drawn up for the reporting of all accidents, and there will usually be a specially prepared accident report form for the purpose.

Security

Security can be a sizeable aspect of any organisation's management responsibility, depending on the nature of its activities. The need to ensure a secure environment necessitates giving attention to security considerations from the design stage of a building when care needs to be taken to minimise the opportunities for illegal entry, to the operational stages where procedures need to be set up to ensure security of information. We are all aware of the term 'computer hacking' and the more recent arrival of computer viruses, so in a high technology age security matters take on added dimensions. They are no longer simply a question of installing burglar alarms and setting up night patrols. They also involve looking into issues which are at a much more sophisticated level and taking the necessary steps to minimise whatever security risks are involved.

Security systems

In organisations where strict security precautions are required it is usual to have established procedures for

- the movement of staff within the organisation
- visitors to the site.
- computer access

Staff movement

Where staff are moving around in high-security installations it will normally be necessary for them to carry, if not wear, identification. It is common practice for staff to be issued with identity cards which show their photograph. These cards should be carried by staff at all times as they can be called upon to produce them for security checking purposes.

Alternatively, staff may be required to wear lapel badges in order to gain easy access to certain restricted areas. In some installations such badges would be fitted with electronic devices which are capable of activating special security locks, thereby enabling ready access to special areas.

With regard to car parking it is also accepted practice that all staff be required to display parking permits on their car windscreens. These assist in recognition of cars entering the site at any time, particularly when there is a steady stream of arrivals, and they also enable the security personnel to identify any vehicle and its owner, should they need to contact that person urgently after the vehicle is parked.

Visitors

Visitors to a large site would normally be stopped at

the gate if travelling by car. Details would be taken by the commissionaire on duty, eg name, company or organisation represented, nature of business and who they wish to see. Clearance may then be required before any visitor is allowed access to the site. Alternatively, entry permits may be sent out in advance when appointments are made. Visitors are often issued with lapel badges which they must sign for, wear at all times on the premises and hand in when leaving. They would then be directed to the visitors' car park.

Visitors arriving on foot would first check in at reception where once again they would be issued with the necessary lapel badges identifying them as visitors.

Such precautions are important not only for security but also for safety on a site where there may be danger of fire or explosion. In such an instance the gate and reception areas would have details of all visitors to the building, so that they could be accounted for if necessary.

Computer access

With so many office personnel now using computing facilities it will be necessary to establish essential safeguards. In respect of access it will tend to require the issuing of individual passwords which can be regularly changed. Certain staff will be allowed only limited access to a centralised system according to the levels of information required to perform their respective jobs. In addition, some terminals may be of the 'dumb' variety which will mean that while information may be accessed on the screen, it cannot be in any way altered or deleted from the terminal.

The system management of a centralised computing facility will also enable terminal usage to be closely monitored as log-in and log-off times will be recorded for each user together with other information in relation to the type of use made of the system. Staff will be allocated individual disk space and this too will need to be closely monitored so that it may be increased or decreased according to requirements. Such arrangements improve general housekeeping as well as tightening up on system security.

Office workers

Office workers are found in support roles within all

departments of an organisation. The range of office jobs will be large and often the content of what appears to be a similar job will vary considerably from department to department. There is always a danger in assuming content from a job title, and it is difficult to speculate or generalise about duties. Hence the need to prepare individual job descriptions (*see* Unit 3).

However, office workers will fall into three broad categories:

- managerial
- administrative
- clerical

At managerial level they include personnel at top management level like Chief Accountants, Company Secretaries and certain other departmental managers, as well as other executives at both middle and junior management levels.

At administrative level they will operate very largely in a supervisory capacity. They act as a filter for higher level management, concerning themselves more with the detail and its implementation. Personal Assistants would fall into this category.

At clerical level, staff deal with the detail of daily work. Such personnel will include all clerical posts, all typists and many secretaries.

Figure 15 is a selection of typical office posts. You should consult office vacancies in the press and judge for yourself how varied the range can be. It is also useful to collect a representative cross-section by way of illustration.

For general quick reference purposes the table given as Fig 16 provides a breakdown of the key words or phrases associated with the duties, responsibilities, skills, competences, qualities and attitudes sought in relation to the more commonly advertised positions. You will see that many of the titles used in typical advertisements combine two or even more of the roles categorised below. For example it is not unusual to see WP Operator/Typist or WP Operator/Admin Clerk or Receptionist/Telephonist/Admin Assistant. Flexibility is the name of the game and the more skills and competences you can acquire, the better your chances of success when applying for a variety of interesting positions.

As far as specific qualifications are concerned it is difficult to be precise although important to stress that a good standard of general education is expected with a qualification in English Language as a

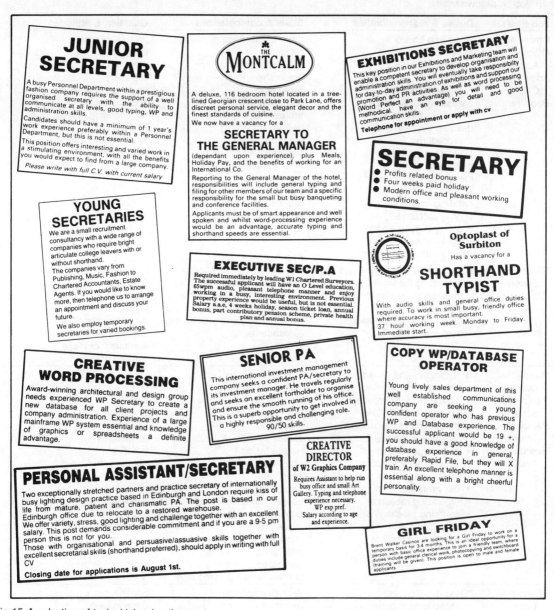

JUNIOR SECRETARY

A busy Personnel Department within a prestigious fashion company requires the support of a well organised secretary with the ability to communicate at all levels, good typing, WP and administration skills.

Candidates should have a minimum of 1 year's work experience preferably within a Personnel Department, but this is not essential.

This position offers interesting and varied work in a stimulating environment, with all the benefits you would expect to find from a large company.

Please write with full C.V. with current salary

THE MONTCALM

A deluxe, 116 bedroom hotel located in a tree-lined Georgian crescent close to Park Lane, offers discreet personal service, elegant decor and the finest standards of cuisine.

We now have a vacancy for a

SECRETARY TO THE GENERAL MANAGER

(dependant upon experience), plus Meals, Holiday Pay, and the benefits of working for an International Co.

Reporting to the General Manager of the hotel, responsibilities will include general typing and filing for other members of our team and a specific responsibility for the small but busy banqueting and conference facilities.

Applicants must be of smart appearance and well spoken and whilst word-processing experience would be an advantage, accurate typing and shorthand speeds are essential.

EXHIBITIONS SECRETARY

This key position in our Exhibitions and Marketing team will enable a competent secretary to develop organisation and administration skills. You will eventually take responsibility for day-to-day administration of exhibitions and support our promotion and PR activities. As well as word processing (Word Perfect an advantage) you will need to be methodical, have an eye for detail and good communication skills.

Telephone for appointment or apply with cv

SECRETARY

- Profits related bonus
- Four weeks paid holiday
- Modern office and pleasant working conditions.

Optoplast of Surbiton

Has a vacancy for a

SHORTHAND TYPIST

With audio skills and general office duties required. To work in small busy, friendly office where accuracy is most important.
37 hour working week. Monday to Friday. Immediate start.

YOUNG SECRETARIES

We are a small recruitment consultancy with a wide range of companies who require bright articulate college leavers with or without shorthand.

The companies vary from Publishing, Music, Fashion to Chartered Accountants, Estate Agents. If you would like to know more, then telephone us to arrange an appointment and discuss your future.

We also employ temporary secretaries for varied bookings.

EXECUTIVE SEC/P.A

Required immediately by leading W1 Chartered Surveyors. The successful applicant will have an O Level education, 65wpm audio, pleasant telephone manner and enjoy working in a busy, interesting environment. Previous property experience would be useful, but is not essential. Salary a.a.e, 4 weeks holiday, season ticket loan, annual bonus, part contributory pension scheme, private health plan and annual bonus.

CREATIVE WORD PROCESSING

Award-winning architectural and design group needs experienced WP Secretary to create a new database for all client projects and company administration. Experience of a large mainframe WP system essential and knowledge of graphics or spreadsheets a definite advantage.

SENIOR PA

This international investment management company seeks a confident PA/secretary to its investment manager. He travels regularly and seeks an excellent fortholder to organise and ensure the smooth running of his office. This is a superb opportunity to get involved in a highly responsible and challenging role. 90/50 skills.

COPY WP/DATABASE OPERATOR

Young lively sales department of this well established communications company are seeking a young confident operator who has previous WP and Database experience. The successful applicant would be 19 +, you should have a good knowledge of database experience in general, preferably Rapid File, but they will X train. An excellent telephone manner is essential along with a bright cheerful personality.

CREATIVE DIRECTOR
of W2 Graphics Company

Requires Assistant to help run busy office and small Art Gallery. Typing and telephone experience necessary. WP exp pref. Salary according to age and experience.

PERSONAL ASSISTANT/SECRETARY

Two exceptionally stretched partners and practice secretary of internationally busy lighting design practice based in Edinburgh and London require kiss of life from mature, patient and charismatic PA. The post is based in our Edinburgh office due to relocate to a restored warehouse.

We offer variety, stress, good lighting and challenge together with an excellent salary. This post demands considerable commitment and if you are a 9-5 pm person this is not for you.

Those with organisational and persuasive/assuasive skills together with excellent secretarial skills (shorthand preferred), should apply in writing with full CV

Closing date for applications is August 1st.

GIRL FRIDAY

Brent Walker Casinos are looking for a Girl Friday to work on a temporary basis for 3-4 months. This is an ideal opportunity for a person with basic office experience to join a friendly team, where duties include general clerical work, photocopying and switchboard (training will be given). This position is open to male and female applicants.

Fig 15 A selection of typical job advertisements

minimum requirement. Employers also recognise qualifications of the major national examination bodies and professional institutions which cater for the particular needs of office-based personnel. Therefore prospective employees are advised to aim for the highest qualification they can get in the particular field of work in which they wish to secure a position.

The question of experience is always a difficult one when seeking a first appointment as, of course, it is only when in a job that real experience can be acquired. However, any limited experience, eg a work placement from school or college, will be taken into account together with other, sometimes less obvious, experience such as participation in group activities or organisations and societies.

Fig 16 Job breakdown table

Job title(s)	Duties & responsibilities	Skills & competences	Qualities & attitudes

Office Manager
Office
  Administrator
Administrative
  Officer
Registrar
	direct and control
	planning
	budgeting
	overall organisation of the
	  office and staff
	assessing requirements
	allocating resources
	devising systems and
	  procedures
	selecting equipment
	delegating duties
	identifying training needs
	arranging training
	handling staff issues
	solving problems
	ensuring a good working
	  environment
	liaising with management
		good communication
		people
		staff management
		leadership
		delegation
		administration
		problem-solving
		decision-making
		team-building
		numeracy
		time management
		negotiating
		advisory
		reporting
		organisational
			professionalism
			integrity
			confidence
			capability
			responsive to change
			approachable
			commanding respect
			firm but fair
			inspiring confidence
			authoritative
			observant

Office Services
  Supervisor
WP Supervisor
	co-ordinating, monitoring and
	  evaluating the work
	  undertaken by a section or unit;
	specific elements of the
	  duties of an Office Manager
	  as outlined above
		technical skills (as appropriate),
		  together with some of the
		  skills listed above, but with
		  the emphasis on supervision
		  and setting and maintaining
		  standards
			conscientiousness
			flexibility
			personable
			loyal
			a good motivator
			able to advise others
			and many of those
			  listed above

Private
  Secretary
Personal
  Secretary
Personal
  Assistant
Executive
  Assistant
	wide ranging and varied
	  dependent on the
	  organisation, the precise
	  nature of the role and
	  the attitude of the boss(es),
	  but likely to include:
	• office organisation
	• general administration
	• correspondence
	• diary management
	• organising meetings
	• servicing meetings
	• arranging travel
	• maintaining records
		oral/aural/written
		  communication
		typewriting
		word processing
		shorthand
		audio
		minute taking
		proof reading
		telephone
		reception
		people/human relations
		numeracy
		researching
		supervisory
		prioritising
		delegation
		perhaps a foreign language
			professionalism
			tact
			loyalty
			discretion
			flexibility
			adaptability
			initiative
			able to work under
			  pressure
			able to accept
			  constructive
			  criticism
			able to anticipate
			  needs
			commitment
			a good memory
			a sense of humour

Shorthand-
  Typist
	taking dictation and
	  transcribing accurately
	basic secretarial duties
		English language
		Shorthand
		Typewriting/WP
		prioritising
		listening
			conscientious
			pride in work
			well organised
			good memory
			able to work under
			  pressure
			flexibility
			minimal need for
			  supervision

Audio Typist	accurate transcription
	  from pre-recorded media
	basic secretarial duties
		English language
		audio typing/WP
		listening
		visualising
			enjoy working with
			  machines
			happy to operate by
			  'remote control'
			prepared to contact
			  the originator with
			  queries

Job title(s)	Duties & responsibilities	Skills & competences	Qualities & attitudes
Copy Typist	production of material (often handwritten) on typewriter or word processor general office duties	fast, accurate typing deciphering poor handwriting proof reading following instructions	prepared to undertake routine, repetitive work high level of concentration
Word Processing Operator	production of varied material on word processor from shorthand audio or manuscript	word processing: text origination text editing file maintenance storage & retrieval proofreading spatial thinking	technology minded happy to work alone logical eye for detail and display happy to work with machines
Clerk Clerical Assistant Clerical Officer	general office work of an administrative nature, including establishing and maintaining record systems	filing and record keeping literacy numeracy telephone skills handling queries	logical systematic well organised painstaking conscientious enjoying routine
Receptionist	receive and direct visitors screen and filter callers identify potential security problems receive hand-delivered packets record and pass on messages maintain an attractive reception area	good communication people/human relations organisational	interest in people pleasant personality outgoing easy conversationalist unflappable attentive to detail discreet tactful alert good memory
Telephonist	receiving and routing incoming calls placing outgoing calls as required	switchboard operation good communication clear speaking voice pleasant telephone manner	helpful interested in people patience able to work under pressure consistent well organised
Office junior	general office duties as instructed by superiors	those already acquired at school or college including perhaps: • typing • telephone • filing • basic business procedures	desire to learn willingness enthusiasm prepared to undertake further training and study

1 What are the main functions of an office within an organisation?

2 What is meant by centralisation of office services?

3 When considering the centralisation of computing facilities what issues should be addressed?

4 Identify **three** specific features relating to work in a large organisation compared with work in a small company.

5 What are the main reasons for considering the appointment of a Facilities Manager?

6 How can computer aided design (CAD) help with office layout?

7 Name **three** important environmental considerations in any office and explain their importance.

8 Explain what you understand by the term 'systems furniture'.

9   What are the principal duties of employers in respect of health and safety at work?

10 What are the most common causes of office accidents?

11 What are the main tasks an organisation can carry out to improve security matters?

12 Outline the duties and responsibilities of a Personal Assistant.

Personal activities

1   Take the opportunity to scan through any business and office equipment magazines which are taken by your school or college library or by your own department/section. Note the latest developments in office layouts, furniture, design and environmental aspects and begin to build a file of useful details and addresses.

2   If you have the chance to visit any offices where friends or relatives may already work, do not pass up the opportunity. Similarly, be particularly observant while on any outside visit or during a work placement. It is always interesting to compare workplaces and to begin to formulate your own ideas of what you think makes for good working conditions.

3   Study your local press and Job Centre advertisements to gain an impression of the types of office jobs which are currently available. Build up a collection of varied job advertisements from the press and compare descriptions in terms of qualifications and skills required, qualities and experience sought and salaries and conditions offered. **Note:** This selection of job advertisements will be required for use in Unit 9.

Group activity

Imagine that you have been given the opportunity to design and equip a new office suite for use during your office and secretarial procedures lessons with a relatively open-ended budget! Draw a plan of your ideal office or suite of rooms, indicating size and shape preferred. Describe the furniture and equipment you would have and how it would be laid out and comment on the colour scheme and accessories you would choose. You should provide a key to your drawing.

Situation-based activities

1   Imagine that your organisation has decided to form a Secretarial Services Unit providing word processing and secretarial support for all members of staff. A new centralised Reprographics Unit is also to be set up to undertake all duplicating, photocopying and print work. Up to now you have worked as Secretarial Assistant in the Sales Department where you have done all the routine typing and photocopying work as well as general office duties for the department. However, in the re-organisation you have been moved to the Secretarial Services Unit. Write a letter to a friend explaining your new position and the changes you have experienced and outline the advantages and disadvantages of the move from your point of view.

2   Imagine that you work as a shorthand typist within Miller & Dobson plc, the company you looked at in Unit 1. A vacancy for a Personal Secretary is soon to come up for one of the parters in a firm of solicitors in your home town and you are considering applying for the position.

    a   What differences would you expect to encounter:
        i   in the nature of the work
        ii in the type of organisation
        iii in working as a Personal Secretary as opposed to a shorthand typist?

    b   What qualifications, skills and qualities would you expect the firm of solicitors to look for in the successful candidate for the position?

3   You work as Secretary/PA for the Senior Partner of a firm of architects and surveyors. Study the traditional cellular office layout currently in use by your firm as detailed in Fig 17. The present staff which totals 30 is listed below:
    1 Senior Partner
    1 Financial Director
    2 Junior Partners
    6 Architects/Architectural Assistants
    5 Surveyors
    2 Clerical Officers
    2 Secretary/Personal Assistants
    1 Typing Services Supervisor
    5 Typists
    2 Reprographics Staff
    1 Mail Room Clerk
    1 Telephonist/Receptionist
    1 Person Friday
    Business is on the increase and bearing in mind the lease on the current building is due to expire,

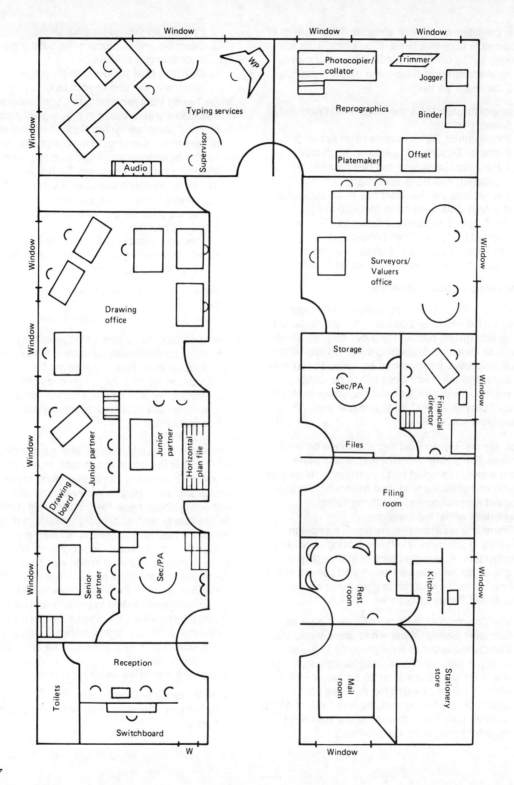

Window Window Window

Typing services

WP

Photocopier/ collator

Trimmer

Jogger

Reprographics

Binder

Supervisor

Audio

Platemaker

Offset

Drawing office

Surveyors/ Valuers office

Storage

Sec/PA

Financial director

Junior partner

Junior partner

Horizontal plan file

Files

Drawing board

Filing room

Senior partner

Sec/PA

Rest room

Kitchen

Reception

Mail room

Stationery store

Toilets

Switchboard

W

Window

Window

Window

Window

Window

Window

Window

Window

Fig 17

new premises have been secured. They consist of a complete floor in a large office block. This will allow great flexibility. In readiness for the move several adjustments have been made in staffing and these are as follows:

- one of the Junior Partners has been promoted to Senior Partner;
- 2 new Junior Partners have been appointed;
- 2 Interior Designers have been appointed;
- 1 Planning Consultant has been appointed;
- 1 Librarian has been appointed;
- 1 new Personal Assistant has been appointed;
- the Architects have been reduced to 5;
- the Typists have been reduced to 4 – now referred to as Secretarial Assistants
- the Typing Services Supervisor has been replaced by a Secretarial Services Supervisor.

The new staff now numbers 36.

Draw up a blank floor plan, basically rectangular in shape. Use whatever scale you find comfortable to work with (graph paper may prove helpful). Draft out your ideas for positioning these 36 staff and their respective furniture and equipment. You may assume that the new offices are to be totally re-equipped with new furniture and equipment. You should provide a key for the furniture and equipment you select.

4 You are the Typing Pool representative on your organisation's Safety Committee, which meets once a month to report on any problems relating to health and safety at work and generally to discuss ways of stimulating and improving safety awareness within the company.

There is a substantial recruitment campaign currently in progress and this will bring about the employment of new members of staff, many of whom will not have worked before and consequently will be unfamiliar with the requirements of the Health and Safety at Work Act 1974.

a The Chairman of the Safety Committee – the Company Safety Officer – has approached you with the request that you contribute to the safety induction programme planned for new staff. He would like you to concentrate on safety in the office. You will be expected to speak for approximately twenty minutes and may, of course, illustrate your talk with appropriate overhead projector transparencies or slides.

i   Prepare an outline for your talk
ii Describe and/or prepare the supporting materials you will use
iii Devise a brief handout which you will provide at the end of your talk.

b As Typing Pool representative your supervisor has asked you to assist in drawing up a code of practice which all Typing Pool personnel should adhere to in an attempt to maximise safe working habits. In addition you are asked to prepare a safety checklist which the Technician should use on a monthly basis to check the electrical equipment in use in the section.

i   Prepare your suggestions for inclusion in the code of practice.
ii Draw up a suitable checklist for the Technician.

c At the next meeting of the Safety Committee, two of the items on the agenda are as follows:

Ideas for a forthcoming safety campaign within the company
A visit from the Safety Inspectorate

As a conscientious committee member you wish to make a worthwhile contribution to the meeting.

i   Suggest two ideas which might be incorporated into the safety campaign.
ii Indicate the sort of preparations which your section will make prior to the visit of the Inspectorate.

5 You work in an organisation where the monitoring of visitors is important at all times. In recent weeks strangers have been found attempting to park their vehicles in the company car park, and also wandering about inside the building. This constitutes an obvious breach of security. In fact, in most instances they had appointments with your personnel but no proper arrangements had been made to ensure that their arrival was expected, that the relevant department or individual was notified of the arrival and that the visitor knew where to go.

You have been asked to prepare and issue a set of instructions which have to be followed by all personnel in relation to the standard procedures which should be taken when visitors are invited on to the premises.

Draw up a suitable set of instructions:

a for visitors travelling by car
b for visitors arriving on foot or by taxi or public transport

3

Understanding recruitment, selection and training

Aim of the unit

The unit provides information on procedures in the recruitment and selection of office staff and offers guidance in applying for positions in an office. It also considers training methods and the appraisal of office staff.

Specific objectives

At the end of this unit you should be able to:

1 Complete application forms.
2 Write your personal curriculum vitae.
3 Compose letters relating to job applications.
4 Prepare simple job descriptions for positions relating to office work.
5 Draft job advertisements.
6 Outline the personal preparations to be made by you prior to attending an interview.
7 Describe the detailed steps leading up to an appointment.
8 Explain the purposes of an induction programme and suggest the likely content of an induction course.
9 Compare and contrast different forms of training.
10 Explain what is meant by 'staff appraisal'.
11 State the advantages of appraisal.
12 Outline the main points of the Data Protection Act, 1984.

Introduction

Any organisation is only as good as the staff it employs, and it will be the recruitment and selection of the right blend of individuals which will help contribute to the effectiveness of the organisation.

Whatever aspect of business life an individual wishes to become a part of, he or she will have to go through the recruitment and selection process which is a vital aspect of the work of any Personnel Department. Personnel performs a unique function within organisations as it has involvement with all prospective employees. It carries the responsibility of forecasting staffing requirements for the future, taking into account technological developments and change as well as economic growth, and thus appointing the right person for the job.

How do vacancies arise and on what ground may they be filled?

Vacancies arise for a variety of reasons, eg retirement, promotion, resignations and increased workloads. They may or may not be filled, depending on factors such as the economic and employment conditions prevailing at the time, the analysis of future requirements and commitments, the availability of likely replacements and the general staffing policy within the organisation.

However, given that it is decided to fill a vacancy, what avenues are open to employers for recruitment and selection? It is common practice for organisations to encourage promotion from within, as this is good for morale and tends to reduce the labour turnover. However, management will normally reserve the right to advertise posts outside the company if it is unlikely that they will be able to make an appropriate appointment from within. The avenues open will be determined largely by the nature of the work and the level of the post, but the following are some of the possibilities:

A company list – this would be drawn up from unsolicited applications from members of the public who have written to express an interest in gaining employment with the organisation.

The press – advertisements may be placed in local and/or national newspapers.

Journals – advertisements may be inserted in specialist journals and magazines.

Local schools, colleges, polytechnics and universities – contact may be made direct to such institutions.

Careers conferences – useful links may be established at such events.

Job Centres

Private employment bureaux or agencies

Radio (particularly local networks) or television

Professional organisations – this would be more likely where the organisation was looking for an employee with a certain professional qualification.

Personal contacts – careful screening is usually necessary.

Via specialist recruitment staff – some organisations employ someone whose job it is to 'sell' the organisation and bring it to the attention of interested parties.

Once the appropriate method has been determined, attention needs to be given to the drafting of any advertisement and to the timing of any insertions in the press.

Guidelines for points to be included in an advertisement

- job title
- level or grade
- key duties involved
- qualifications required
- experience required
- any special skills required
- any special working conditions
- some indication of the image and style of the organisation
- some indication of the salary
- details of how application should be made

In all instances an advertisement should leave prospective candidates in no doubt as to what is required of them.

Application forms

The majority of large organisations will have their own printed application forms. A specimen is given in Fig 18. The purpose of an application form from the point of view of an organisation is to ensure that candidates provide *all* the information the organisation requires and to simplify comparison between candidates by having all the information in the same order. The design and preparation of application forms is something which needs to be handled carefully and professionally. Forms should be logical, simple to follow and allow sufficient space for completion.

From the point of view of an applicant, it is desirable to complete a form as well as possible. It is the only means of advertising to a potential employer exactly what qualifications you hold and what you are likely to be capable of doing. A carefully completed application form could well be the passport to an interview.

Some general advice on completing application forms

1 Read through the form carefully first of all and make sure that you are clear in your mind about what is required and what is to go where.

2 It can be useful to make a photocopy of the blank form. You can then fill this in first to see how much space you have. It will also provide a useful record of what you have written, and you should check through it before an interview – if you secure one. Also it will prove useful when you come to complete other forms or prepare CVs in the future.

3 Write clearly and legibly, using black ink (application forms are often photocopied for the use of members of an interview panel).
Alternatively you may type if it is appropriate.

4 Aim to be concise but clear.

5 If there is insufficient space on the form, refer, in the space provided, to a numbered appendix and supply the information on a separate sheet which should be attached to the form.

6 Try to complete all questions to the best of your ability. However, avoid completing a section for completion's sake if it does not apply to you.

7 Always be truthful.

8 Make sure that you supply the correct details and addresses of any referees. Be sure to obtain their permission beforehand.

APPLICATION FOR EMPLOYMENT

Vacancy ....

SURNAME (block letters)	FORENAMES
	Mr/Ms

ADDRESS

Tel no

Age last birthday	Date of birth	Nationality	If registered under Disabled Persons (Employment) Act YES/NO
		Place of birth	

EDUCATION Schools attended		From	To	Examinations passed (state subject, board, level and grade attained)
Colleges, university attended				Qualifications attained
Training courses attended				

Membership of professional or other similar associations

Hobbies/sports/other interests

Fig 18 Application form

DETAILS OF PREVIOUS EMPLOYMENT (Please commence by stating your present employment first. Use an additional sheet if required)

Name and address of employer	From	To	Brief description of duties

Earliest date at which you could take up this appointment	Present salary £ per annum

Names and addresses of *two* persons to whom reference may be made in relation to your experience and suitability for this post

ADDITIONAL INFORMATION in support of your application. You may continue on a separate sheet if necessary

Signature	Date

Fig 18 Application form (contd)

Curriculum vitae

An increasingly popular alternative to an application form is the curriculum vitae (CV). Here the applicant for the post supplies his or her own details rather than filling in a form as supplied by a prospective employer. Where an individual is making an unsolicited approach to an organisation in the hope of establishing interest and perhaps gaining an interview if a suitable vacancy arises, it is established practice to prepare a CV which would be sent with a covering letter.

Basically the same sort of information will be included in a CV as would be given when completing an application form. However the CV does allow flexibility of approach and unlimited space. Figure 19 provides an example of the order in which one might be set out.

Shortlisting

Shortlisting is the first step in the selection process and must be a methodical exercise. It is important that prior consideration is given to the criteria for shortlisting candidates for interview, particularly in situations where a large number of applications are received. It is common practice to prepare an assessment grid in the form of a matrix with candidates along one axis and qualifications and special requirements listed along the other. This shows instantly those applicants fulfilling the requirements for the post as well as highlighting those who in no way 'fit the bill'. From the possible candidates a selection of the most likely ones is made and these people are then called for interview.

Note: At this point it is good practice to send a short letter to unsuitable applicants thanking them for their applications and saying that they have not been selected for interview on this occasion. This is often preferable to waiting until the final selection interviews have been held, particularly when there are many applicants for the job and where the time span between the advertisement and the final appointment can be several weeks or months.

Interviewing

The purposes of an interview are as follows:

- to find out what sort of person the applicant is
- to check the factual details supplied on the application form
- to fill any gaps in the information supplied
- to supply the candidate with information about the job
- to enable the candidate to ask questions about the job
- to compare the applicant with the personnel specification for the job and assess the applicant's suitability for the position
- to select the best person for the job

Remember that an interview is a two-way activity and both parties need to be prepared.

The organisation's preparations

Interviewing is a costly and time-consuming operation, and organisations will try to ensure that everything is done to assist the selection of the right candidate for the job. Points of detail will include the following:

Notifying applicants – candidates should be informed of the date, time and place of the interview well in advance. They should also be supplied with adequate directions, and be given a name and telephone extension number to contact if they require further information or find that they are unable to keep the appointment and wish to try to arrange an alternative one.

Timing appointments – appointments should be arranged at convenient times, with due consideration given to travelling. Sufficient time should be allowed between interviews so that the interviewer(s) can make notes on the person just interviewed and prepare for the next candidate.

Notifying reception – candidates should be welcomed on arrival and made to feel that they are expected.

The waiting area – this should be attractive, comfortable, well lit and airy, with ample reading material provided. Tea or coffee should be offered where candidates are expected to wait for any length of time.

Interview room – this should be quiet and offer a relaxed atmosphere. Consideration should be given to the seating arrangements and chairs should all be of the same height. It is also important that candidates should not be expected to face into the sun or other light. There should be no interruptions (telephone calls, visitors) during the interview.

Briefing – where a panel interview is to be conducted interviewers should be well briefed in

CURRICULUM VITAE

Personal Details

Name _____

Address _____

_____

Telephone No _____

Age _____ Date of birth _____

Educational Background

Secondary School attended _____
(with dates)
_____

_____

Further education details _____
(with dates)
_____

_____

Qualifications

Subjects	Examining Body	Grade	Date

(include examinations taken but indicate if results are awaited)

Relevant Business Experience (if any)

_____

_____

Hobbies and interests

_____

_____

Referees (Name, address and tel no)

1. _____   2. _____

   _____   _____

Fig 19 Curriculum vitae

advance and have prearranged times/points for questions.

The candidate's preparations

Candidates have only one opportunity to create a favourable impression and present the appropriate image. Attention should be given to the following:

Time – make sure that you allow ample time to arrive at the building and prepare for the interview. Allow, too, for unexpected problems or delays.

Directions – be sure that you know precisely where to go and how to get there. It is advisable to have a practice run if time and distance permit.

Homework – see that you have done any possible 'homework'. It is useful to do any reading or research about the organisation which might supply useful background information.

Appearance and dress – give careful consideration to general appearance: first impressions tend to be lasting! Aim to look smart and businesslike and avoid extremes of dress.

Avoid clutter – do not burden yourself with extra bags, cases, coats and umbrellas. If you have taken such things with you, leave them in the waiting area when you go in for the interview.

Try to relax – it is natural to feel nervous, but try to relax and gain composure before going into the interview. Deep, slow breathing can be helpful. Try not to get too involved in conversation with other candidates. Keep any conversation general in nature. Never discuss the job. You may gain wrong impressions and may unwittingly reveal your own strengths and weaknesses to your fellow candidates which could be to their advantage and your own detriment.

Prepare any questions you may wish to ask – where you have a definite question to ask do not let the opportunity slip by. Have your questions ready and do not be afraid to ask them when the occasion arises.

Testing

Testing in the course of an interview is usually kept to a minimum. Where it is known that candidates will be expected to undergo a test, notification should be given in the letter outlining the date and time of interview. The purpose of testing is usually to provide candidates with an opportunity to demonstrate a particular skill (eg shorthand or the opera-

tion of a machine) and to check that the standard of performance is in keeping with that indicated in the application form and required by the job.

Arrangements for testing should be such that candidates are not subjected to undue stress. All necessary materials required should be provided, instructions should be given clearly and the test should have been validated in advance to ensure that it is capable of completion. The applicant is unfamiliar with the organisation and is likely to be nervous, and should be assured that this will be taken into account and that it is simply potential which is being assessed. It is usual to supplement any practical test with theoretical questions during the interview.

Medical examinations

Some organisations require successful candidates to undergo a medical examination before being formally appointed. Once again notification of any arrangements should be given to candidates in advance.

Assessment

Most interviewers create a set of criteria for interviewing prospective employees, with special emphasis on essential skills required for the job, desirable skills and areas of knowledge. It is important to distinguish between 'skills' and 'knowledge'. 'Skills' are what the interviewee is expected to demonstrate at the interview while 'knowledge' is something which may be developed in the course of time.

Assessment forms

During the course of an interview the interviewer(s) may complete assessment sheets (Fig 20) for the candidates. These assessments are sometimes referred to as 'quality ratings' and operated on a grading structure. This may be numerical (say 1 – 6) or alphabetical (say A – F), with standards allocated for example as excellent, very good, average, fair and unsatisfactory. The purpose of completing assessment forms is to rate qualities which are brought out during the interview. Different forms would be prepared for other posts where different qualities need to be assessed. Obviously such a technique is open to criticism and cannot be abso-

POST	DEPARTMENT
NAME OF APPLICANT	DATE
NAME OF INTERVIEWER	

Details	Remarks	Grading
Age Educational background suitability Educational qualifications Training Skill qualifications Language communication skills Present post (if appropriate) Present job title Present job content Any special experience Present salary Previous general experience		
Suitability for the department Appearance Personality Self-confidence Courtesy/manners Voice Facial expressions Image		
Suitability for the job Understanding/comprehension Speech Fluency		

Fig 20 Interview assessment sheet

lutely accurate because it is bound to be subjective. However, it can be useful particularly where applicants are interviewed by a panel rather than an individual.

Testimonials

A testimonial is a general document from a private individual or business source, testifying to the character, integrity and general competence of an individual. It used to be standard practice for such a document to be given to an employee on leaving an organisation so that it could be produced later if required or considered necessary. It would usually be addressed 'to whom it may concern'. Being an impersonal document it would normally, if considered relevant, need to be followed up by a specific letter or telephone call to the author.

References

Nowadays it is more likely that candidates would be required to supply the names of referees. This ensures that the reference is up to date. Referees will sometimes be provided with background information on the organisation and sufficient job details to enable them to supply appropriate references.

Some organisations prefer to contact these ref-

Details	Remarks	Grading
Suitability for the job (cont) Interest Knowledge of the organisation Relevance of questions asked Attitude to training Knowledge of current affairs Reason for applying for the post		
Special requirements Unsocial hours Occasional overtime Necessity for travel Domestic commitments Travelling distance from home availability of transport		
Other information		
Key for grading A Excellent B Very good C Good D Fair E Poor F Very poor		

Fig 20 (cont'd)

erees prior to the interview, while others make the appointment conditional on the receipt of satisfactory references. It is not uncommon these days for organisations to contact referees by telephone. This can save time and may also reveal much more valuable information than would be gained from a letter.

Letter of appointment

Once the most suitable candidate has been selected, an offer of appointment may be made verbally at the end of the interview or in writing later. Where the offer is made verbally and accepted in the same manner it should be followed up promptly by a letter of confirmation, incorporating the terms and conditions of employment or enclosing an actual contract of employment.

An employer has a duty under the Employment Protection (Consolidation) Act 1978 to issue each employee who works for more than 16 hours a week with a written statement about his main terms of employment. This should be a personal copy which the employee can keep and it should be issued within 13 weeks of starting work. It should include the following information:
- name and address of employer
- name of employee and location of his employment

- job title
- starting date
- salary scale or rate of pay and intervals at which payment is made, including incremental date
- working hours
- details of entitlement to paid annual holidays
- details of entitlement to paid sick leave
- details of rights in relation to pensions and pension schemes
- notes on disciplinary rules with reference to some other document (eg Staff Handbook) which provides full details
- a note of person, by name or job title, to whom grievances or complaints should be addressed
- a note explaining the steps in the employer's disciplinary and grievance procedure
- the terms of notice required by both parties
- reference to any specific points made at interview

Confirmation of acceptance of the appointment in accordance with the terms outlined should be received in writing from the new employee (sometimes this may take the form of a signed copy of the conditions of service). At this point the new employee may also be sent any company literature not given at the interview, together with any other relevant literature and material relating to fringe benefits and general conditions of service.

Unsuccessful applicants

Once the final selection has been made and confirmed, unsuccessful candidates should be informed at the earliest opportunity. Prompt and courteous notification can only be good for an organisation's public image. Applicants not shortlisted may have been informed earlier: see 'Shortlisting'.

Documentation for the new employee

When a new member of staff is appointed, a personnel file will be opened providing a detailed profile of the individual for the duration of their employment with the organisation. This file will be kept by the Personnel Department and will contain the following:

1 The new member's letter of application and/or application form or curriculum vitae
2 Any references.
3 The interview assessment form (if one was used).

4 Details of any test undertaken and the results/assessments.
5 A copy of the contract and letter of appointment if relevant.
6 A letter confirming acceptance.
7 A copy of the job description (Fig 21).
8 A personnel record card for use during the period of employment. (Fig 22).

Thereafter all documentation relating to this new member of staff will be added to the personnel file and so made easily available for reference purposes.

Job descriptions

A job description is an outline of the duties required of an individual employee. It should form the basis of all future dealings with the person appointed to that job. This document is not for all time; it should be revised at regular intervals, probably following an appraisal interview. (**Note:** An appraisal interview is a periodic review of an employee's progress and performance in a job. It is an opportunity to discuss any work problems, identify any deficiencies, assess potential and consider an employee's ambitions for the future. See also later in this unit.)

In the recruitment stages its purpose is to provide a broad statement as to what a particular job involves, and a basis on which to recruit the best candidate for the job.

A job description should include the following:

1 The job title.
2 The aim or function of the job, ie what objectives the person is expected to achieve through the performance of given duties.
3 To whom the employee is responsible (ie the immediate superior), the job title and where it fits into the hierarchical structure (see Unit 1).
4 For whom the employee is responsible, ie person or persons answerable to them and whose work they must supervise.
5 A broad statement of the duties to be undertaken and an indication of what constitutes a satisfactory standard of performance.
6 Any special conditions, specific information or limitations which apply to the job and which the employee should be aware of. (These would apply to things like decision-making and financial responsibilities.)

```
                    JOB DESCRIPTION

Title               Junior Secretary

Department          Sales (18 staff)

Location            Regional Office

Responsible to      Sales Manager

Job summary         Shorthand, typing and general office duties

Essential education 4 GCSEs, including English language
                    Minimum 80 wpm shorthand
                    Intermediate typewriting

Hours of work       0930 - 1730 hours   Mon to Fri

Promotion prospects Senior Secretary/Personal Secretary
```

Duties and responsibilities

1   To take and transcribe dictation from Sales Department
    personnel, including detailed sales report material of a
    confidential nature

2   To maintain appropriate files and records

3   To undertake essential photocopying for superiors

4   To prepare outgoing mail for despatch

5   To answer telephone calls and answer general enquiries
    or reroute as required to appropriate personnel

6   To receive personnel from Head Office

7   To liaise with Travel Department in preparing travel
    arrangements and essential documentation for sales
    personnel

8   To deputise at meetings for the Sales Manager's
    secretary if and when requested to do so

9   To generally assist the Sales Manager's secretary at
    peak work periods

Fig 21 Job description

Surname	Forenames	Date of birth	Nationality	Name change	Sex
Address		Change of address			
Tel no		Tel no			
Education		Dates	Qualifications		
Date interviewed		Nat Insurance no		Record of illness	
Job offered	Job accepted	Bank account no			
Department/section		Union membership			
Occupation		Disablement reg no			
Further training details		Appraisal record		Transfer of employment Date Reason	
				Termination of employment Date Reason	
Employee number	Surname	Initials	Date of birth	Present post	Grade

Fig 22 Personnel record card

There is no set pattern for setting out a job description. Some begin with duties and responsibilities in general and then go on to list specific tasks. Others begin with an analysis of the individual's function within the organisation. For example, a secretary's job description may be closely linked to the manager's job description and mode of operation.

Taking up a new appointment

Whether you are starting your first job or moving from one job to another, the first few weeks or months will be a period of settling in both for you and your new colleagues. In a small firm the process will most probably be simply 'allowed to happen' with little or no formal procedure to help it on its way. Existing staff will be expected to be supportive and to answer whatever queries you may have and 'show you the ropes'; you will keep your eyes and ears open and 'get the feel of the situation'.

Induction

In a larger organisation, however, you may take part in an induction programme, most likely together with others who have been newly or recently appointed. Induction is the process by which new employees are introduced more formally into an organisation and given an insight into the organisation's policies and practices as well as an idea of where their jobs will fit into the overall scheme. It is also an exercise in ensuring good morale and stimulating general interest. Conditions of employment, salary, pensions, welfare, recreational facilities and so on are often included on the agenda, and on completion of the programme staff handbooks are often issued which reiterate all the information given during the induction sessions.

How are induction programmes organised?

This will vary considerably. Some may be relatively short, informal affairs, consisting perhaps of a morning or day set aside near the beginning of a period of employment when the Personnel and/or Training Officer will formally welcome new employees and provide them with all the necessary information. During this time employees may, in addition, be given a guided tour and introduced to

other members of staff. This programme may be scheduled after a few weeks rather than immediately, as new staff are initially more concerned with their immediate surroundings and their precise duties. It is usual practice to try to put on a programme for several people at once, so an organisation may wait till a few appointments have been made. This also has benefits for new personnel, as they will have the opportunity of meeting other new employees.

Alternatively some organisations may arrange an elaborate induction programme extending over several days or even weeks. This type of programme will not, of course, be continuous but will have set aside for it say a particular afternoon over a number of weeks. Where longer programmes are designed it is likely that the organisation will be a larger one and that it has an active recruitment programme and ample resources. The content of such a programme will be likely to include the following:

- a welcome by the Managing Director
- background information relating to the organisation as a whole and the nature of its business, possibly even supported by a film or slide presentation
- a tour of the works where appropriate
- a breakdown of the organisation, with talks given by senior personnel on different aspects of work and procedures
- full details on aspects relating to employment, eg salary, contracts of employment, benefits, sickness procedures, promotion policy, training and welfare services
- an introduction to the social side, eg staff facilities, recreational activities
- a talk, possibly accompanied by a film, on safety matters
- the inclusion of some form of social activity, eg a luncheon or cheese and wine party, where new employees have an opportunity to meet others and generally circulate in a less formal atmosphere
- the issue of staff handbooks

Any general programme will then be followed by specific sessions on the nature of the work which new employees are expected to undertake, together with any necessary preliminary training.

Thus induction may be very minor aspect organised on an *ad hoc* basis, or a highly structured activity organised by the Training Department and viewed with the utmost seriousness.

Training

Once a new member of staff has been appointed, the personnel interest does not stop there. Another very important function of personnel work is the analysis of training needs within an organisation and the consequent setting up of appropriate training programmes. It is only when an organisation has a properly trained workforce that it will be in a position to achieve its goals and meet the challenges imposed from outside in terms of competition and response to change. Also adequate training will be essential to the job satisfaction and motivation of individual workers. This sort of approach to training will be routine, but sometimes it is necessary to set up training courses in response to particular needs as they arise. The following are some likely examples:

- the installation of new equipment and systems
- a change in working methods, perhaps following an Organisation and Methods (O & M) investigation
- the introduction of a new product and the consequent need to revise strategies, eg marketing plans
- an attempt to improve performance generally
- an increase in staff turnover
- promotion or transfer of existing staff
- an increase in accident figures.

Any of these instances would be likely to raise the question of training and how it should be carried out.

What sort of training is available?

Different methods of training exist, and will depend upon the employee's needs, the demands of the job, the availability of suitable programmes and the resources at an organisation's disposal – financial and otherwise. Broadly speaking training may be undertaken in two main ways: on the job and off the job.

On the job

On-the-job training is given during normal work. Employees receive instruction in the actual procedures to be undertaken, using any necessary equipment in the actual environment in which they will ultimately operate. This method has the advan-
tages of being less costly and more job specific, but can be disadvantageous in that the instructor (possibly a supervisor or other worker) may not be skilled in teaching techniques, might be resentful of the encroachment into other duties, and may pass on bad habits and faulty practices. Also the situation may be stressful because the time taken to give instruction may impinge on normal work time and the normal work activities may cause distraction. These disadvantages can be alleviated to a certain extent by using external trainers (often the case for word processing training), who are paid for their services and allocated the necessary time allowance to complete the job satisfactorily.

On-the-job training can also be undertaken within an organisation's own training school with both in-company and external tuition.

Off the job

Off-the-job training takes place away from the normal working environment, usually at a college or training school (company or other), and on either a full-time or a part-time basis, depending to a large extent on the nature of the training. The advantage is that the training is provided by specialists who should have the time and patience to ensure that each stage of the training is satisfactorily completed before progressing to the next; there is no conflict of loyalties between the job of work and the training responsibilities. However, such training will be more costly and is less likely to be job or machine specific – hence the possibility of transfer of learning difficulties. Also it may be more difficult to monitor progress with any degree of satisfaction or to gauge an employee's reactions to the training.

Devising a training programme

Whether the programme is being developed within an organisation or by some outside agency, certain fundamental points will be considered in its design and implementation and certain questions will need to be answered:

- What sort of training is required?
- How many people will be on the course?
- How long will the course last?
- What will be the course content?
- How will it be arranged – in what order will topics be presented?

- How much will it cost and how much can be allowed?
- What training methods can be used?
- How will the programme be staffed?
- How will it be advertised, if at all?
- How will course members be selected?
- What records will need to be kept?
- How will progress be monitored?
- How will performance be assessed?
- What sort of feedback will be sought?

The need for validation and evaluation

Whatever form training takes it is essential that it is properly **validated**, ie looked at with a view to its success in achieving its aims, and **evaluated**, ie assessed as to whether the new knowledge, skills and attitudes acquired by the trainees are of financial benefit (cost effective), to the organisation. These factors, particularly the latter, can be very difficult to assess, certainly in the short term.

At the conclusion of certain courses, performance can to some extent be measured by results in a test or examination or by the comments made by tutors and assessors. However, in other types of course, for example at supervisor or management level, it can be difficult to determine whether improvement has occurred as a direct result of the course or simply because the course member is now older and wiser! Whatever the training offered, it will be desirable to attempt to monitor results in some way and to receive feedback on the programme with a view to making improvements or implementing changes next time round.

Appraisal

What is meant by 'appraisal'? It is the assessment of an employee's performance in the job. It is based not purely on productivity but on the quality of the work, the co-operativeness of the employee and the degree of dependability shown. When appraising office workers, the term 'merit rating' is often used and appraisal takes the form of a periodic assessment of how the employee is doing in the job. It is a subjective exercise whereby an employee can be assessed for a pay rise or for transfer or promotion or even for some form of training. Therefore it is useful from the viewpoints of both employer and

employee. Such an exercise can help the employer reach decisions about an individual's prospects or training needs and help establish where and how well he or she fits in. The employee is given some knowledge of how he or she is faring in the job, the opportunity to discuss work with superiors, and possibly the motivation to do better in the pay and promotion stakes.

How is appraisal carried out?

There are many ways in which appraisal or merit rating exercises can be carried out, but generally they will fall somewhere into the following four patterns:

Ranking – where a manager simply ranks subordinates in order of merit. This may work reasonably well with small numbers but becomes increasingly difficult with larger staff numbers. The method may be satisfactory in terms of allocating work and deciding pay but will do little to identify training needs or improve motivation.

Grading – where employees are placed in predetermined merit categories, usually about five in number. A typical distribution would be:

Poor 10%	Below average 20%
Average 40%	Above average 20%
Exceptional 10%	

However, like ranking this technique does little to distinguish between the above average and average categories.

The rating scale – this is the most common technique and consists of a list of personal characteristics which would then be rated on a five-point scale. The main problems can be the reluctance of managers and supervisors to give extreme ratings (they prefer to stick to the middle range), the difficulty in determining standards and the definition of what is meant precisely by the different characteristics specified. Also it can be difficult not to be influenced by a particularly obvious strength or weakness and by recent actions rather than overall behaviour.

The open-ended method – this is the most recent technique, and arises out of dissatisfaction with the other methods. The general pattern here is for a manager or supervisor to write a general report on the work of a subordinate over the year, highlighting strengths, weaknesses, promotional prospects and training needs, and suggesting ways in which performance could be improved. Some organisations require subordinates to prepare their own version at the same time, and the documents would then be exchanged prior to an appraisal interview.

The publication of appraisals

There is little argument as to the desirability of having appraisals or merit rating exercises, and despite criticisms to the effect that many such exercises can degenerate into form-filling routines, it is generally felt that subordinates can only benefit from having their work reviewed annually and having their efforts formally recognised. However, there is considerable controversy over the question of whether or not employees should be told of their ratings. The following provides a breakdown of the arguments for and against publication:

For
1 Employees have the right to learn of their progress.
2 Secret reports are bad for morale.
3 Only when faults are made known do employees have the opportunity to improve themselves.

Against
1 It can lead to arguments and bad feeling with employees.
2 It can only assist management.
3 It can dishearten the average employee.

Like any such scheme there will be those in favour and those against, and it may be wise for management to try to strike a compromise in which only exceptional reports (ie very good or very bad) are commented upon, while the others are simply recorded.

Advantages of appraisal

1 It recognises workers who show above-average ability.
2 It compensates for some of the disadvantages of job grading. Several staff may occupy the same grade after an analysis of the actual work involved in respect of qualifications needed, skill required, degree of difficulty and responsibilities incurred, but no allowance may have been made for the personal attributes and qualities brought to the job by the individual.

3 Employees know where they stand and can do something about weaknesses.
4 It makes promotion exercises easier and fairer.
5 It encourages managers and supervisors to take a more subjective view where individual reports are required.
6 It motivates employees to do their best.

Disadvantages

1 It cannot rule out favouritism.
2 It is difficult to retain objectivity.
3 There is no way of validating its effectiveness.
4 No precise units of measurement can be applied to something like 'merit'.
5 There is difficulty in assessing personal qualities.
6 Where unpublished, ratings may act as a disincentive to employees.
7 There is always a likelihood of recent events colouring assessments.

Finally it is important to note that the primary purpose of personnel work in any organisation, large or small, is to secure, as far as is practicable, a working environment conducive to the maintenance of staff morale and consequently staff commitment to the enterprise in the achievement of its overall aims or objectives. A workforce which feels that the organisation cares about the aspirations of individual workers will certainly tend to be efficient and more effective.

Data protection legislation

Any section on personnel matters would be incomplete without reference to the safeguarding of personal information stored on computer. Under the **Data Protection Act 1984**, which became fully enforceable in November 1987, employers holding computerised data, including personnel records, need to register as '**data users**'.

Employees ('data subjects') have a statutory right to access all computerised information held on them and may claim compensation for damage and distress if the information is found to be inaccurate. It should be noted that manual records are not covered by the Act provided any reference to the records is for purely factual information.

Data users are supervised by the Data Protection Registrar and they are required to disclose the nature of data held, why it is held, how and from whom it has been obtained and to whom it will be disclosed.

There are eight principles, which together form a standard against which the Registrar will seek to ensure compliance and these are as follows:

1 'The information contained in the personal data shall be obtained and the personal data shall be processed fairly and lawfully.'

2 Personal data 'shall be held only for one or more specified and lawful purposes.'

3 Disclosure shall not be 'in any manner incompatible with that purpose or with those purposes' for which the personal data is held.

4 Personal data held shall be 'adequate, relevant and not excessive' to the purpose or purposes.

5 Personal data held shall be 'accurate, and where necessary, kept up to date.'

6 Personal data shall 'not be kept for longer than necessary.'

7 'An individual shall be entitled:
   a at reasonable intervals and without undue delay or expense:
   i to be informed by any data user whether he holds personal information of which that individual is the subject; and
   ii to access any such data held by a data user; and
   b where appropriate, to have data corrected or erased.'

8 Appropriate security measures shall be taken against 'unauthorised access to, alteration, disclosure or destruction of personal data and against accidental loss or destruction.'

1 Why is it important to select good staff?
2 What are common sources of recruitment for office staff?
3 What are the main points to be included in a job advertisement?
4 What are the important things to remember when completing application forms?
5 What is a curriculum vitae?
6 What is the purpose of an interview?
7 What sorts of preparations are likely to have been made by the firm conducting the interview?
8 What is a reference?
9 What sorts of things should be included in a letter of appointment?

10 What is a job description, and what should it include?
11 What is meant by 'induction'?
12 What do you understand by 'on-the-job' training?
13 What is meant by 'appraisal'?
14 What are the advantages of appraisal:
   a to employers
   b to employees?
15 What piece of legislation deals with safeguarding interests in respect of personal information held on computer?

Personal activities

1 Prepare your own curriculum vitae. Try either to type a very good copy or, better still, if you have access to a word processor, place it on disk.

2 Compose suitable letters to accompany your CV:
   a for one of the positions in your collection of advertisements
   b to an organisation of your own choice as an unsolicited enquiry.

3 Open a job file with the advertisements you have been collecting as recommended in Unit 2. Devise a system of classification for the different advertisements you have collected, eg according to job title, qualifications required, type of organisation, age range stipulated, or according to salary – it's up to you to choose!
Paste the advertisements on to plain paper, leaving ample space around them for your own notes and comments. Compare the style used, the requirements specified, the modes of application sought (eg application form, CV, letter, telephone).
Note: You will need to consult this information to tasks in Unit 9.

Group activity

Select an advertisement which appeals to the members of your group. Discuss the following, making notes as appropriate:

- How you would dress for an interview if granted one
- The sort of questions you might expect to be asked at interview and why they might be asked
- The sort of questions you would ask and why

Situation-based activity

1 Imagine that you have just read the following advertisement in your evening paper.

Naturana Health Products

require a

Junior Secretary

for their expanding Sales Department based in pleasant offices in the city centre.

Good standard of general education essential, together with appropriate secretarial skills. This post would be ideal for a suitably qualified school or college leaver.

Holiday arrangements honoured. Salary negotiable. LVs.

For further details and an application form contact Miss Hanson, Personnel Department, Lord Street, Anycity.

You send for further details as requested – write a suitable letter – and receive the following information together with an application form.

Details accompanying the application form
Naturana Health Products is a fourishing company engaged in the preparation and distribution of health foods and associated products. It has four branch offices in the United Kingdom, one in France and one in Germany. Its manufacturing outlet is in the Midlands.

The operation started as a one-man (one-woman actually!) business in the early 1960s and such was its early success that a partnership was soon formed, which was later to develop into a limited liability company. In 1978 the company went public and has been going from strength to strength ever since.

The company is progressive in its thinking and working conditions are excellent.

Job description

Title	Junior Secretary
Department	Sales
Immediate superior	Personal Assistant ot the Sales Manager
Responsible to	Sales Manager
Authority over	Two departmental typists, one clerical assistant and one officer junior
Job function	To perform such secretarial duties as outlined by the

Sales Manager or his Personal Assistant, consistent with the efficient operation of the Sales Department of this branch of the company, and oversee the general support work of junior staff as and when considered necessary

Promotion prospects	Senior secretary within the company secretarial structure
Working hours	A 38-hour week. Flexitime in operation

Specific duties/responsibilities
1 To receive dictation from the Sales Manager or his Personal Assistant and transcribe accordingly.
2 To attend meetings in the absence of the Personal Assistant.
3 To prepare non-confidential mail for distribution within the department: to ensure that all outgoing mail is ready for dispatch at the end of the day.
4 To maintain an efficient filing system.
5 To receive incoming telephone calls and take messages as necessary.
6 To supervise and check the work of junior staff as necessary.

2 For this series of tasks assume that you work in the Personnel Department of Naturana Health Products.
   a Draft an advertisement for a receptionist. This advertisement would appear in the local evening paper.
   b Prepare a suitable job description for this Receptionist.
   c Draft an assessment grid which might be used for shortlisting candidates for the position of Receptionist.
   d Jayne Briggs is one of the candidates shortlisted for the Receptionist's post. Write to Jayne asking her to attend for interview on an appropriate date two weeks from now.
   e Compose a letter to be sent to Jayne's referees.
   f Devise a checklist which can be used by you and the Personnel Department in preparing to interview the *six* candidates you have shortlisted.
   Note: Each candidate will be expected to undergo a telephone test.
   g Devise a suitable assessment form to be used by the interview panel in conducting these interviews.

h Compose a letter offering the position to Jayne Briggs.

3 Assume that you are once again working for Miller & Dobson plc referred to in the previous units. As a practising secretary within the company you have been asked to contribute to the induction programme arranged for new office staff. You have been specifically asked to talk about your own job as secretary (select the department of your choice from Fig 12) and about the training you have undertaken since joining the company.

    a Prepare notes on the content of your talk under the following headings:

      i the work of my department
      ii where I fit in
      iii details of my work
      iv my personal training programme at the local college of further education and in the company

    b Imagine that you are approached shortly after the induction programme by one of the newly appointed secretaries. During the induction session she did not fully understand the merit rating system used in Miller & Dobson and feels worried about it. Explain to her in simple terms. what is involved and what you think is good about such a system.

4

Communicating effectively

Aim of the unit

The unit emphasises the importance of effective communication within an organisation and with the outside world. It identifies the different media available, examines recent developments in data and telecommunications and highlights the secretary's role.

Specific objectives

At the end of this unit you should be able to:
1　Identify the different communication media available.
2　Select the most appropriate communication method to use in a given circumstance.
3　Recognise common barriers to effective communication.
4　Identify factors which influence the selection of communication media.
5　Write suitable business letters.
6　Compose memoranda.
7　Prepare reports.
8　Compile written messages.
9　Design a formal invitation
10　Reply positively and negatively to formal invitations.
11　Prepare a notice for a noticeboard.
12　Write an article for a house journal.
13　Prepare messages for transmission by telex.
14　Provide guidance on the use of the telephone.
15　Devise a message for a telephone answering machine.
16　Compare and contrast different methods of communication.
17　State the advantages and disadvantages of different methods of communication.

18　Outline recent developments in telephone systems and services.
19　Explain the operation of electronic mail.
20　Outline the principal Post Office mail services and those provided by independent couriers.

What is communication?

Communication takes place between individuals and can be said to be the conveying of ideas from the mind of one person to the mind of another. Effective communication is essential to life itself and imperative if businesses are to prosper and survive in a competitive environment. Within organisations communication of information is what the work of offices is all about and a variety of communication media is required for both internal and external purposes.

At a personal level

To communicate well you need to learn and develop the following skills and competences:

- clear thinking
- clear speech
- resisting the desire to speak on impulse
- intelligent listening
- ensuring that you are being understood
- recognition of barriers to effective communication (*see* below)
- selection of the appropriate media (*see* below)
- logic
- consistency
- timing
- choosing appropriate words
- obtaining feedback
- writing clearly and concisely

- appreciation of the benefits of technology
- understanding the operation of appropriate technological support systems.

Barriers to effective communication

Any form of communication will fail to be effective if there is any form of barrier between the person sending the communication and the person or persons receiving it, irrespective of the particular means used. For example, if an envelope is inadequately addressed a letter may fail to reach its destination or if the handwriting is illegible it may fail to be accurately deciphered. Similarly, where an audience cannot hear a speaker or where there is interference in a telecommunication link the communication will fail.

Other factors which act as barriers include:

- unfamiliar accents
- unaccustomed vocabulary, eg too technical
- distracting physical mannerisms (body language)
- previous experiences
- educational and cultural backgrounds
- pre-judging an issue
- resistance to change to the extent that listeners hear only what they want to hear
- stereotyping, ie giving someone a label before they have been heard
- putting two and two together and making five.

Any of these factors can seriously affect the likelihood of successful communication taking place and individuals need to be aware of possible pitfalls in preparing any form of communication and in selecting the most suitable media to use.

Factors influencing the choice of media

There are many alternatives to choose from, but essentially it will be a matter of deciding whether to use some form of oral communication or whether to write. There are, however, many other possibilities which can also be used, as shown in Fig 23 which provides a breakdown of the types of media commonly found in business today.

The first factor to consider in deciding which method to use will be to reduce the need for communication to basic human terms by considering *'who needs to ask what of whom?'*

It will then be necessary to take account of the following:

- degree of urgency
- whether for internal or external purposes
- organisational structure if internal
- distance
- time of day
- the need for accuracy
- the importance of a written record
- legal requirement – must it be in writing?
- legal evidence at a future date
- confidentiality
- security
- credibility
- complexity of the material
- legibility
- choice of media available
- level of technology available to both sender and receiver
- impression it is desired to create
- status of the recipient
- nature of the message, eg good news or bad news
- consideration for the feelings of the recipient
- protocol
- convenience
- speed
- cost

These may seem like a lot of things to bear in mind but due consideration to such points will help ensure effectiveness.

Written communication

As can be seen from Fig 23, written communication can take many forms and will range from the informal note made to pass on a message to a colleague to the formal report prepared for submission to shareholders and perhaps publication in the press. It will also include the accurate completion of *proforma* letters and a vast array of business documentation necessary for the completion of a business transaction.

Written communication has the following advantages and disadvantages:

Advantages

- Written record for future reference
- In-depth explanation possible

Written		Oral/Aural
Internal	*External*	face to face encounters
memoranda	letters	interviews
notices	invitations	briefing sessions
bulletins	circulars	seminars
agendas	estimates	meetings
minutes	quotations	conferences
reports	advertisements	telephone
house	orders	teleconferencing
journals	invoices	intercom
contracts	debit notes	public address systems
manuals	credit notes	radio
handbooks	invoices	
	statements	
	export	
	documents	
	promotional	
	literature	
	press releases	
	articles	
	reports	
	information	
	booklets	
Visual/Physical		**Telecommunication/Technological**
charts		Telex
diagrams		teletext
graphs		teletext (Ceefax/Oracle)
photographs		facsimile transmission
slides		electronic mail
films		voice mail
television		videoconferencing
video		viewdata
overhead projector		local area networks (LANS)
models		wide area networks (WANS)
conveyor belts		cellular radio/telephone
chutes		cable television
messenger/courier services		satellite transmission

Fig 23 Breakdown of principal communication media

- Visual support for complex ideas
- Identical copies can go to different sources
- Back-up or confirmation of oral communication
- Legal foundation for contracts or agreements

Disadvantages

- Time consuming in terms of production
- Difficulties of interpretation
- Can be expensive in preparation
- No instant feedback possible
- No scope for modification once sent
- Time gap between originating ideas and the response to them

House styles

Organisations all have their own house style for written communications and it is important that you adopt that style and quickly become accustomed to using the preferred layouts and conventions. As far as layouts are concerned much will depend on the design of letterheads, memoranda forms and any other *pro formas* used, while the presentation of reports and minutes can be easily ascertained by looking through previous examples in the files.

Business letters

Many types of letter are required to suit a wide

variety of business purposes ranging from those providing information or confirming details of some kind to those making a complaint, offering an apology or conveying thanks. Additionally there are letters required for more specialist purposes such as checking creditworthiness or advertising goods and services, while it should not be overlooked that certain occasions require letters of a personal kind as for example where it is desired to extend congratulations or express sympathy. The writer must always bear in mind the purpose of the letter and the nature of the person to whom it is being written.

Content and style

Like most forms of written English, a good letter requires careful structuring. Basically it needs a beginning to place the message in context and set the scene, a middle to develop the message and an end to state the action taken or required of the recipient.

The style should reflect the tone of the letter and should be chosen with the intention of conveying the message to effect. Remember that a letter is a written record and as such must be carefully worded and logically presented to avoid any misunderstanding or possible ambiguity.

Some basic do's and don'ts

1 *Do* try to be concise, but *don't* be brief to the point of abruptness.
2 *Do* keep content simple but *don't* use cliches, eg use 'Thank you for your letter of . . .' rather than 'We acknowledge receipt of your communication of . . . .'
3 *Do* try to be helpful and positive but *don't* be over-familiar or vague and ineffectual.
4 *Do* try to be relevant in what you write, but *don't* use jargon or officialese.
5 *Do* try to be tactful and courteous and *don't* forget you are writing to another feeling human being.
6 *Do* check spelling and punctuation – *don't* send out letters with uncorrected errors.
7 *Do* remember that the letter provides a written record. *Don't* forget it is a permanent reflection of you and your organisation.

Memoranda

Memoranda, or memos as they are usually called, form a widely used communication channel throughout an organisation, operating in all directions – vertically, horizontally and diagonally. They differ in style and content depending upon the status of the originator and that of the recipient, the content of the message and the degree of urgency attached to it. It may be couched in very formal terms or be of a quite informal and personal nature. Its most important function is that it provides a *written* record for future reference. It will usually be handwritten or typed on a printed form designed to company specifications but usually containing the following:
Heading – 'Memorandum' or 'Inter-office Memorandum' (sometimes the organisation's name may appear above the heading)
To – with a blank space for the addressee
From – with a blank space for the sender's name and/or title
Date – with a blank space left for the date

Reference ⎫ These items are not always
Subject   ⎬ printed on memo forms, but they
Copies to ⎭ can be useful. The subject is sometimes filled in simply at the top of message.

Memo forms tend to be printed on both A4 and A5 paper. They may be set out traditionally across the page, or they may be fully blocked to the left-hand margin.

Memos are usually initialled rather than signed.

Purposes of memoranda

- to convey information, instructions or requirements
- to put forward suggestions or ideas for consideration
- to ask for assistance or co-operation
- to seek information
- to clarify something
- to outline current progress or lack of it
- to make modifications to existing methods or practices
- to confirm oral communication
- to outline policy decisions
- to augment existing oral agreements

Reports

Like memoranda, reports vary in format, style, content and length, depending upon their purpose and the audience. They may be little more than short internal communications (like memoranda) between persons or departments, as for example in reporting on a minor departmental complaint. At the other end of the scale they could extend to very formal documents of hundreds of pages, as for example the report of a Royal Commission. It will be important, therefore, to distinguish clearly the sort of report required and prepare it accordingly.

Where it is of the shorter more informal nature it will normally be broken down into three main component parts:

1 The introduction (background details, a description of the current situation and the reason for the report).
2 The findings (information gathered on the subject).
3 The conclusions (recommendations as to what action ought to be taken).

Note: It may be even less formal in that it may be presented in a memo form under an appropriate subject heading, with such subheadings as are considered necessary.

On the other hand a formal report would be prepared along the following lines:

1 Title page (including the author's name and the name of the person/body commissioning the report, together with the date of presentation).
2 Contents page.
3 Terms of reference.
4 *Modus operandi*: the procedure or method of tackling the investigation.
5 Findings: often sectionalised.
6 Conclusions.
7 Recommendations or suggestions for action.
8 Appendices.
9 Bibliography.

Note: Sometimes a lengthy report includes a synopsis after the contents page.

Report writing style

Reports should always use impersonal constructions, ie 'It was evident' rather than 'I noticed' or 'I observed'. The absence of 'I, we' and 'our, my,' lends objectivity to a report, which should always confine itself to the facts and be devoid of any suggestion of bias, emotion or self-interest. Where it is necessary to supply opinion, as in the conclusions section, it should still be possible to produce these in an informed manner, free from subjective value judgments as far as possible.

Special points for the secretary in relation to the preparation of reports

1 Always be sure that you understand the terms of reference. It is important that you stick to them. The report will be unsatisfactory if you fail to work up to the terms of reference, and similarly if you overstep them. Working to a brief is a very important aspect of many jobs which a secretary will undertake.
2 The tone of the report will also be flavoured by whether you are writing it and submitting it personally or producing it for someone else to submit.
3 Be sure of the time available. It is important to work to any deadline.
4 Ascertain the length of report required. Any word restriction may limit the level of research which it is feasible to pursue.
5 Be sure that you have identified your audience. This will affect the level of language you use and the degree of background information you need to provide.
6 Find out how formal a report is required. It is important to strike the right note of formality.

An example of a short report is given in Fig 24.

Minutes (*see* also Unit 8)

The production and presentation of minutes is an important task in any secretary's work. The minutes must be a true record of what has taken place at a meeting, and be capable of being called upon for future reference. Good minutes are essential to the effective operation of any committee or working party in that they provide a source of precedent and an accurate written record of what has previously been debated and agreed upon. Minutes may be recorded in different ways. Where they are used purely to record decisions reached, the minutes written are 'resolution minutes', but where the outline of discussion prior to a decision is also recorded they are 'narrative minutes'. Sometimes it

REPORT ON OFFICE SAFETY

For the attention of the Managing Director   10 March 19..

A   TERMS OF REFERENCE

On Thursday 23 February, in response to a series of minor accidents in
the offices of Miller & Dobson plc during a three month period, the
Managing Director requested that the Company Safety Officer carry out an
investigation into the nature and cause of these recent hazardous incidents
and make recommendations to improve the safety awareness of office personnel.

B   PROCEDURE

In order to ascertain the precise nature of the accidents and the attitude
of staff towards safety matters generally, the following investigatory
procedures were adopted:

1   The Accident Book was studied and an analysis made of accidents listed.
2   All personnel who had sustained injuries were interviewed.
3   Supervisory staff in the sections concerned were interviewed.
4   Safety questionnaires were sent to all offices within the company to
    obtain information on staff knowledge on safety procedures and attitudes
    to safety generally (see Appendix 1).
5   Current safety procedures were evaluated (see Appendix 2).

C   FINDINGS

1   The nature of accidents

    Accidents fell into three main categories:

    a) Falls
    b) Strains
    c) Electric shocks

2   The extent of injuries

    Injuries were of a minor nature, only two incidents requiring absence
    from work in excess of 3 days.

3   The nature of supervision and training

    Supervision was on the whole adequate given the relatively straightforward
    nature of the work undertaken and the equipment used. However,
    new staff often received no formal training on machine use and operation.

4   Staff knowledge and awareness of safety matters

    a) This varied considerably from an in-depth knowledge to a very
       superficial awareness.
    b) Very few office staff were qualified in the use of first aid.
    c) Some staff were totally unaware of the provisions and staff
       requirements of the Health and Safety at Work Act 1974.
    d) Reference was made to the inadequacy of information on office
       safety contained in the Company Handbook.

Fig 24 A short report

```
     5    Existing safety procedures

          These were felt to be in keeping with the recommendations made during
          the last company safety inspection. The system used to evacuate the
          offices in the event of fire was found to be particularly efficient.
          Observation of several offices and work programmes indicated the need
          for changes in layout and accommodation.

  D    CONCLUSIONS

          The principal conclusions drawn were that the minor office accidents
          which did occur resulted from the individual negligence of office staff,
          that one office in particular (the Accounts Office) was badly laid out
          and somewhat overcrowded, and that responsibility for safety matters rested
          too long in the hands of the same personnel. Office accidents would
          continue to take place unless appropriate avoiding action was taken and
          staff were encouraged to be more safety conscious.

  E    RECOMMENDATIONS

          In order to improve the situation urgent consideration should be given
          to implementing the following:

          1    An immediate update of the Office Safety section in the Company
               Handbook.
          2    A management initiative to encourage office staff to gain proficiency
               in first aid techniques.
          3    The rotation of staff safety representatives on the Safety Committee.
          4    An O & M investigation to look into the safer operation of the
               Accounts Department.


  Signed




  Company Safety Officer
```

Fig 20 A short report (contd)

is usual for a combination of the two to be implemented, perhaps with the addition of details of the persons delegated to act upon decisions reached. These would be described as 'action minutes'.

Style and form

Minutes are always written in the past tense using reported speech, eg 'The Chairman raised the question of . . .', 'The Chairperson asked the Secretary to . . .', 'The Treasurer drew the attention of the meeting to . . . .'.

Layouts vary, although it is usual to begin by stating the type of meeting and where and when it was held, followed by the names or the numbers of those present. Names normally begin with the Chairperson, follow in alphabetical order, and conclude with the Secretary. Sometimes minutes are numbered, and the numbers may even follow on sequentially from one meeting to the next. Numerical referencing can be of great assistance where committees have occasion to refer back frequently to previous meetings and decisions reached.

As with reports, spacing and the use of headings and subheadings will play an important part, and their effective use will greatly facilitate reading and comprehension. The sequence of minutes will follow that outlined in the agenda (*see* Unit 8). It is important to use correct names and designations and to report what has been said accurately. Where a decision is reached the resolution should be worded in verbatim form, eg:

'IT WAS RESOLVED THAT the company should operate a scheme of flexible working hours on a three month trial basis as from 1 February next.'

Bulletins and notices

Bulletins are used to announce forthcoming events, changes in policy and other matters to all interested parties. Bulletins and notices are effective forms of communication in that their very arrival on desks or in pigeonholes heralds the arrival of something important or of relevance, worth reading by all personnel in terms of events to happen or reports on matters of general interest.

Bulletins are often several pages long and can refer to several topics, whereas notices are normally much shorter and refer to one thing.

Either form of communication can be posted on a noticeboard. The important thing to ensure is that noticeboards are accurate and neatly and attractively displayed, and where the same board is used for various sorts of notice they should be arranged under appropriate, well-labelled subheadings. Another vital aspect of maintaining noticeboards is that all obsolete material is removed and logged for a short time in a book in case it is required for reference.

House journals

House journals are really extended bulletins and are usually produced within the company several times a year. They fulfil a twofold purpose in that they provide staff with details and often pictures of past events and successes and a diary of future events, while at the same time providing a useful public relations outlet for distribution to customers and outside agencies, and for display in reception areas. Secretaries often find themselves actively involved in the collection and editing of material for the journal.

Press releases

Press releases are announcements made to the press and other mass media regarding important events of an organisation. They do constitute a form of free publicity but require careful advance preparation if they are to secure maximum impact. There are different categories of release:

a *news* releases – here the time factor is vital
b *features* releases – less urgent and requiring some research
c *general* releases – general summary of a subject, possibly prior to a more detailed article featured later.

Preparation and presentation

This is usually the task of the Public Relations Officer (PRO) if there is one, but secretaries often have their part to play in both the preparation and follow-up activities. It will be important to determine the following:

- the subject – in precise detail
- the audience
- the deadline for copy
- the length of the copy
- supporting materials – drawings, photographs, diagrams

Content and style

The content must be absolutely accurate, and must therefore be proofread and checked prior to submission for publication. The material should be appropriate, logically presented and free of surplus detail. Wording should be clear, precise and economical as paper space is expensive, and it must fit in with the style of the overall publication. Some publications are quite technical while others are quite informal, and these distinctions must be respected at all times.

Desktop publishing (DTP)

In recent years there has been a surge in the sale of DTP software as a major business application for personal computers (PCs). For organisations which prepare a lot of text, particularly of a prestigious nature, desk top publishing (*see* Fig 25) can offer significant benefits.

What is DTP?

Strictly speaking the term 'publishing' is misleading, as what DTP does is improve the design and pre-

Fig 25 Desktop publishing; *Reproduced by kind permission of Aldus PageMaker*

sentation of printed material. It helps remove much of the complexity and specialisation associated with designing documents and producing complicated layouts incorporating artwork. A DTP package can help produce the sort of professional image that many organisations seek for their publications without the need to call on the services of designers, layout artists and typesetters, while eliminating many of the proof and layout stages which lead up to the preparation of what is termed 'camera ready artwork or copy'.

DTP saves time on the many checks and revisions necessary to reach this stage and dispenses with the need to employ many expensive specialists by enabling relatively unskilled personnel to come up with their own layouts using a personal computer.

What components are needed?

Basically, the four requirements are:

- a PC with a hard disk facility (where diagrams and photographs are incorporated into the text too much memory space is taken up to make floppy disks a viable option)
- word processing software
- page make-up software
- a laser printer.

Also, regular users of DTP systems may wish to have additional software to enable them to create or modify illustrations and photographs, while a desktop scanner would enable drawings and photographs to be converted into digitised computer files which can then be stored and manipulated on a PC. Briefly what a scanner does is capture line drawings, photographs and printed text by scanning the image with a light-sensitive detector and converting it into digital 'bits' which are the electronic pulses that computers use to store and represent data. Previously this facility has been very expensive and very much the province of professional printers who have long used scanners to convert photographs to halftones for printing purposes. However the recent arrival of low cost desktop varieties has brought scanners into the realm of small users.

Other additional features would be input devices such as a mouse for controlling the cursor on the screen or a drawing tablet and light pen to make preparation easier. A large screen, providing a full page display would also be a useful feature.

Some uses of DTP

The essence of any aid to communication is its ability to help the originator to get his message across more clearly and effectively. With DTP even complex ideas can quickly be translated onto paper by incorporating diagrams and appropriate illustrative material. Examples of instances when DTP could help improve written communication include the preparation of:

- general reports or those following a consultancy exercise;
- catalogues
- information booklets
- business forms
- instruction manuals
- notices
- advertising and publicity material
- conference and seminar publications
- technical and engineering specifications
- bids, proposals, tenders, and contracts
- market research projects
- training materials (OHP transparencies and slides can usefully be prepared using DTP originals as a basis)

Advantages of DTP

- high quality documents
- reduced production time in comparison with the traditional printing processes
- cheaper than securing the services of designers, layout artists and professional typesetters (however it should be noted that the volume of usage would need to be relatively high to justify the investment and benefit from the consequent savings)
- helps retain in-house confidentiality
- the disk holding DTP documents could be sent to a bureau which handles typesetting, where

contents could be typeset to achieve the very best end product, without the investment in typesetting equipment
- easy to amend layouts as everything which appears on the screen is stored electronically
- late changes and typographical amendments are possible right up to the final storage or print phase.

Disadvantages of DTP

- costly to install initially
- compatability problems in that not all hardware and software will function together
- more than basic computer skills are required of an operator who needs design ability and creativity which not everyone possesses
- specialist staff needed to get the best out of a system
- training required for even casual users.

DTP can produce impressive documents but should not be viewed as the answer to all presentational problems faced by an organisation. Nor is it a substitute for word processing. It is rather something to complement word processing's constantly improving systems. It should be borne in mind that many of the new generation word processors (*see* also Unit 10) have a wide range of specialist features and that DTP, given the cost implications and the need for user training, really comes into its own where there is a substantial need for high quality design work and the production of a high volume of specialist publications.

Distribution procedures for written communication

All organisations will have established systems and procedures for handling written communication and ensuring its efficient collection, internal distribution and outward despatch. Systems and procedures adopted will depend on the size of the organisation, the nature of its business operations and the physical layout of its accommodation.

By way of example the following is a typical step-by-step procedure which might well be adopted by a medium-sized company for handling and distributing incoming mail. Staff involved in opening mail will usually report for work approximately one hour before the office staff.

1 Mail arrives in the Mail Room (it may have been delivered by the Post Office, collected by a messenger or picked up from a locked postbag/box service). It should be noted that some mail will require to be signed for on receipt eg recorded delivery or registered mail.

2 Some form of preliminary sort is usually made, eg separate basic letter mail from other mail like advertising materials, printed matter and packages.

   Note: Regrettably it is now common practice to scrutinise mail for possible letter bombs. This would be done at the central sorting point but where secretaries work for a top executive or influential public figure, they too should take special care with all incoming mail passing through their hands.

3 Separate all personal, private and confidential mail. Whatever the standard procedure regarding the opening of mail, such correspondence should always reach the addressee's desk *unopened*.

4 Open all other mail – usually with the aid of a letter opening machine. In some organisations mail will only be opened when addressed to the company/organisation in general. Specifically addressed mail will go unopened directly to the individual or department concerned.

5 Remove all contents.

6 Check enclosures (a note should be made on relevant letter or any missing enclosures).

7 Attach enclosures to letters (normally with a semi-permanent staple).

8 Enter any remittances (cheques, postal orders etc) in a Remittances Boook which should be signed and checked by someone in authority.

9 Date stamp all incoming correspondence.

10 Make any extra copies necessary or attach appropriate circulation/routing slips.

11 Sort mail into appropriate departments/sections/individuals for distribution.

12 Retain envelopes for a few days in case of queries (if considered important at the time of opening, the envelope should be attached to the rest of the correspondence).

Mail may be distributed departmentally by Mail Room staff or it may be lodged in collection baskets/pigeonholes for collection by departmental staff.

The secretary's role

As a secretary you may find yourself doing all or any of the things mentioned above. In a small organisation you may even have the total responsibility for dealing with incoming mail. However, it is perhaps more likely that you will be involved only with mail for the executive you work for and then you will have the responsibility of ensuring that mail is on the desk when they arrive at work. Then you will take receipt of the mail from the Mail Room and sort it out in rough order of importance. You can also, at this stage, select any files and papers which may be needed to deal with the correspondence.

You should read all incoming mail thoroughly except of course, that marked personal or private and confidential. Some executives will authorise you to open confidential mail, as you will inevitably learn of its contents in the course of your work. A sound knowledge of all business affairs will enable you to perform your work more effectively. You can often take the pressure off your executive by being able to answer routine telephone calls and queries, assess priorities and intercept minor matters at an earlier stage. Very routine correspondence may not even require to be seen by the executive and can be dealt with by you, quite independently.

Internal circulation of mail during the working day

In large organisations it is likely that there will be several collections/distributions of mail at scheduled intervals throughout the day. Also hand-delivered letters, packets and telex messages may arrive on your desk, and it will be your responsibility to ensure that you have a procedure for dealing with such correspondence and that it is given appropriate attention – dealing with it as a priority where necessary. In/Out baskets should always be clearly marked to assist Mail Room personnel and should be checked frequently for new items.

Outgoing mail – the secretary's role

It is important that you as a secretary are totally conversant with the procedure for processing outgoing mail and that you are mindful of the time schedules. It is worthwhile establishing good working relations with the Mail Room personnel, as any secretary for a busy executive is likely to need to take emergency mail to the Mail Room at the last minute on occasions. It is, of course, important to ensure that the majority of mail is signed and sent to the Mail Room for processing in good time. It is bad practice to rely on the goodwill of the mailing staff in dealing with perpetually late mail. This can present a problem for some secretaries, particularly perhaps those operating on a time-sharing basis for several executives. Some may try to short-circuit the system by leaving their mail till the last minute and expecting it all to be treated as urgent. This practice must be discouraged quite firmly as such abuse of the system will ultimately contribute to its failure.

Where a secretary may unavoidably have regular late mail to deal with it will be advisable to have a personal set of letter scales and a supply of postage stamps so that you can process such mail personally after normal hours, when necessary, without troubling the Mailing Department.

General points relating to outgoing mail

1 Efficiency depends on individuals and departments being conversant with the procedures.
2 All mail should be signed in good time.
3 All mail should be placed in appropriate envelopes and appropriately and adequately addressed.
4 Any special instructions relating to posting, eg first class, recorded delivery, air mail, should be given clearly.
5 The Mail Room should be notified in advance of any special bulk mailings or large despatches requiring special attention.
6 Mail should be assembled in the appropriate out baskets or taken to the collection boxes (some large organisations have these situated on all floors to facilitate collection), throughout the day where possible, and in ample time for the last collection of the afternoon.
7 All staff should be aware of the 'deadlines' for collection.
8 In a large organisation, outgoing mail can be a highly mechanised activity.

Mail Room machinery and equipment

Any textbook on office practice or office machinery will provide comprehensive details of the sort of machinery, equipment and accessories you can expect to find assisting procedures in a modern Mailing Department. Briefly this is likely to include the following:

- sorting tables
- letter opening machines
- stapling machines
- date stamping machines
- photocopying equipment
- shredding machines
- delivery trolleys
- collating machines
- joggers
- punches and perforators
- binding machines
- addressing machines
- folding machines
- inserting machines
- sealing machines
- parcel tying machines
- letter and parcel scales
- franking machines

Note: Many of these machines can be linked together to perform a continuous automated process for handling outgoing mail, particularly where an organisation sends out frequent brochures and circulars to customers on a mailing list.

Post Office postal services

A wide range of postal services is available from the Post Office and full details are supplied in the *Royal Mail Guide* which is published annually. Alternatively, useful up-to-date leaflets on the individual services are available from most Post Offices or on application to the Head Postmaster for the district who will also be able to supply details of the current charges in operation.

The following is a list of the principal services with which you will need to be familiar:

- First and second class mail
- Recorded delivery
- Registered mail
- Certificate of posting
- Advice of delivery
- Parcel post
- Datapost
- Freepost
- Business Reply Service
- Poste Restante (To be called for)
- Air mail/overseas mail

Courier services

Any section on communication systems and services would be incomplete without reference to the many courier services which operate to deliver physical office data quickly and safely to local, regional, national and international destinations. Such services include:

- special messenger services including those operated by the Post Office and the independent agencies, often using high speed motor cycles as in the London area
- the Post Office Datapost service
- Securicor and other specialist agencies
- Red Star (a British Rail Service)
- air courier services such as Express Air Ltd, Transworld Couriers and World Courier (UK) Ltd.

All such services have their own conditions and charges which need to be studied carefully in the light of the service required.

Oral communications

Advantages

- direct means of communication
- fast
- two-way
- instant feedback
- allows the participation of all present
- creativity may result from spontaneous reactions

Disadvantages

- lacks the security of the written word
- often no record of what has been said
- can be difficult to control discussion where it involves a lot of people
- spontaneity may result in inferior, ill-considered decisions
- less easy to hold ground when opposed (thinking on one's feet)

Oral communication includes all the methods listed in Fig 23 but falls largely into three categories:

- person to person or face to face
- meeting situation
- over telephone lines

Person-to-person

Person-to-person or face-to-face techniques will be used during interviews of all kinds, in briefing situations, during business discussions and on occasions where requests are made or instructions given. This is effective, particularly in terms of improving personal/public relations, but it can be extremely time consuming. Speaking directly to someone enables an individual to make use of four important facets:

a   choice of words
b   tone of voice
c   facial expression
d   gesticulation.

It is, therefore, usually the easiest way of communicating and conveying exactly the right information, but there is no permanent record and great difficulty in referring to verbal communication at a later date. Also it may be slow and impractical if several people have to be seen and any physical distance is involved.

Meeting

Meetings have the advantage of being a direct method of communication, and can partly solve the time problem in that a group activity can serve to kill several birds with the one stone. Also it permits two-way communication between the originator of the meeting and the group, and most likely horizontal communication within the group itself.

Meetings provide a useful form of oral communication and will be dealt with in detail in Unit 8. It is, however, important that they should not become burdensome, by becoming too many, held too frequently and lasting too long.

Telephone

The telephone may be second best to person-to-person contact, but it can none the less be very effective where used correctly and can take the place of several letters passing between two individuals. It provides immediate feedback and is relatively inexpensive where properly used. In addition, it can be an advantage to be able to conceal emotions which would be revealed by facial expression and gesture.

Switchboard techniques

The switchboard operator is very often the first contact an outsider will have with an organisation. The operator's technique and manner are, therefore, of the utmost importance. Often a secretary, particularly in a small firm, will have to act as temporary operator, and the following are points to remember:

1 Answer promptly saying 'good morning' or 'good afternoon'.
2 Announce the name of the firm or organisation clearly and not so quickly that the caller has to ask for it to be repeated.
3 Where a call is unable to be routed immediately and the caller chooses to 'hold', keep the caller informed as to what is happening by reporting back frequently.
4 If it is within the operator's brief to take a message (often this is not possible in a large organisation where the board is busy and where any messages would be taken at departmental level) be sure that you have a pad and pencil available and proceed in the normal way (*see* 'Message-taking').
5 Be polite and patient at all times.
6 Try to be helpful whenever possible.
7 Cultivate a pleasant, reassuring tone of voice. It is important to inspire confidence in the caller.
8 Be organised. This is particularly necessary where the operator may be required to place a lot of outside calls as well as receive and route incoming ones.
9 Don't let yourself become flustered – keep calm.

Extension techniques

As a secretary you will be one of many extension users, and as such should develop your own technique and observe certain simple rules.

1 Always answer your telephone promptly.
2 Announce yourself by stating either your name or position, the name of the department, or the extension number.
3 If you are in the vicinity of another extension, be prepared to answer the telephone and take a message.
4 Speak clearly and not too quickly.

5 Listen carefully to what the caller has to say – this can save a lot of time!
6 Be prepared to make notes as the call progresses. This can save time when it comes to taking a coherent message.
7 When placing a call, be organised. Have any necessary papers to hand and generally follow the time-saving formula outlined below.
8 Where you may not be able to dial directly, try to assist the switchboard operator by having the correct number ready. You should not expect the switchboard operator to search for a number for you unless it is an emergency.

A word of advice

The telephone forms a very vital part of a secretary's daily work, and it is essential that you are totally conversant with the particular telephone system in the organisation. You may also find that you are required to master a sophisticated electronic telephone system which enables elaborate call switching to take place as well as teleconferencing, ie the connection of numerous extension users simultaneously.

Whatever the telephone arrangements in existence, it is important that the secretary is familiar with its most efficient use. This may also require mastery of a system whereby all the boss's calls are screened prior to switching them through. In some offices there may be more than one instrument on each desk, so adding an extra dimension.

It will be worth your while to acquire informative literature from British Telecom and some of the competing telephone companies which are now on the market, with the purpose of studying the wide range of systems and facilities now available.

A time-saving formula for using the telephone

1 Know who it is you wish to speak to, preferably by name.
2 If that person is not available, try to have an alternative ready.
3 Find out the telephone number (remember this is your job, not the switchboard operator's).
4 Have the department or extension number ready when you are connected to the answering

switchboard (if you do not have these details for a first call, make a note for future reference).

5 Have brief notes prepared on the subject of the call. This will prevent any omissions during the conversation.

6 Have to hand any papers which might be required for reference during the call.

7 When you get through, state who you are and the general nature of your business.

8 Always be prepared to leave a message – sometimes with an answering machine! (This tends to be a daunting experience first time round, but such machines are becoming increasingly used.)

9 Where an immediate contact is unavailable, avoid holding on. Suggest ringing back after an agreed interval.

10 Always have a pad and pencil ready to make notes.

Note: STD (Subscriber Trunk Dialling) call charges vary according to the time of day and day of the week, as well as distance. Less important STD calls should be made during 'off peak' times. Refer to your telephone directory for further details.

Message-taking

Accurate message-taking is important in any organisation. Staff should always be willing to accept messages for their colleagues, and they have a responsibility to ensure that the message is accurate and can be clearly understood by the recipient. Some organisations favour preprinted message forms, whereas others simply utilise scrap paper. The main advantage of the former is that it will be instantly recognisable as a message and may, therefore, receive more prompt attention.

Rules for taking messages

1 Always be ready and prepared to take a message.

2 Make sure that you have elicited sufficient information to formulate an understandable message.

3 Be sure to take the caller's name and address (where appropriate) together with the telephone number and extension (if there is one).

4 Always ensure that messages are dated and timed and that they contain the name of the person taking them. These points may all prove useful later for reference purposes, and will enable the recipient to contact the message-taker for clarification should it prove necessary.

5 Always repeat the message to the caller for confirmation or alteration.

Telephone systems, services and features

Since the liberalisation of telecommunications following the Telecommunications Act 1981 and the formation of British Telecom (BT) as a separate body from the Post Office which now controls mail services only, there have been many changes. The following are the principal ones:

- now two competing telephone networks operate in the UK in the form of BT and Mercury Communications;
- increasing digitisation of the network;
- an increase in the amount and types of equipment available and the emergence of many competing suppliers;
- the choice of different telephone systems and the increasing number of special features available;
- the growth of cellular phones;
- the emergence of two cellular network providers.

Let us now consider these points in a little more detail.

Mercury – is it a realistic alternative to BT?

Mercury Communications is part of the Cable and Wireless Group and was licensed to compete with BT in 1982. While still a relative newcomer when set against BT's long-standing and well-established market, Mercury has put forward an ambitious programme in order to expand business and has based its telephone network on a system of fibre optic cables running alongside railway lines. Its main benefit over BT at present is cost, with Mercury claiming savings of 20 per cent on a telephone bill and even greater savings on local calls. It is also interesting to note that while BT charges by the minute Mercury charges by the second. Mercury also provides a comprehensive itemised bill which can be very helpful to a company in monitoring and managing its telephone system.

Mercury offers three main services for the business and domestic user as well as the Centrex service which is available to customers on the

London network. Each service is slightly different and involves a different cost. The main one is the 2100 service which is available in most areas, needs no special equipment and is geared to large companies.

The 2200 service is geared towards small to medium sized businesses with users requiring what is termed a 'smartbox' – an interface between the telephone system and the public exchange in order to access Mercury lines. This 'smartbox' is, however, an 'intelligent' device so there is no need for the user to make a decision to use the Mercury network nor is there a need for any special code to be applied.

Finally the 2300 service is designed mainly for domestic users who need a Mercury-compatible telephone and are required to press a special M button to route trunk calls onto the Mercury network.

Digitisation

It is important to remember that analogue is the traditional method of transmitting telephone calls. Digital, on the other hand, relies on a binary method of transmission like that used by computers. It is faster, clearer and more reliable than analogue and being based on fibre optics can carry more traffic than the copper cables used for analogue systems. (Two strands of fibre optic cable can handle up to 2000 calls at the same time.)

Currently the UK network still relies on analogue technology although both BT and Mercury are investing large sums of money into digitising their networks. Nevertheless, we are still some way from a fully digitised network and even where an organisation may have opted for and invested in digital equipment there is no guarantee that all the benefits will be automatically secured. For example, where digital equipment is used to make a call to a telephone not served all the way by a digital network, the system will 'default' to analogue standard to complete the call and so benefits will be lost.

Equipment and suppliers

There is more telephone equipment available than ever before and a wider range of suppliers to choose from. Equipment can be bought direct from the manufacturer, particularly in the case of large PABXs (private automatic branch exchange systems),

although most sales are made through dealers and distributors.

The installation of a telephone system is a costly business and a wrong decision can have serious consequences. It is important that companies do their homework, investigate thoroughly, identify their needs and estimate future requirements as accurately as possible. Otherwise ill-advised, short-sighted decision-making can result in a system which is below capacity in terms of the business's growth potential and future needs

Organisations need to explore all avenues, including the pros and cons of renting and leasing, installation and maintenance matters and the competing services offered by different suppliers.

Telephone systems and features

Basically there are two types of telephone system for business use – the key system or the PABX. Key systems are geared more to smaller businesses. They have special handsets, proprietary to the system in use, which carry a range of special function keys as well as 'line keys' (all of which have a light accompaniment to indicate when a line is busy) for the exchange lines available to the system. The handsets are relatively expensive in comparison to the simpler types which come with a PABX.

Private automatic branch exchange systems are generally thought of as switchboards with their own operators, although key systems with a number of outside lines (30 is currently the maximum a key system can support) will also require a designated member of staff to deal with the incoming calls if transfer chaos between extensions is to be avoided.

Where installations have in excess of 60 extensions, PABXs dominate the market. No special handsets are required although it is possible to provide superior versions for staff with special needs, eg instruments used between the secretary and boss for screening calls.

Larger PABX systems, ie those catering for in excess of say 250 extensions, will be computerised and highly programmable with many special options available. Such systems will come under the control of someone like a Telephone System or Services Manager who will be responsible for everything relating to the PABX and its use. The TSM will have a duty to provide the best possible service by identifying the number of lines needed, monitoring extension usage and generally advising on specialist features required and the efficient and effective operation of the system.

As far as features are concerned, a wide range is available and manufacturers struggle to compete with one another. Features tend to have somewhat jargon-based names and it is necessary to master the terminology associated with any particular system used. Unfortunately many of the special features are rarely used in some systems largely due to the problems staff have in recalling the access codes. However, where certain features are used a more effective and efficient service should be provided. Some of the more common features are as follows:

- **abbreviated dialling** particularly useful for frequently used numbers eg international ones, with many digits
- **automatic call distribution (ACD)** ie first come, first served by the first available extension
- **call back** where an extension is busy the caller can replace his receiver and be called back automatically when the extension becomes free
- **call barring** ie restrictions on calls made from certain extensions, eg local calls only may be dialled
- **call forwarding** rerouting to other extensions at selected times
- **call logging** monitoring the cost and nature of telephone usage
- **camp-on busy** the same as call back
- **conference call** a call set up between two or more extension users
- **direct dialling in (DDI)** outside callers can by-pass the switchboard to go direct to designated extensions;
- **distinctive ringing** difference in tone of the ring between internal and external calls
- **extension group hunting** enables the system to search around among designated extensions for a free phone – useful where lots of people will be able to supply the same information, eg in sales or service situations
- **follow-me** call forwarding from one extension to another on a temporary basis
- **last number recall** system automatically redials the last number following the pressing of a code (Note: this does not include abbreviated dialling numbers)
- **LED/LCD displays** upmarket handsets let you see what you have dialled or perhaps the duration

of your call or enable you to receive a brief message on the line display
- **music on hold** synthesised music while you are waiting lets you know that you are still connected
- **night service** reroutes incoming calls to a designated extension outside normal office hours
- **paging** on a PABX this is a separate tannoy system accessible from certain extensions; on a key system it comes through the loudspeaker of all extensions not in use
- **waiting return** on a PABX, calls which have not been answered are returned to the switchboard after a predetermined programmable period of time, so no call is forgotten!

Cellular phones

Mobile phones (*see* Fig 26), whether for use in a car or elsewhere, are growing in popularity. There are three main types:

- **mobile** permanently fitted in cars and occupying the largest segment of the cellular market;
- **hand portable** small, lightweight, battery-operated (so frequent need to re-charge) handsets which can be used anywhere;

Fig 26 A cellular telephone; *Reproduced by kind permission of British Telecom*

- **transportable** hybrid of the previous two (ie can be fitted in the car or carried), a larger, heavier, battery-operated portable telephone (but holds the charge longer as batteries are larger capacity).

All cellular phones, like any other telephone equipment, need to be BABT approved. Cost is based on a monthly charge for air time rental plus a charge per minute dependent on whether the call is made at peak or off peak time. Many special features are available similar to those listed in relation to telephone systems in general. Additionally it is important to note that in car phones there is likely to be 'hands free' speech. Otherwise, according to the Highway Code drivers, should, in the interests of safety, pull off the road to make their calls. Where 'hands free' speech is in operation a small microphone will be fitted to the dash board or sun visor. Some sophisticated systems will also accept voice-activated dialling instructions ensuring totally 'hands free' operation.

Cellnet or Vodafone?

Two rival networks operate in the UK – Cellnet (a joint venture between BT and Securicor) and Vodafone (owned by Racal). Neither company sells systems and equipment direct, both working through distributors. Cellular phones tend to be expensive with those for cars also incurring an installation charge on top of the purchase or lease price and in addition to the charge for calls made.

Other communication media

So far we have emphasised what are considered to be the traditional methods of oral and written communication, which are still widely used throughout business today. Such skills will be essential acquisitions for anyone occupying a secretarial support role. However, other communication media are also available and may play an important part in the effectiveness of communications within an organisation, and you should be aware of them and their possible uses. As indicated in Fig 23, they fall into various categories. Their use will be largely dependent upon the size of an organisation, its location and the nature of its business.

Intercom

As the name suggests, an intercom is simply a device which enables communication to take place between two or more locations without interfering with the main telephone system. Extensions on the system are called simply by pressing a button. An intercom unit provides a useful link between offices (often the secretary and the boss), and its advantages over the telephone are that it frees the hands of both caller and receiver during talking or listening and, of course, saves movements between offices.

Abbreviations and acronyms associated with telephone services

BABT	British Approvals Board for Telecommunications
BSI	British Standards Institution
BT	British Telecom
BTMC	British Telecom Mobile Communications
CCITT	Comite Consultatif International de Telephonie et de Telegraphie
IDA	Integrated Digital Access
IPSS	International Packet Switchstream
ISDN	Integrated Services Digital Network
ISO	International Standards Organization
MHS	Message Handling Service
OFTEL	The Office of Telecommunications (Government watchdog body)
PABX	Private Automatic Branch Exchange
PCI	Pre-connection Inspection
PSS	Packet Switchstream
PSTN	Public Switched Telephone Network
PTO	Public Telecommunications Operator
SCVF	Single Channel Voice Frequency

Note: Not all of the above are contained in the text of this book but are likely to appear in any supplementary reading which you may choose to undertake in order to familiarise yourself more with advances in telecommunications.

Often it incorporates a flashing or buzzing device to attract immediate attention.

Public address systems

Public address systems are useful where it may be necessary to make public announcements, and they can be invaluable in the event of emergencies, as for example in the event of a bomb scare or fire where it is necessary to evacuate a building quickly. The system simply operates through loudspeakers connected to a microphone – often an integral part of the private branch exchange (PABX) network. The disadvantage is that, when used frequently, it can be ignored and may be the cause of great distraction and irritation. Also it is essential that the person making the announcements has a very clear voice.

Paging system

Paging is simply a variation on the use of a public address or loudspeaker system. The intention is to call the attention of a particular individual and to then direct that individual to a particular location to be given a message or further instructions. Such systems are commonly used in places like airport lounges or the foyers of large hotels during conferences and other functions.

Bleeper systems

Where executives are constantly on the move and yet may need to be contacted while out of the office, they may be issued with personal radio receivers which fit comfortably into the pocket. These 'bleeps', as they are commonly referred to, send out high-pitched, readily audible signals which are activated from a central control point – usually the switchboard. When the signal is picked up by the individual member of staff issued with the 'bleep', they report to the nearest telephone. Such devices are unobtrusive and widely used by people such as doctors in hospitals and executives in large organisations. Unlike other paging devices they cause little disturbance and enable confidential messages to be related once the individual has gone to the telephone.

The main problem associated with bleeper systems is a human one, viz forgetfulness. The system is rendered useless where a bleeper is left in a briefcase, on a desk or in a jacket pocket when the jacket is left in the office hanging over the back of a chair!

Radio paging

This operates over a much wider area than the bleeper system. In the UK BT's rental service currently handles around 80 per cent of the market in radio pagers in that it operates a nationwide area paging network. A variety of paging devices is available ranging from the basic 'tone only' type which merely bleeps, signalling to subscribers the need to dial a relevant number from a normal telephone, to more sophisticated models which incorporate a small light-emitting diode (LED) which can display a brief message. Full details of all BT's paging services are available from BTMC.

Telephone answering machines

Telephone answering systems are growing in popularity and there are many different systems and suppliers to choose from. Basically there are three types of machine:

1 those which answer only and play the caller a recorded message, eg they may announce that the office is closed until a particular time or provide an alternative number to call;
2 those which answer and record, ie enable the caller to leave a message, eg name and telephone number so that the call may be returned when the message is played back;
3 those which are dual purpose, ie operating as a telephone and answer machine combined, so enabling calls to be answered personally or left for the machine to record.

Some of the more sophisticated systems also incorporate a remote control facility which is either bleeper or voice-activated and which enables a user to contact his own machine and listen to any messages which have been left or perhaps alter a pre-recorded message from the distant location. Some systems also use special security codings which prevent unauthorised access to messages.

Telex

Telex, which was first introduced in 1932, is the largest worldwide text transmission system, serving nearly 2 million subscribers in 200 countries. Based on the original telegraphic network (it transmits over telegraph *not* telephone lines) it offers a round the clock service both for the despatch and receipt of written messages, provided machines are switched on and have a supply of paper, (where memory machines are not in use) regardless of whether the machines are attended.

What equipment is needed?

Several different options are available:

1 The most common is a dedicated terminal specifically designed for the purpose and justifiable where telex traffic is heavy.
2 Where telex is required but volume of use is relatively low, a microcomputer may be used if equipped with appropriate conversion software and a modem.
3 A memory typewriter may be upgraded by adding what is known as a telex box.
4 High volume users with several telex lines and terminals may operate a multi-user whereby a message switching system automatically routes incoming messages to free terminals and outgoing messages to free lines.
5 A microcomputer attached to a telex machine via a special interface enables the microcomputer to gain direct access to the telex line. This eliminates the need to re-key messages. This can also operate on a large scale where microcomputers are linked to a centralised telex message switching system via a local area network (LAN) (*see* page 75).

Using bureaux services

It is also worth noting that low volume users may prefer to opt for the services of a telex bureau, perhaps even transmitting their messages to the bureau via an electronic mailbox system (*see* page 75).

Special telex features

Since BT's loss of monopoly over the supply of equipment telex systems have undergone major improvements in line with the electronic age. Messages can now be prepared on screen and are no longer interrupted by the arrival of incoming ones.

These can now be stored in the system's memory for later retrieval unlike the old system in which the two processes could not operate simultaneously and incoming messages took precedence. In addition modern systems include the following special features:

- abbreviated dialling
- automatic re-try, ie re-dialling of engaged numbers
- batching of messages to the same destination
- multi-addressing (telex's version of list processing or mail merge in word processing applications)
- editing facilities
- enhanced storage potential on hard or floppy disk so enabling records to be kept of messages sent and received
- low noise level when compared with the early teleprinter machines.

The disadvantages of using telex

- telegraph lines are more expensive to rent and generally less sophisticated than telephone lines
- transmission speed of about 70 wpm is slower than more modern alternative services such as fax (*see* below)
- the network is overworked, causing delays in urgent messages due to engaged lines
- only upper case characters and a limited number of other numbers and symbols are used in print-outs which come on continuous stationery and are less than letter quality in standard
- it can be difficult to obtain numbers and answer-back codes for foreign subscribers.

How are messages sent?

Telex operation is simple. All that is needed is a little practice to enable you to send a message. The following are the general steps required:

- find the number from the *Telex Directory*
- type the message on the screen, checking its accuracy very carefully
- call, type or dial the number (depending on the system)
- an answerback code or a service signal such as ABS (absent – meaning the machine is switched off), DER (derangé – French for out of order) or OCC (occupied) will be supplied.

- if answerback code (this is also supplied in the *Telex Directory*) is given correctly you supply your own answerback code prior to supplying the message (answerback codes are safeguards in respect of avoiding sending messages to the wrong destinations and are indicators that both machines are ready to transmit and receive)
- at the end of the message answerback codes are exchanged again
- the message is then transmitted and either printed simultaneously at both ends or stored electronically in both memories for record purposes or later access.

An example of a telex message is given in Fig 27.

Facsimile transmission (fax)

Fax refers to a system of transmitting exact copies of documents quickly and accurately over telephone lines to another fax terminal. Distance is no object and charges are based on the time taken to transmit the message and are at exactly the same rate as normal phone calls. In appearance the end product is like a photocopy of the original but it is there the similarity ends as the process is very different.

Facsimile is a process of scanning, encoding and reconstructing. It involves converting digital signals to analogue for telephone transmission (most of the existing telephone networks are still analogue) and back to digital via built-in fax modems.

```
89-09-01  09:07
Msg 550 Title:


261367  MILLER + DOBSON
33160  H + P OFFICE EQUIPMENT

NO: 0498  01-09-89  10:21
TO: MILLER + DOBSON
FM: H + P OFFICE EQUIPMENT

ATTN: MR ROBINSON
--------------------

RE: DAMAGED EQUIPMENT ORDER NO 51067

APOLOGIES.  NEW EQUIPMENT ON ORDER.
DELIVERY EARLY NEXT WEEK.  WILL
CONFIRM THIS.

ENDS+++

33160 H + P OFFICE EQUIPMENT

261367  MILLER + DOBSON
MMMMMM
```

Fig 27 A telex message

Facsimile transmission is a growth area in tele-communications and owing to the high volume of users in Japan there are, in fact, more fax users world wide than there are of telex. Fax machines come in various sizes and in various levels of sophistication and the supply market is extremely competitive. At the bottom end of the market there has been an explosion in terms of low-priced, semi-portable machines (*see* Fig 28) while at the top end there are high level memory machines capable of fax networking, ie the setting up of networks of compatible fax machines locally or at a distance. The linking of fax machines into microcomputers (PC-fax) is also an area of high activity.

Compatibility

Early in fax's history there were compatibility problems between one manufacturer's machine and another but now that they conform to international industry standards set by the CCITT, which is based in Geneva, all faxes can communicate with each other regardless of manufacturer. These industry standards are referred to as 'Groups' and there are four currently in operation, although the majority of machines fall into Group 3 which can transmit an A4 document in about 20 seconds, while groups 2 and 1 take much longer. (Group 4 standard has been designed with digital telephone networks in mind and is capable of transmitting a page in as little as 3 seconds.)

While users may have machines which fall into different groups it is still possible for them to communicate, but the speed of transmission is determined by the lower group machine. The technical term for this is 'talking up' and talking down' and, of course, the cost will always be based on the slower machine. It is also worthwhile noting that transmission speeds are affected by the quality of telephone lines.

Fig 28 A fax machine; *Reproduced by kind permission of British Telecom*

Special features

Like much of today's electronic equipment, fax has its own range of special features and the following are typical examples:

- **auto-dialling** using the keyboard on the machine to dial the number
- **auto re-try** when lines are busy
- **abbreviated dialling**
- **delayed send** which saves money by using cheap rate times for transmission
- **group codes** to handle multi-destination transmissions
- **security features** to restrict access to machine use and avoid abuse
- **reduction and enlargement facilities**
- **improved paper quality** for end copy in that plain paper is beginning to make an impact over the traditional flimsy thermal paper
- **error detection and correction** which provides automatic cut-off after a certain level of error is reached
- **'fine mode'** transmission which improves the quality of the copy although transmission takes longer.

Advantages over telex

- easier to use – as simple as a photocopier
- cheaper – it uses telephone lines which are less expensive to rent and have off peak periods
- faster in terms of both preparation (no need to key or re-key) and transmission
- more flexible – accepts graphs, diagrams, handwriting etc
- better quality end product.

Datacoms

An efficient method of communicating information is to do so between electronic workstations such as word processors or microcomputers. All that is needed with modern compatible machines, in addition to the terminals and telephone lines, is the necessary communications software and modems. You then have the basis of electronic mail.

The modems deriving from the words **mod**ulator and **dem**odulator) are needed to convert the digital signals of the sending terminal to analogue for transmission down phone lines and back to digital

---

Other British Telecom services

Full details of the many services and their charges are available from BT via the Freefone service. Useful outline information is also provided in general telephone directories. The following are some of the main services available via the operator:

- alarm calls
- Advise Duration and Charge Calls (ADC)
- Credit Card calls
- Fixed Time calls
- Personal calls
- Subscriber controlled transfer
- Transferred Charge calls
- Freefone calls
- Telemessage
- International Telemessage to the USA
- International Telegrams
- Maritime Services
- Conference calls

Additionally a comprehensive Directory Enquiry is provided by dialling 192 and stating the town and the name and address of the subscriber required.

Yellow Pages also provide a full classified directory where numbers are arranged according to trades and professions.

---

for the receiving terminal as indicated in Fig 29. It should be noted, however, that compatibility problems, varying transmission speeds, system protocols and other technical factors have severely inhibited what on paper looks like a simple means of message transmission.

Teletex

Based on internationally agreed standards set up by CCITT to ensure the sort of compatibility of inter-communicating equipment and designed to transmit and receive electronic mail via PSTN or PSS, Teletex (not to be confused with Teletext which is the generic name for Ceefax and Oracle, the BBC and IBA viewdata information services) was introduced in 1981. However, despite the seemingly attractive possibilities offered by the system such as letter quality text, faster transmission speeds and ease of operation, Teletex has proved something of a disappointment in the trade. This is due to a variety of factors including:

- the expense of equipment

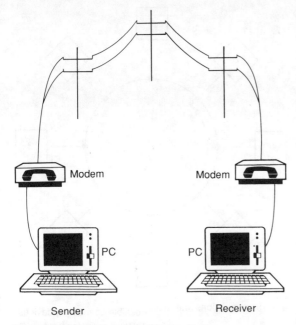

Fig 29 Communicating electronic terminals

- initial delays in the testing arrangements
- restricted international link-ups
- uncertainty about the legal status of documents while telex is accepted as legal evidence
- the arrival of another standard which would provide still greater flexibility
- general lack of support from the business community.

What is electronic mail?

Electronic mail is the term used to describe a range of electronic transmission services but is commonly applied to either a company's internal mailbox system operated via its own computer or to one of the services provided by bureaux such as BT's Telecom Gold.

As an intra-company facility, electronic mail can improve message sending and help eliminate the need for a considerable amount of paper, particularly where many staff have personal terminals on their desks. A message is keyed in and addressed by code to relevant mailbox users. It is then received by the host computer and held in memory storage until accessed by the addressee (s) who may then read it, transfer it to personal storage, forward it to someone else, reply to it via the mailbox system,

print it out for hard copy retention purposes or delete it altogether.

Local Area Networks (LANs)

At its simplest a LAN is a means of linking together, via coaxial or fibre optic cable, a number of electronic devices over a restricted geographical area, eg within a building, for communication purposes. The fact that transmission is over relatively limited distances helps ensure high speed and greater efficiency.

The technology

Like other areas of IT LANs have their buzzwords. As far as the technology associated with the operation of networks is concerned they will be served by any of the following:

- **twisted pair wiring** as used in telephone lines so there are limitations in both capacity of handling devices and in transmission speed.
- **baseband single channel cabling** which is the simplest and most economic but enables only one device at a time to transmit data, so is more suitable for smaller office complexes or for use within a specific area of a larger company. It is best suited to high speed computer-to-computer traffic but slower and more problematic when needed to support audio or video transmission.
- **broadband multi-channel cabling** Here cable is broken into channels so more users can transmit many different communications simultaneously. In future with the developments in fibre optic cabling, and the virtually unlimited bandwidth, most LANs will be broadband, enabling a network to support thousands of users rather than the hundreds which can be served with baseband. However, initial investment and maintenance charges are much greater on a broadband network.

Uses and alternative configurations

All types of compatible electronic device may be interfaced to the LAN including microcomputers, word processors, telex terminals, printers, OCR machines and auxiliary storage. Each device can operate independently within the network but where necessary, one device may communicate with another via the LAN to accomplish a particular task. For example, a word processor could contact a remote printer and instruct it to print the text sent to it.

Networks also enable user terminals to share information and from this point of view they represent a viable alternative to a traditional mainframe or minicomputer facility within an organisation. This not only decentralises the provision of computer held information but can help reduce some of the mystery surrounding complex centralised computer facilities.

There are three main types of architecture or topology (to use the technical term) for linking devices in order to transmit data via a network – star, ring or bus, *see* Figs 30, 31 and 32).

The star is similar to the operation of the telephone network with a central controller (switchboard) and consequently the network is totally dependent on the operation of the central hub.

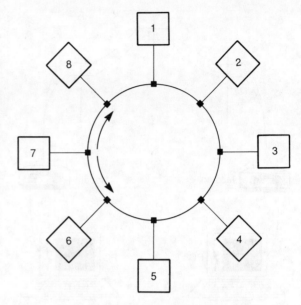

■ = communications interface Possible connecting devices

1 Word processor
2 Microcomputer
3 Management workstation
4 Phototypesetter
5 Intelligent copier/printer
6 OCR
7 Data processing terminal
8 Communications terminal
  eg Telex

Fig 31 Ring topology

The ring's main problem, on the other hand, is that breakdown anywhere on the ring will affect other users.

Therefore, the bus tends to be most popular in that malfunction of any terminal or connection on the network does not incapacitate the entire network as could be the case with the other two configurations.

Telecom Gold

Where an organisation subscribes to a service like Telecom Gold it is allocated mailbox space rather like electronic 'pigeon holes' and other subscribers can collect and leave messages for forward transmission. In addition the system has:

● direct access to the telex network
● many office automation facilities
● access to certain on-line database services (*see* also Unit 9)

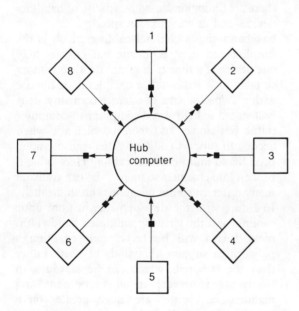

■ = communications interface Possible connecting devices

1 Word processor
2 Microcomputer
3 Management workstation
4 Phototypesetter
5 Intelligent copier/printer
6 OCR
7 Data processing terminal
8 Communications terminal
  eg Telex

Fig 30 Star or hub topology

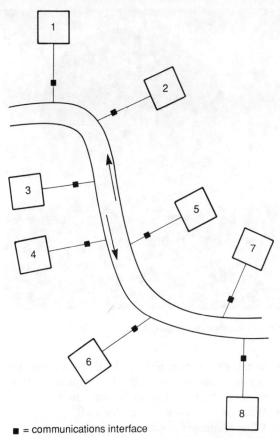

■ = communications interface

Possible connecting devices
1 Word processor
2 Microcomputer
3 Management workstation
4 Phototypesetter
5 Intelligent copier/printer
6 OCR
7 Data processing terminal
8 Communications terminal
  eg Telex

Fig 32 Bus topology

- a paging facility whereby subscribers can keep in touch while out of the office
- diary and appointments scheduling facility
- a record keeping system
- access to a wide range of business data services.

The advantages of electronic mail

- speed
- cost effectiveness particularly with the rises in postal charges

- time saving
- prevents interruptions
- paper saving
- efficient in that it enables flexible working patterns, eg from home or even abroad
- enables individuals to have better control and management of their own time
- extends the range of potential services an individual can utilise
- facilitates wide message distribution where used intra-company
- can provide a useful written/memory held record when used as an alternative to a phone call
- enables messages to be date-activated which ensures that they are delivered automatically at pre-determined future dates.

Disadvantages

- initial expense of installation
- staff reluctance to use it
- the need to train staff in its use if they are to maximise its potential
- system breakdowns
- the likelihood of receiving 'junk mail'
- the possibility of unauthorised access to the system causing security worries
- internally they are not suited to the preparation and transmission of lengthy documents
- can invite information overload
- do not alleviate poor communication habits
- can encourage time wasting via the exchange of personal and nonsense messages internally (usually a teething problem only!)

Voice mail

Voice mail refers to the storage in digital form of verbal messages for later delivery. Voice messaging is becoming increasingly used and many sophisticated PABX systems now incorporate the facility. It differs from electronic mail in that it is the voice which is stored and the recipient can, therefore, listen to rather than read the messages. Voice systems have the following advantages:

- very user friendly – speech is learned from infancy
- eliminate the need to continually return or re-try unsuccessful calls
- enable a comprehensive message to be left

- enhance the accuracy of messages and eliminate the need for physical message taking by others
- telephones are more easily accessible than terminals for electronic mail
- easier to use a telephone than a terminal – virtually no training needed
- users can dial own extensions and dictate memos and reminders for themselves
- verbal delivery is faster than handwriting or keying in
- inessential chit-chat is reduced
- messages can be relayed to multiple destinations
- messages can be left or accessed at any time
- in some organisations there can be substantial reduction in long distance telephone charges

In terms of disadvantages these tend to be restricted to the reluctance (often only initial) to talk to machines and the need for users to organise their thoughts carefully before transmission (as with telephone answering machines).

Satellite communications

Satellite transmission is used for long distance communications, the principle involved being that used for satellite television. The data, voice, facsimile or pictures travel from an earth station to a communications satellite (*see* Fig 33) from which they are bounced back to one or more earth stations elsewhere for transmission to the ultimate destination. This form of transmission is both fast and cost effective where vast distances require to be covered.

The questions to be answered when considering datacoms

To introduce a successful datacommunications system within any organisation much careful planning and homework must be done. This will include finding answers to the following questions:

- What purposes must the system serve?
- What kinds of data will flow throught the system?
- What is the degree of urgency?
- How significant is accuracy?
- What protocols are to be used?
- What expansion flexibility needs to be built in?
- How much will a system cost to purchase and install?
- How will it be serviced?

Fig 33 Communication satellite

- What existing expertise is there within the organisation to smooth the implementation, monitor usage and identify problems?
- What are the implications for staff?
- What training would be required?
- How and by whom would essential training be carried out?
- How well can any system selected be upgraded to take benefit of new developments?

There will be continued research and development in the areas of voice recognition, long distance transmission, artificial intelligence and expert systems – all geared to increasing information handling potential, enhancing decision-making and generally improving overall organisational efficiency and effectiveness.

Self-test

1 What are the essential features of effective communication?
2 What elements can act as barriers to effective communication?
3 What factors influence media selection?
4 What are the advantages and disadvantages of oral communication?
5 What are the advantages and disadvantages of written communication?

6 What technological developments have been introduced to help ensure more efficient communication?
7 What are some of the special features to be found on a computerised switchboard?
8 How does radio paging operate?
9 What kinds of cellular telephone are available?
10 What is telex and how does it work?
11 What are the advantages of fax over telex?
12 What special telephone services does BT provide for subscribers?
13 What are the disadvantages of electronic mail?
14 What are the main advantages of voice mail?
15 What other communication media and services are available to businesses?

Personal activities

1 Try to improve your telephone technique. Listen to your own voice on a cassette recorder. How does it sound? Could it be improved?

2 Contact BT and other suppliers to find out more about equipment and services available to businesses today.

3 Where appropriate, always write thank – you letters. They do not take long to write and are always appreciated – often much more than a quick telephone call.

Group activity

Form a panel of four for 'Question Time' and appoint a Chairperson to accept questions and guide discussion. The remaining members of your group should form the audience and put questions to the panel through the Chair. Questions should be concise but clear and varied in content. The question should be repeated by the Chair who should then request the views of the panel by asking each member to speak. The Chair should then bring in audience views and finally summarise conclusions drawn and views expressed.

Note: This is a good exercise for building confidence and will be even more valuable if filmed on video for later playback and constructive criticism.

Situation-based activities

1 Imagine you are Secretary to Jason Winthrop, the Managing Director of Markland Plastics plc, a manufacturing company with plants throughout the United Kingdom. You are based at the head office in Southampton. The following are tasks which require your action and attention:

a Mr Winthrop wants you to send out, on his behalf, a memorandum to all departmental heads advising them of the new car parking arrangements which are due to come into effect in two weeks' time. He wishes you to stress that unauthorised parking will lead to problems for the many large lorries which deliver raw materials and collect finished goods from the site. Staff must be instructed to park *only* in the areas indicated on the plan (which you should prepare and attach to the memo). Staff must also display *blue* permits at all times.

   The memo should also explain the procedure for visitors. Visitors to the site must report at the gatehouse on arrival. There they will be issued with *yellow* permits and directed to the visitors' car park. Heads of department should instruct their staff to notify the gatehouse, in advance if possible, when they are expecting a visitor.

Materials required
1 A4 memo form
1 A4 site plan which you should draw from your imagination!

b Draft a report on the effects of the introduction of flexitime within Markland Plastics. Assume that this system has been on trial for two months and that you have been requested to submit a report on how it has been received by staff and whether it ought to be implemented permanently. The report will be submitted for consideration by the management at the next full meeting of the board next month.

Materials required
This task should be submitted on A4 paper – typed if possible.

c Mr Winthrop has asked you to notify Fiona Robinson in the Typing Pool that she has been awarded the David Markland Prize for consistent progress in her studies.
   You should also prepare an entry for inclusion in the company house journal.

d Mr Desmond Crawford, Sales Director of Paramount Packaging in Birmingham (tel 021 727/9656) telephoned while Mr Winthrop was out. He would like to receive details of Markland's latest developments in clear plastic self-cling packaging material and to meet Mr Winthrop at the earliest possible opportunity. Your conversation with Mr Crawford led you to believe that Paramount could be a valuable potential customer, so you have tentatively made a luncheon appointment with him when he is in Southampton next Thursday. Will Mr Winthrop please confirm. Compose a suitable message, inventing suitable dates, places and times.

e Write a letter to Information Processes Limited, 29 Duke Street, Southampton complaining that their representative failed to keep an appointment to demonstrate a new record processing application of their microcomputer which you are considering installing in the Personnel Department. Assume that the appointment was confirmed by Information Processes several weeks ago and that you had made all the necessary arrangements at your end to release staff from their duties and to set up a room for the demonstration, as well as booking lunch in the staff restaurant.

f Design an invitation card for the opening of the new sports and social complex attached to Markland Plastics. The opening is to be marked by a party in the foyer of the building in six weeks' time on Thursday from 1930 to 2100. All members are invited to attend and to bring one guest each, and replies are required.

g Write a suitable article announcing the opening of the sports and social complex for insertion in the local newspaper. The article should be between 200 and 300 words in length. Your copy should be presented – typewritten if possible – in double line spacing.

2 Imagine you are a secretarial assistant with Trans-Continental Holidays plc, a travel company in Lincoln. Your duties are extremely varied, but much of your work involves placing and receiving telephone calls. The company has recently taken on a junior assistant who has been put in your charge. In this role please complete the following tasks:

a Design a telephone message form to be used within the company by all personnel taking messages.

b Write a letter to Mr and Mrs J Henderson, 22 Saville Crescent, Lincoln confirming their booking of a two-week Italian holiday (one week in Rome, one week in Sorrento) and acknowledge receipt of their £60 deposit – the balance to be paid eight weeks prior to departure. Add any other information which

you consider might be helpful and relevant. The holiday reference is RS/BA 7214/JUL.

c Trans-Continental Holidays have just had a telephone answering machine delivered. This is to be used to provide a 24-hour service for customers. This means that it will be set up with a prerecorded message for people calling after office hours, and it will also enable callers to leave their names and numbers and details of their enquiries so that they can be dealt with promptly the next day. Prepare a message to be recorded by you for the machine.

d Prepare a memorandum notifying all staff of the installation of the new telephone answering machine.

e As part of your job you are occasionally asked to attend meetings of local societies and talk about holidays. On this occasion you have been particularly asked to talk about bargain break weekends in England. Prepare a talk which will last about twenty minutes. You should talk about the idea in general and then select two different weekends and provide details on them. You should also prepare a brief handout for distribution at the end of your talk.

f Among your tasks for today you have set aside half an hour to speak to the new office junior on the importance of good telephone technique. What sort of things would you stress, and how would you ensure that she has your uninterrupted attention while you are talking to her?

g Devise a mock telephone exercise which you can try out with the new junior to help assess her present technique and point out any obvious weaknesses she might have. Assume that the telephone equipment you have will enable you to carry out such a test in privacy.

h Prepare a guidance sheet on telephone usage to give to the junior.

3 Assume that you are Personal Secretary to Mr Geoffrey Firbank, a partner in the solicitors' firm of Briers, Firbank & Taylor in Poole, Dorset. Mr Firbank has many outside interests including the presidency of the local golf club for this year and the chairmanship of the Rotary Club. As well as carrying out your work for the firm you often oblige Mr Firbank by attending to matters relating to these activities.

The following tasks have to be dealt with by you today:

a Prepare for Mr Firbank's signature a business

```
                                        652 Ringwood Road
                                        Parkstone
                                        POOLE
                                           Dorset
                                           BH14 4NA

                                        18 September 19..

        Briers, Firbank & Taylor
        Solicitors
        Lloyds Bank Chambers
        POOLE  Dorset
        BH7 9LT

        For the attention of Mr Geoffrey Firbank

        Dear Mr Firbank

            I very much regret the necessity of having to write this letter
        but feel obliged to remind you that I have a very busy schedule and
        consequently consider it vital that all my appointments are honoured.
        Your failure to keep our appointment of yesterday resulted in my
        wasting the major part of the afternoon when I could very easily have
        spent the time in a constructive way.

            Also I feel that it is amiss of your office not to notify me
        should you be unable to keep an appointment.

            Your firm came highly recommended to me and I am extremely
        disappointed that our first encounter should end in this way. I have
        a lot of very important business for which I require sound legal
        guidance and am anxious to establish a relationship which will be
        fruitful to both parties.

                                Yours sincerely

                                Charles Delamere

                                C Delamere
```

Fig 34

letter to Mrs Geraldine Hilary of 29 The Grove, Branksome Park, Poole, Dorset BH 13 6JS informing her that the drafting of her will has been completed and is ready for her approval and signature. Suggest a suitable date and time, one afternoon towards the end of the week.

b Reply to a letter of complaint which the firm has received from Mr Delamere of 652 Ringwood Road, Parkstone, Poole BH 14 4NA (Fig 34). Mr Firbank's car broke down on a country road on the way back from Wimborne and by the time he managed to telephone the office Mr Delamere had gone. The letter should be suitably apologetic as Mr Firbank did hope to secure Mr Delamere's business!

c Mr Firbank has received the two invitations shown in Fig 35. He has asked you to accept the invitation from Lymington Golf Club to attend their annual dinner and to send an apology to the Wareham Antiquarian Society. Write suitable replies on his behalf.

4 You work for Mrs Forsythe, the Personnel Manager of a large company. She has been receiving a series of complaints from Mr Wilkes, the Senior Mail Clerk, about the late arrival of mail to the Mail Room and the consequent need for staff to work late in order to clear this mail before the next day and the arrival of large quantities of incoming correspondence. Mr Wilkes has made specific reference to several points in his complaints:

```
┌─────────────────────────────────────────────────────────────────┐
│                                                                   │
│              WAREHAM ANTIQUARIAN SOCIETY                          │
│                                                                   │
│         requests the pleasure of                                 │
│                                                                   │
│           MR & MRS G. FIRBANK                                    │
│         .............................................            │
│                                                                   │
│         at a Cheese and Wine Party to be held                    │
│                                                                   │
│         at Major & Mrs Dewhirst's, The Steading, Grange Road on  │
│         Friday 25 October 19.. at 2000 hours.                    │
│                                                                   │
│                                                                   │
│         RSVP                                                      │
│                                                                   │
└─────────────────────────────────────────────────────────────────┘


┌─────────────────────────────────────────────────────────────────┐
│                                                                   │
│                     LYMINGTON GOLF CLUB                           │
│                                                                   │
│         requests the pleasure of                                 │
│                                                                   │
│             GEOFFREY FIRBANK                                     │
│         .............................................            │
│                                                                   │
│         at their ANNUAL DINNER to be held on                     │
│                                                                   │
│         Friday 25 October 19.. at Peasford House                 │
│         Hotel, Lymington - 7.30 pm for 8.00 pm.                  │
│                                                                   │
│                                                                   │
│         RSVP                                                      │
│                                                                   │
└─────────────────────────────────────────────────────────────────┘
```

Fig 35

a the fact that mail is often poorly addressed

b the lack of essential instructions from certain offices which use special postal services like recorded delivery

c the failure of staff to adhere to collection times

d his shortage of trained and dedicated staff

e the inadequacy and poor condition of some of the equipment.

Mrs Forsythe has asked you to investigate these complaints over the next two weeks and to report your findings and recommendations to her in the form of a report which she will use as the basis of her submission when the problem is considered at the next meeting of the Management Committee. (For this activity you will need to use your imagination. The five points raised by Mr Wilkes provide you with a starting-point, but do not hesitate to suggest other reasons for the problems and to elaborate on the five already given.)

Additional exercises on telephone technique

Study the following telephone conversations. Compare and contrast them, indicating the principal differences in technique. Be critical in your comments and point out any errors and omissions you notice.

Conversation A

Secretary Good morning, Mr Robinson's office, his secretary speaking.

Caller Could I speak to Mr Robinson please?

Secretary I'm sorry, Mr Robinson is out of the office this morning. Can I help you or take a message?

Caller Well, he and I were chatting the other evening at the squash club about microcomputers, and he suggested that I should have a demonstration of your new one here in our office and that if I could get a suitable date and time organised at my end he would bring a machine along and do the demonstration.

Secretary I see, and you are?

Caller Phillips of Winston & Green.

Secretary Have you settled on a date and time Mr Phillips?

Caller Well, yes, as a matter of fact I have. Next Tuesday morning would be perfect if you can manage that?

Secretary I am looking at Mr Robinson's diary for next week and it does seem alright for that time, but I shall have to confirm it with him. May I call you back later when I have spoken to Mr Robinson?

Caller Yes, that would be fine.

Secretary Could I have your telephone number, please, Mr Phillips?

Caller Sorry, of course. It's 837 6511 extension 279.

Secretary Thank you. That's 837 6511, extension 279. I'll call you back later, Mr Phillips, and we can finalise all the details then.

Caller Thank you very much. Goodbye.

Secretary Goodbye, Mr Phillips.

Conversation B

Office Junior Hello.

Caller Is that the Sales Department?

Office Junior Yeh.

Caller Could I speak to Mr Fowler please?

Junior He's not here. He went out to lunch a couple of hours ago and I haven't seen him since. He should have been back ages ago.

Caller Could I leave a message for him?

Junior Yeh, if you like.

Caller Could you ask him to call David Symonds about the arrangements for next week?

Junior OK. Hang on a minute, though, till I get a pen. (*Long pause*) Who did you say you were again?

Caller My name is David Symonds and I would be grateful if he could call me as soon as possible about the arrangements for next week.

Junior Right oh. Bye. (*Hangs up*)

Now rewrite Conversation B as it ought to have taken place.

Go back to Conversation A and prepare a message for Mr Robinson, assuming that you are his secretary.

5

Applying the secretarial role

Aim of the unit

This unit examines the aspects of secretarial work which comprise the secretarial role and provides the opportunity to enact this role via a series of integrated tasks and assignments which a practising secretary could realistically expect to encounter as part of the daily routine.

Specific objectives

At the end of this unit you should be able to:
1   Complete a diary accurately.
2   Keep an appointments book.
3   Devise a suitable bring-forward system.
4   Prepare briefing notes for a junior member of staff who will stand in for you in your absence.
5   Indicate how you would deal with a persistent newspaper reporter.
6   Outline the arrangements you would make for an informal buffet luncheon in the committee room of your organisation.
7   Prepare a brief talk to be given to the secretarial students at your local college.
8   Make travel arrangements.
9   Prepare an itinerary.
10 Book hotel accommodation.
11 Identify the priority task from a selected in-tray.
12 Suggest how you would handle a difficult situation in the office.
13 Give advice to a fellow secretary.
14 Indicate how you would attempt to establish a good working relationship with your boss.
15 Indicate the problems you could expect to encounter when taking on the work of an additional executive.

Introduction

Before we can begin to look in detail at aspects of secretarial work, it is necessary to consider what we mean by a 'secretary'. The term 'secretary' will mean different things to different people, and a glance through the advertisements in Fig 15 (page 27) will indicate the varied descriptions to be found.

As far as we are concerned, the important thing to recognise is the distinction between the duties and responsibilities of someone appointed as a secretary and those of someone appointed as, for example, a shorthand typist. There is, or certainly should be, a difference, and it is this difference that will be emphasised throughout this unit.

What distinguishes a secretary from other office workers?

In simple terms, someone holding the post of secretary will be expected to possess additional skills, qualities and attitudes to someone employed as, for instance, a shorthand typist, to adopt a career approach to the job and demonstrate abilities in keeping with a support role. Aspects of a secretary's duties must necessarily reflect attitudes and qualities which an employer could not reasonably expect to find in those office workers who are appointed largely to perform very specific duties.

What are the additional skills required?

In addition to the basic technical skills of typewriting, word processing, shorthand, audio and a good standard of English language, a secretary will be expected to possess the following extra skills:

- telephone skills
- keeping diaries
- scheduling appointments
- greeting visitors
- arranging meetings
- taking minutes
- maintaining files and records
- making travel and accommodation arrangements
- processing figures and simple statistics
- handling simple financial matters
- researching information
- proofreading and checking
- identifying priorities
- making decisions

Many of these skills will be elaborated upon later in this unit.

What qualities and attitudes are sought?

Prospective employers seek to employ individuals not only with capabilities over and above the basic technical skills but also with certain qualities and attitudes in keeping with the role and function of a secretary and which are considered desirable by managers today.

What are these qualities and attitudes? Obviously the range will vary considerably according to the nature of the work and the demands of individual employers, but the following will provide an indication of the types currently specified by employers when considering secretarial staff:

Qualities
- common sense
- tact and courtesy
- loyalty
- poise
- efficiency
- good memory
- enthusiasm
- versatility
- reliability
- organisational ability

Attitudes
- the ability to anticipate needs
- the ability to work under pressure
- the ability to accept constructive criticism

- good human relations
- diplomacy
- flexibility
- adaptability
- willingness to try out new ideas
- initiative
- a sense of humour

Obviously many of these things will only come with experience, but anyone aspiring to become a good personal secretary would do well to cultivate them. Much of this comes down to what could be termed 'professionalism'. Professionalism applies to all aspects of a secretary's work including appearance that reflects and projects the company's image, and the quality and appearance of work produced, which should be well presented, error free and produced as quickly as possible. It also includes the ability to deal with people at all levels and in all types of situation, both formal and informal. A true 'professional' must always be ready to adapt to change, adopt new ideas and flourish in new circumstances.

Routine secretarial tasks

Many of the tasks performed by secretaries are part of a regular routine. The following provide a typical selection.

The diary

The diary is the linchpin of the day-to-day organisation of the office, as well as the basis for all forward planning.

The maintenance of diaries is an extremely important part of any secretary's work. The plural 'diaries' is stipulated as there will usually be more than one, even where the secretary works for only one executive (an increasingly less common circumstance these days, as emphasised later). As well as the boss's desk diary there may be a pocket diary (often the fly in the ointment!) and the secretary's own desk diary or diaries if the nature and complexity of the work makes it easier to operate from more than one. Wherever possible, however, it is preferable to restrict the number of diaries handled to one. Otherwise, considerable confusion can arise and discrepancies will occur.

What are the likely reasons for discrepancies?

1 One party may make arrangements without informing the other.
2 One party may alter or cancel something without notifying the other.
3 There may be failure on the part of either party to seek confirmation of a tentative arrangement.
4 There may be errors in relation to places, dates or times.
5 There may be lack of frequent (daily) coordination and checking.

Types of diary

A browse through any large stationer's shop before Christmas will give you some idea of the wide range of diaries available, certainly of the pocket variety, covering every conceivable speciality or interest. Executive desk diaries also come in many formats and can be purchased according to the nature of a company's business. Various organisations produce their own, with information, facts and figures relevant to the particular profession: for example, Lloyd's produce a special one for insurance personnel. Education diaries may operate on the academic rather than the calendar year.

The selection of a suitable diary requires careful consideration as some rulings will be more appropriate than others. Also the tightness of an executive's typical daily schedule and the average number of different appointments will make certain layouts preferable or to be avoided.

Likewise a secretary may find certain layouts better than others; some secretaries even prefer to devise their own ruling and have it prepared by the Reprographics Section for insertion in a looseleaf book. This also has an advantage in that completed pages may be removed and filed separately. It would then also be possible to incorporate different coloured pages where a secretary works for more than one executive and yet prefers to operate from a single diary.

Diary/planners

Many executives who schedule their time weeks or even months ahead, and perhaps undertake much international travel, find it invaluable to operate from a planner which enables them to see at a glance their commitments for the months ahead. Such a device helps avoid 'bunching' appointments and enables users to identify the optimum time for appointments, meetings, and visits. Planners are designed to provide an overview only and consequently it will be necessary to supply more detailed information in a standard diary. It should be noted that many pocket diaries and personal organisers incorporate a fold out planning page to serve the same purpose.

Points to consider in keeping diaries

1 Write clearly, printing names and initials, taking return telephone numbers where possible.
2 Make tentative arrangements in pencil, seeking confirmation as soon as possible and finalising in ink.
3 Detail all essential information. (Nothing is worse than inadequate information!)
4 Where a lot of additional information is taken or received in relation to an appointment, cross-reference to an appropriate file or reminder system.
5 When booking appointments, give consideration to the appointment picture for the whole day and perhaps even the remainder of the week.
6 Do *not* book appointments too close together – allow breathing space and time for routine work.
7 Where outside appointments are made, allow travelling time (particularly at peak times or in bad weather) and be sure that the precise location is noted.
8 Always make allowance for the unexpected.
9 Don't book your boss so tightly that you leave no time for yourself! You must allow time to take instructions, receive dictation and plan ahead.
10 Try to allow times at convenient points during the day to co-ordinate diaries. Where more than one operates, add any extra entries and get confirmation on any tentative arrangements you may have made.

Note: It is important to remember to transfer certain annual reminders when starting a new diary. For example, you might include membership reminders (although many are now catered for automatically by means of the direct debit banker's authorisation system: *see* Unit 7) as well as passport renewal, inoculations (where your boss travels overseas a lot) and perhaps items like family birthdays and anniversaries.

Some secretaries, in addition to using special checklists and countdown calendars (*see* later in this unit) also like to preview forthcoming events and deadlines in the diary as an added reminder.

Personal organisers

In the age of the Personal Organiser or 'Filofax' it would be remiss not to mention its usefulness in keeping together in one place varied information. The great advantage of such organisers is the fact that they are **personal**, ie the loose leaf arrangement enables the contents to meet individual needs. Infils are interchangeable within the many different types and costs of covers, and all manner of rulings and special purpose inserts are available, ranging from basic diary, addresses, expenditure sheets, project planners and reminder sheets to road maps, calorie counters, metric conversion tables, business card holders and endless other specialist requirements. It is even possible to buy loose-leaf versions of popular fiction for reading while commuting by train!

Desktop organiser software

An extension of the personal organiser is the inclusion of a specialist applications package for use with a personal computer (PC). Several packages are appearing on the market aimed at improving the organisation of desktops by eliminating the clutter caused by scraps of paper, address books, message pads, diaries and so on.

The idea is to provide what are termed 'memory resident pop-up utilities' which provide the sort of information normally contained in the aforementioned desk 'clutter' without needing to leave the particular application, eg word processing, in use on the PC. Basically the software operates a series of windows which open up on screen providing such information as would normally be held on paper.

Electronic diaries (*see* Fig 36)

More and more organisations are harnessing technology to effect and one other useful application is in terms of diary management. Where executives' appointments are keyed into the computer by their respective secretaries, details can be accessed easily for future updating or coordination purposes.

For example, where a secretary is required to arrange a meeting for a manager with several other executives in the same company, it will be possible, if an electronic diary system is in operation, to access all the relevant information in respect of all the managers' commitments at the VDU and decide upon a suitable time. Alternatively the computer can be instructed to check on the basis of the dependent variables which apply and come up with a selection of possible alternative dates and times. Once a selection has been made it can be sent via electronic mail to the other parties for confirmation.

Some systems incorporate a reminder system whereby the appointments themselves are signalled on the screen or a symbol appears to remind the secretary to check the appointments calendar. While such systems can improve general efficiency by saving considerable amounts of time, it should be remembered that there is still a constant need to update, coordinate and monitor. The system will only be as good as the information which is fed in and the extent to which it is up to date.

A special word about making appointments

Making appointments may be a major part of your secretarial duties. In addition to entering them in a diary it may be desirable to prepare daily or weekly typewritten lists for your executive(s). Such an exercise can also be helpful in terms of enabling essential preparations to be made. Many executives like to prepare themselves for certain meetings and interviews by reading through the relevant files and gathering their thoughts well in advance.

It may also be helpful in reminding you of any additional preparations or arrangements you may need to make, eg ordering or serving refreshments, booking tables for lunch, arranging transport, reserving parking places or notifying Reception.

Receiving visitors

Receiving visitors is likely to be one of the pleasurable social aspects of a secretary's day and should be done in a warm, friendly and courteous manner. In a large organisation it will be likely that they will

Appointment Schedule

J Marston

04/05/ - 08/05/

	April							May							June					
S	M	T	W	T	F	S	S	M	T	W	T	F	S	S	M	T	W	T	F	S
		1	2	3	4	5						1	2	1	2	3	4	5	6	7
6	7	8	9	10	11	12	3	4	5	6	7	8	9	8	9	10	11	12	13	14
13	14	15	16	17	18	19	10	11	12	13	14	15	16	15	16	17	18	19	20	21
20	21	22	23	24	25	26	17	18	19	20	21	22	23	22	23	24	25	26	27	28
27	28	29	30				24	25	26	27	28	29	30	29	30					
							31													

MONDAY   04/05/-

09:00	17:00	i NEW SALES REP STARTS TODAY
12:00	14:00	i LUNCH WITH SALES DEPARTMENT
NOTES:		v SARAH - 1 DAY HOLIDAY
		v JANE HARPER - HOLIDAY 4TH-8TH INCL.

TUESDAY   05/05/-

09:30	11:30	i PREPARATION FOR MANAGEMENT MEETING
11:30	12:30	m DEPARTMENTAL MEETING
14:00	17:00	m VISIT TO FACTORY
NOTES:		v JANE HARPER - HOLIDAY 4TH-8TH INCL.

WEDNESDAY   06/05/-

09:00	09:05	i REMINDER -- AG TO TELEPHONE BOROUGH COUNCIL
09:30	13:00	m MANAGEMENT MEETING - BOARDROOM
14:00	17:00	i KEEP FREE - POSSIBLE VISIT - time to be confirmed
NOTES:		v JANE HARPER - HOLIDAY 4TH-8TH INCL.

THURSDAY   07/05/-

| 13:00 | 10:45 | m LUNCH WITH PRODUCTION MANAGER |
| NOTES: | | v JANE HARPER - HOLIDAY 4TH-8TH INCL. |

FRIDAY   08/05/-

10:00	10:45	m SPEAK FOR INDUCTION COURSE
12:00	12:05	i REMINDER - TELEPHONE P COLLINS RE: MONDAY REVIEW
NOTES:		v JANE HARPER - HOLIDAY 4TH-8TH INCL.

KEY: i - INFORMATION   m - MEETING   v - VACATION

Fig 36 Electronic diary

have reported in the first instance to Reception and then been directed or taken to your office. Alternatively you may have gone to Reception to meet them and escort them personally.

Within a large organisation it is usual, for security reasons, for all visitors to be vetted at Reception and perhaps issued with the necessary visitor's identification before being conducted to the relevant offices by security staff. Either way, as a secretary you will have received from Reception notification of their arrival.

Whatever the size of the organisation it is the secretary's duty to ensure that visitors are greeted appropriately: first impressions can be lasting. Where visitors have travelled some distance they are likely to appreciate being directed to the cloakroom prior to their appointment. Visitors should not have to ask about such facilities; the secretary should take the initiative. You should also offer to relieve them of any bags and cases with which they may feel encumbered, and where time permits offer refreshments.

Where visitors may be very early for an appointment and may be waiting in your office you should be prepared to make casual conversation to at least a limited extent, bearing in mind, however, the necessity of getting on with your own work if you are busy. You should not, however, permit yourself to be drawn into conversation on any topic which may be considered to be of a leading or confidential nature.

The art of 'small talk'

Small talk comes more easily to certain individuals, but can be made by anyone with experience. What is important is that the secretary is capable of showing genuine interest in what the visitor has to say and is capable of being a good listener. Such deviation from the normal routine can be very welcome during a demanding day and it is surprising how much useful and interesting information may be gleaned during such conversations.

Where visitors are frequently required to wait in your office it will be a good idea to have your own coffee/tea-making facilities available together with a suitable selection of newspapers and magazines. It will also be appreciated by callers if you are in a position to keep them notified of any delays and to reassure them that they have not been overlooked or totally forgotten.

Where you are aware of the visitor's schedule you may also be in a position to provide useful assistance in terms of calling for a taxi or perhaps recommending a suitable restaurant or making hotel reservations where necessary.

Performing introductions

An extension of receiving visitors can be the need to make introductions. There is an established etiquette for this, and it is easy to get it wrong.

Basically men are introduced to women, for example 'Mrs Williams, may I introduce Mr Steele, our General Manager – Mr Steele, Mrs Williams.' Where people are of the same sex, juniors are introduced to seniors.

Incidentally, when you are the person being introduced, the usual response is a firm handshake and 'How do you do'.

The secretary as a host

No secretary wishes to be seen as a glorified coffee-maker. On the other hand, where this task does form an integral part of the duties, it is well to perform it gracefully. Only when its prominence over other duties is greatly exaggerated will it be reasonable to discuss the essence of your role with your boss and come to some suitable compromise.

It is important to mention here that many senior secretarial positions do involve a considerable amount of what could be termed 'hosting activities', particularly where the nature of the employer's work necessitates much business entertaining. However, where this is likely to be the case it will normally have been specified in the job description.

Visitors without an appointment

Persons arriving to see your boss without an appointment always pose a problem. This is one area which requires careful discussion with your boss and the laying down of guidelines for your use. It is all very well to attempt to stipulate that no one is seen without an appointment, but there may be extenuating circumstances, and it is important that these can at least to some extent be identified and anticipated. In large organisations this will, of course, be a problem which is dealt with first at Reception. However, even then it is likely that they refer to you for a final ruling.

Where the unexpected visitor is a sales representative, for example, it is extremely unlikely that they would be received without an appointment. Many firms have very strict rules about this. Only certain personnel ever see representatives (even those with appointments) as only these people will have the authority to place orders.

On the other hand, the caller may be a valued business associate or client who happens to be in the vicinity and is calling 'on the off chance', or the reason for the call may be personal, or the result of some form of emergency which your boss would wish to be advised about. Therefore, in certain instances the decision made will depend on your assessment of the degree of urgency and importance. In such circumstances the power which secretaries are in a position to exert is considerable; this is something that all secretaries should readily acknowledge and take care not to abuse or misuse. You should always be prepared to cater for eventualities in organising your boss's daily programme, otherwise you could 'protect' to such an extent that a vital business opportunity is missed or insufficient time is given to an important matter which may have serious repercussions at a later date.

Dealing with the press

One special sort of 'visitor' who may confront you on your arrival at the office in the morning could well be a representative of the press. Reporters can be extremely persistent and certain types of business activity can attract considerable interest and attention and, if you are not careful, much unwanted and sometimes harmful publicity. Great care must be exercised, therefore, in giving information to the press or other representatives of the media. It should be emphasised that the only information supplied should come from an authorised source, probably the Public Relations or Press Officer.

Having said this, it is of course desirable in many organisations to cultivate good relations with the media. They can be in a strong position to provide help and the right sort of publicity on, for example, special occasions or during promotional exercises, where a write-up or 'spot' on radio or television could be worth its weight in gold.

Taking dictation

An important aspect of every secretary's daily routine will be the time spent taking dictation or receiving briefing for the compilation of material on the boss's behalf. Some executives like to try to set aside a particular period each day for this purpose, while others will simply take the opportunity as and when it presents itself.

Either way, the secretary must be prepared. You must be ready to go into your boss's office immediately when you are called and you must have pad, pens and pencils to hand. Some bosses even choose to dictate material over the telephone or via the intercom. There is no set pattern and secretaries must be ready to adapt accordingly.

Where you are required to take a lot of dictation you must organise yourself in a way that facilitates the art of writing. Films regularly portray secretaries taking dictation from pads on their knees, but in reality this is often far from ideal. It is preferable, if at all possible, to have a flat surface to lean on and to be seated directly opposite the dictator so that hearing is not impaired in any way.

The date and the dictator's initials (where more than one executive's material is recorded) should be detailed at the foot of the page of the shorthand notebook. Many experienced secretaries keep elastic bands round their notebooks so that they can isolate the next blank page immediately and be ready to begin writing at once. It is also advisable to draw a diagonal line through material which has already been transcribed. How you organise your notepad will, of course, be very much a matter of personal preference, as will your choice of writing implement. Some people prefer a pen to a pencil; others favour a ballpoint pen. The important thing is to adopt your own system, make sure that it works for you and stick to it. You should also devise your own system of 'flagging' or 'signalling' particular pieces of dictation which require some form of special or immediate attention. Possibilities for your consideration might be coloured pens, some sort of symbol or code, the insertion of paper clips or perhaps a fold on the page. While taking dictation it is also helpful to place any documents given to you by the boss face down on the desk so that they will be in an order compatible with the dictation when you return to your desk to transcribe the session's work.

When a shorthand notebook is filled it is a good idea to date the front cover with the period of its use, eg from 15 March to 19 April. This can be useful where you may wish to trace a piece of dictation at a later date. It may also be advisable to store all old notebooks in chronological order for say a two-year period, dependent upon the nature of your work.

Methods of preparing correspondence

Different individuals will favour different ways of preparing correspondence. Some will still prefer to draft much of their correspondence by hand, perhaps even at home, and will utilise a secretary's shorthand skills more in meetings. Others will have mastered the art of dictation to a shorthand writer and will require fast, accurate speeds as a consequence. Some might favour audio preparation, while others might leave the vast majority of the actual composition to the secretary, choosing only to provide the briefest of general guidelines.

Whichever method is adopted the secretary will need to fulfil the role satisfactorily. Where you work for more than one executive, each may use a different technique, so making it essential for you to exercise all your skills and perhaps operate at different levels for each one.

Interruptions

One problem which will affect all forms of preparation is that of interruptions. These may come in the form of personal interruptions, telephone calls, external noise or disturbance or some form of emergency, like a fire alarm. Whatever the method of imparting the information, interruptions of any kind will break the flow and cause lapses in concentration (sometimes on the part of both parties). This is perhaps one of the main arguments in favour of audio dictation/transcription. Dictators can plan their time and have the benefit of being able to play back as often as necessary without unnecessarily wasting the secretary's time. In turn, the secretary can transcribe the material when convenient and save any time that might otherwise have been spent waiting for the dictation to be completed.

Bring-forward systems (tickler files)

Many secretaries make extensive use of bring-forward systems or 'tickler' files as they are sometimes called. These are used where a topic cannot be dealt with instantly or where additional information needs to be gathered. For instance, a letter may be received asking a question which cannot be answered until a committee has met in the following week. In such a circumstance the procedure would be to acknowledge receipt of the letter and assure the writer that the question will be answered following the relevant meeting. (This could well be one of the instances in which a secretary has the authority to process this correspondence without reference to the executive.) While awaiting the meeting the correspondence would be placed within a bring-forward system, rather than filed and perhaps forgotten.

A typical bring-forward file consists of a concertina file with numerical divisions for the days of the month. Therefore if a communication is received on 3 March but cannot be dealt with satisfactorily until after a meeting scheduled for 15 March, the letter would be acknowledged briefly and then placed in the pocket for 16 March. On that date the secretary would, as a matter of course, check the bring-forward system for any items appertaining to that date.

Follow-up systems or aide-mémoires

A secretary may find it helpful to initiate other follow-up systems for many different purposes and in many different situations. A good memory is a very useful attribute but none of us is infallible, and most of us would do well to devise some sort of follow-up or reminder system other than a knot in one's handkerchief or a cryptic note on the back of a cigarette packet or envelope!

What sort of systems could be set up?

Inclusions in diaries – some diaries have special sections for reminders and notes.

Special stationery – this is becoming increasingly popular, and many firms specialise in producing special eye-catching stationery for this purpose. The important thing here, of course, is to restrict such pads to their intended use, and this is often difficult.

Special files – where the topic is of major significance and likely to involve considerable correspondence, it may be desirable to open a special file and perhaps allocate a different colour to it and retain it at the desk while it is in use. Its existence could also be noted in the diary.

Make lists – where the follow-up may be initiated after a dictation session where large quantities of notes may need to have been made in a shorthand notebook, or perhaps where specific 'actions' were requested and noted during a meeting, it will be advisable to make itemised lists and to tick off the items as they are dealt with.

Special 'reminder' books – where a secretary or the executive has many things to remember, of both a personal and a business nature, it may be advisable to keep a separate book or folding card in addition to the normal diaries. Just as it becomes second nature to consult the diary on at least a daily basis, so too will it become a habit to consult the reminder book.

Making arrangements

Much of a secretary's work may come under the general heading of 'making arrangements'. These arrangements may include any of the following:

- setting up meetings
- booking meals
- organising working lunches
- organising briefing sessions
- organising seminars
- organising conferences
- organising company public relations visits
- organising social activities and functions
- organising collections
- arranging presentations

All such activities will tend to have certain points in common, and the organisational skills employed in one area can often be easily transferred to another.

What will be the common features?

1 All will have to be done within a predetermined time.
2 All will involve other people.
3 All will involve the exercise of some form of communications skills.
4 Most will require arranging a suitable venue.
5 Most will require the opening of a special file and the maintenance of records of some kind.
6 Some will require considerable paperwork.
7 Some will necessitate handling money.
8 Some will require decisions to be made or taken.

9 Some will require careful monitoring as they progress.
10 Some will involve the use of transport.

When making any sort of arrangements you are operating on behalf of your boss, and will need to establish firmly your terms of reference and liaise closely as the arrangements get under way.

Successful arrangements require meticulous attention to detail and the sound operation of checklists and countdown calendars, otherwise it can be remarkably easy to overlook an important detail or essential ingredient or find that you are in grave danger of running out of time.

However, a successfully organised event or meeting can give any secretary considerable personal satisfaction and the opportunity to demonstrate organisational abilities and administrative flair, and hopefully receive positive feedback afterwards.

Travel arrangements

Another aspect of a secretary's duties, and certainly one which is frequently highlighted by examining bodies, is that of making travel arrangements on behalf of your employer.

People are now much more prepared to travel in order to do business, and such is the progress in the means of travel at an individual's disposal and its increased speed that distance becomes less of a problem.

Travel will, of course, be of various kinds and will involve arrangements for both home and overseas. Once again attention to detail is the key factor to be observed.

Travel departments or the use of agents

Where a number of travel arrangements require to be made, organisations may have their own travel departments. Only in this way can a large international organisation rely on having the necessary expertise readily available and to secure the best deals. A top rate travel department can make a substantial contribution to the efficient and economic operation of a company's foreign and domestic business, where considerable time and energy are spent by high-ranking personnel in different locations and on the move throughout the world.

When the scale of travel within an organisation does not warrant a special department, arrangements will normally be left totally to the secretary, who will then liaise with a reputable travel agent (one who is a member of ABTA, the Association of British Travel Agents). Where arrangements need to be made frequently, it will be worth while for the secretary to cultivate the services of a particular agent and to establish a rapport with one of the clerks there.

The planning

Identify the objectives

Whether the journey/visit is to be at home or abroad, the first thing to be discussed is the objectives. Any journey or visit, whatever its purpose, must be undertaken with a view to achieving the desired objectives irrespective of what they might be. Their identification will, therefore, have considerable influence on the arrangements which are drawn up. For example, is the visit a routine one to perhaps a subsidiary company in this country, or an exploratory one to a previously unvisited Middle Eastern destination with a view to establishing an overseas outlet, or one to a European trade fair or of a lecture tour of the USA? Obviously each of these visits will be undertaken with totally different objectives in mind, and will consequently require very different arrangements to be made.

Ascertain the mode of travel

Sometimes there will be little or no alternative in respect of the mode of travel. However, where viable options do exist it will be necessary to take individuals' personal preferences into consideration and these should always be clarified before making definite reservations and plans. Also where arrangements are made, in-company checks should always be made with the airline company to be used or with British Rail as well as ensuring that timetables and other reference sources are up to date.

Travelling by air

Much business travel is done by air and the following are points to remember and consider if the benefits of flying are to be maximised:

- distance involved and the likelihood of jet lag
- duration of the business trip
- comfort – first class travel need not be viewed as a luxury for a busy executive
- availability of special on-board facilities for business travellers
- the desirability of direct rather than stopover flights
- time savings to be gained by using Concorde on a trans-Atlantic crossing
- distance of the departure point and appointment venue from the respective airports
- implications of delays in making flight connections or perhaps changing airports
- airport facilities
- baggage restrictions
- the benefits of membership of British Airways Executive Club, *viz* priority check-in, special lounges, business facilities, insurance, security baggage tags, hotel benefits
- shuttle services for domestic flights

London City Airport

With the business world shrinking and the approach of 1992 and the 'open market' in Europe, increasing numbers of business transactions are being made between European cities. To cater specifically for the needs of the business traveller, City Airport situated in London's booming Docklands and only 6 miles from the Bank of England, provides 'short-hop' services to Charles de Gaulle Airport in Paris and to Brussels and Amsterdam and the Channel Islands, with further plans to extend the service to include Rotterdam and Dusseldorf.

Despite initial problems with local authorities and residents over approval to operate the services in the heart of London and the current restriction to prop-type planes, it is anticipated that approval will be gained to operate a jet service. Also the lack of an underground station in the immediate vicinity seems to have been overcome by alternative transport. This takes the form of a London City Airport Riverbus which departs from Charing Cross Pier and after one stop at London Bridge travels direct to the airport in 35 mins.

The advantages of the City Airport services are its flight frequencies, its convenient location, its fast check-in times, good support services, such as secretarial help, fax, room hire and good catering.

- travelling at peak holiday periods
- booking difficulties on certain routes.

Note: Where companies own or charter their own planes, arrangements need to be made in respect of securing pilot and crew, as well as take-off slot and other flight information.

Travelling by train

Many business people choose to travel by train, particularly on the Inter-city routes which are fast and frequent, in order to remove the strain of driving, while enabling them to get on with work while travelling, if desired. In respect of making train arrangements the following are some points to remember and consider:

- duration of journey
- services available on train, including meals (Pullman Service)
- the fact that many cities have more than one station
- the need to book seats and to distinguish between smoking and non-smoking compartments and seat facing directions
- the benefits of an executive ticket, *viz* reserved car parking at the departure station, reserved seat, first class travel, refreshment vouchers and free underground rail travel in London
- the possibility of sleeper accommodation on longer journeys
- the possibility of taking one's car on the train for use at the destination
- the possibility of hiring a special executive saloon where a group of executives may be travelling a distance and wish to hold a 'meeting on the move'
- the benefits of opening a British Rail account whereby travellers simply present a BR Travel Warrant at the booking office
- the convenience of maintaining a supply of prepaid tickets for emergency use.

Travelling by car

Possession of a company car is still viewed by most business personnel as a perk and many cover thousands of miles every year on business. When taking a car to Europe there are, however, certain special factors which need to be remembered, including the following:

- booking ferry crossings (perhaps also cabin accommodation) sufficiently in advance, particularly during holiday periods
- the existence of certain concessions offered by ferry companies to shareholders
- the need to stipulate car size and details of passengers at the time of booking
- the need to display a GB sticker
- the need to carry a warning triangle to use in the event of an emergency stop
- tinted headlight requirement (removeable covers are an option here)
- headlamp convertors to alter the direction of the beam when driving on the right hand side of the road
- first aid kits are obligatory in some countries
- the advisability of carrying spare parts
- the need for adequate, up-to-date road maps
- the services provided by the AA and RAC
- essential currency for toll charges where using autoroutes
- necessary driving documents (whether using own car or hiring) – some countries still require an international driving licence
- knowledge of driving and insurance restrictions and regulations for the countries in question
- where an executive's own car is to be used a green card is required.

Electronic navigation systems

Technological advances are becoming increasingly common in respect of assistance with road travel. Map reading can pose a problem, particularly when driving in strange territory, alone and where it is difficult or even impossible to pull in to read a map.

Modern electronic navigation systems are being developed using mini computers and electronically digitised copies of the UK Ordnance Survey road maps. The idea is that once a driver enters the town of his destination a VDU in the dashboard of the car will display a line map of the main roads between the current position and the destination, with the scale enlarging as the driver closes in on the destination. Street names appear within the last few miles making it easier to compare progress.

As an alternative to using their own cars, many business people opt for the convenience of the hire car. These can often be hired on a 'rent it here, leave it there' basis within countries for a minimum 48 hours, which can be particularly useful where combined with flight arrangements. Additionally when travelling by car in winter weather conditions it is always advisable to carry a shovel, as well as some food and a flask of tea or coffee and a travelling rug. In this situation, of course, a mobile telephone could be particularly useful.

Booking hotel accommodation

Secretaries undertaking frequent travel arrangements will build up useful reference files containing comprehensive details and where possible leaflets and current tariffs for hotels used by executives. When booking hotel accommodation it is important to remember the following:

- ascertain personal preferences in terms of type of accommodation, eg bath or shower, quiet room
- ascertain preferred size of hotel
- select suitable location, eg city centre or outskirts
- check facilities available, eg quality of restaurant, parking, sports facilities, secretarial support
- check room availability by telephone
- provide written confirmation by letter, telex or fax (traveller should have personal copy of the confirmation)
- try to be precise about requirements and duration of stay (where there is no set itinerary but a lot of movement is envisaged, eg travel throughout a country, many of the hotel chains offer a useful advance booking service within their group).

Organising the necessary paperwork and documentation

Foreign travel requires certain essential documents which need to be carefully checked in terms of their validity as well as the completion of certain paperwork. The following are the main items requiring attention:

- **Passports** These must be up to date and valid for the type of trip envisaged. Full 10 year passports are available from one of the UK Passport offices but take time to be processed, renewed or amended. British Visitor's Passports are

available from main Post Offices but are not valid world wide and can only be used on trips of up to 3 months' duration.

- **Visas or entry permits** These are necessary to secure entry into some countries and it is important to check the regulations applying at any particular time as they change frequently. Information is obtainable from the appropriate embassy or from the International Air Transport Association (IATA). Again sufficient time should be allowed to arrange the visas.
- **International Driving Licences** These are available from the AA or RAC. Charges are minimal and licences are issued to any current holder of a valid UK licence on production of two passport size photographs and the appropriate fee.
- **Health Certificates** Some countries require travellers to have certain inoculations/vaccinations. Again current health regulations are available from IATA. The main health risks are in respect of cholera, malaria, typhoid, polio and yellow fever and any necessary inoculations/ vaccinations should be had well in advance of any trip in case there are side effects to overcome. Emergency vaccinations can be carried out at British Airways Medical Centres in London.
- **Insurance certificates** Travel can be hazardous and adequate insurance cover is essential. This should cover all contingencies from death, personal accident, medical expenses, loss of money and personal property including luggage.

All paperwork should be completed prior to a trip and kept in a convenient place so that it may be produced or consulted when necessary.

Arranging foreign currency

Checks should always be made into any currency regulations or restrictions which might exist in respect of money taken into or out of countries to be visited. Arrangements should be made well in advance as to the manner and amount of currency to be taken. Several possibilities exist dependent on the nature of the trip and whether business deals may be anticipated, in which case additional arrangements with banks in respect of Banker's Drafts or currency transfers may have to be made. This, however, would be likely to fall within the remit of a company's finance department. The country or countries to be visited will have a bearing on which options(s) are to be advised. However, in general it will be a matter of choosing from the following options:

- cash in the relevant currency or currencies
- Eurocheques supported by the appropriate card
- traveller's cheques in an appropriate currency and in denominations of a suitable size
- credit cards.

Whichever variations are used it is important that records are kept of all cheque and card numbers in case of thefts. Also where credit cards are to be used, expiry dates should be examined.

The preparation of an itinerary

An itinerary is simply a document referring to the details and plans for a journey or trip, including timing of events and information on modes of travel, departure and arrival times, accommodation and other items of information which may be useful to the traveller. Itineraries can come in various forms. On a long, complex business trip it is likely that the traveller will have a fairly detailed, itemised version in his briefcase, and a very brief version containing only essential information (perhaps on cards) in his pocket.

When preparing itineraries it will be customary for a secretary to prepare several copies – one for personal use, one on file and others as considered necessary. Fig 37 is an example of an itinerary.

Points to consider when preparing an itinerary

1 Do *not* make the schedule too tight – allow breathing space.
2 Bear in mind time changes and the international date line.
3 Consider factors such as political unrest and strikes.
4 Note weather conditions – dramatic changes in temperature can cause fatigue and add to the problems of jet lag.
5 Remember that holiday times are always busier.
6 There may be local holidays or religious festivals in the countries to be visited.
7 Always use the 24-hour clock to avoid confusion.
8 Always include check-in times in your calculations.

9 Allow for changes between stations and airport terminals.
10 Include flight numbers.
11 Allow free half days during lengthy trips for catching up and relaxation.
12 Include a set time for contacting the home base or vice versa.

Other preparations

Maps

Where the executive is not familiar with the area it will be helpful to organise suitable maps, including street maps and perhaps a local sketch map. Sometimes where they may be attending an organised conference these will be sent automatically together with the conference programme and any other items of possible local interest.

Phrase book

Where someone is visiting a foreign country and is unfamiliar with the language, a simple phrase book can prove invaluable.

Briefing documents

These may take the form of providing any relevant facts or information relating to the visit. There may, for example, be a synopsis of the company(ies) to be visited, general policies, financial positions, future plans and personnel. Such details will enable an executive to 'do his homework' or 'revise' prior to a visit. This advance knowledge is likely to be useful during meetings and interviews and will also serve to impress clients or prospective customers.

Speeches

Where an executive is required to make a speech at a function or give a formal lecture at a conference, he should be well prepared. The speech may have to be vetted in advance by the organisation, and it will be customary to have determined the content and have it typed up prior to departure. Likewise, any supportive documents or visual aids should be ready.

Sales literature

Where a trip is planned as part of a sales promotion

```
                        ITINERARY

            Trip of Miss C D Jenkinson to Valencia
                     6 - 8 June inclusive



    Tuesday, 6 June

    1430 hours      Company car from office to airport
    1540            Arrive London Heathrow, Terminal 2
    1645            Depart Flight IB 615 for Valencia
    2005            Arrive Valencia (1 hour ahead)
                    Taxi to Hotel Rey Don Jaime



    Wednesday, 7 June

    0800 hours      Breakfast meeting with Sr Hernandez
    0930            Car collect to take to Lladro
    1000            Meeting with Maria Duarte
                    Tour of Factory
    1530            Return to hotel
    1700            Meeting with Juan Jimenez
    2000            Dinner booked for self and 5 guests
                    (Los Viveros, Jardines del Real - seafood
                    a speciality)



    Thursday, 8 June

    1030 hours      Meeting at Museo Provincial de Bellas Artes
                    (Sr Carlos Ferrar)
                    Suggest lunch at El Condestable
                                  (Tel 369 92 50)
    1535            Depart Valencia Flight IB 614
                    (minimum Check in 20 minutes)
    1655            Arrive London Heathrow, Terminal 2
                    (take 1 hour off)
                    Company car will collect.
```

Fig 37 Itinerary

exercise it will be necessary to have ample supplies of sales literature, preferably prepared in the language of the country. This will indicate the necessity of forward planning as such materials are not produced overnight and in order to create a favourable impression it will be important to secure accurate translations and presentations that can in no way cause offence. This latter point can be vital in certain Middle Eastern countries, where European advertising and promotional techniques would be unnacceptable to their culture.

Specimens and samples

Sometimes, depending on the nature of the product being promoted, it will be possible to take actual samples. Where these are electrical it will be important to check plug types and voltage, which vary from country to country.

Display equipment

On certain trips, particularly those made by marketing executives, support material in the form of professionally prepared audiovisual presentations may be desired. Where travel is within the UK, cars can easily be loaded accordingly. However, lightweight travel packs available nowadays also make presentations abroad relatively simple to include in a promotional programme.

Visiting cards

An executive who does a lot of travelling and meets many potential clients and other influential contacts should always have an adequate supply of printed business cards to hand out. These should be appropriate to their status within the organisation they represent and include all relevant information.

Checklists

During a lengthy trip involving many meetings and appointments, it will be useful for an executive to have a summary card printed for each day. These will provide details of all appointments set out in chronological order, together with names, addresses and telephone numbers. Such cards can be easily carried in a pocket.

Addresses and telephone lists

Where a trip may spread over several days or even weeks, it will be advisable to prepare a detailed list of all possible business contacts in the area of the visit, in case opportunities present themselves for extra contacts to be made. Some organisations will alert all business contacts in the area of the visit or the presence of 'their person' together with their arrival and departure dates and hotel details during the visit, thereby maximising the potential for useful contacts outside those specifically scheduled for the trip.

Emergency Information

Where a person is travelling in a foreign country for the first time and no relevant foreign language knowledge is possessed, it is a good idea to have things like the name and address of the host company and hotel details written on cards in the language of the country. These can be useful to show to taxi drivers or to police and other officials should any difficulties be experienced.

Useful reference books

Travel is obviously an area where use can be made of a wide range of reference books. These are fully detailed in Unit 9. It is important that any books used in connection with travel plans should be fully up to date.

Medical advice

The Departments of Health and Social Security will be able to provide full details of the health agreements in operation within the EC and with certain other countries. Arrangements vary considerably from country to country and it is always advisable to have full details well in advance of departure.

Where a traveller is currently undergoing any form of medical treatment, they should obtain a letter from their personal doctor outlining their case history and detailing any medication they are receiving. They should also ensure that they have adequate supplies of any essential medication which may be difficult to obtain at their destination.

It will, of course, be advisable for any traveller to carry such general medical requisites as are considered necessary, eg aspirin, stomach pills, antiseptic ointment or lotion and perhaps salt tablets and anti-malaria pills if travelling in certain countries, together with any particular 'favourite personal remedies' which may not be readily available at the destination.

One other wise precaution will be the inclusion of a spare pair of spectacles or contact lenses or a copy of any complex prescription for these: loss of or damage to spectacles or lenses could prove quite disastrous on an important business trip.

Countdown preparations

Making preparations for a trip requires careful advance planning and provides an ideal opportunity for initiating follow-up systems. Where a secretary regularly makes travel arrangements on behalf of staff confidential personal travel files should be opened in respect of each individual. These should contain comprehensive information of all personal details, passport and visa documentation status, health matters and vaccination certificates held and details of all credit cards, together with all personal travel and accommodation preferences. Such information will save a great deal of time and help avoid errors, last minute panics or disappointments and dissatisfaction on the part of travellers. Certain things will need to be done by certain dates, and depending on the nature of the trip preparations may be under way many months in advance in order to secure flights and accommodation and to coincide with particular events.

It may be necessary also to begin to gather literature, to set up files, to do research and prepare speeches and presentations, and to organise incidental transport (car rental).

The schedule for home events will also require to be built up around any trip out of the country. This may require the rearrangement of meetings or the briefing of stand-in personnel where appropriate.

Last-minute details

Prior to the departure the following things will need to be checked. (A checklist would normally be drawn up by the secretary and checked off with the executive.)

1   Flight times, where appropriate
2   Transport to the airport or railway station
3   Documentation – passport, visa, vaccination certificates, insurance, driving licence
4   Tickets and/or travel warrants
5   Currency – foreign and sterling
6   Credit cards
7   Travellers' cheques
8   Hotel reservations
9   Itinerary
10 Personal papers, notes, briefings, addresses etc
11 Medical supplies
12 Hand luggage in addition to briefcase
13 Baggage labels

Note: On short business trips many executives favour carrying a spare suit/outfit, shoes and so on in one of the popular folding traveller packs which are accepted as cabin luggage, rather than taking a full suitcase and having to wait for it at the baggage collection point, so wasting perhaps valuable and limited time.

In the boss's absence

In addition to the checklist for the actual trip, decisions will have to be made relating to the smooth running of the office during the executive's absence. These will include the following:

1   How has correspondence to be handled?
2   To whom are emergency decisions delegated?
3   Who will supply any technical advice if it is required?
4   Have anticipated visitors been contacted or alternative arrangements made?
5   Have apologies or substitutes been noted for scheduled meetings?
6   How can the executive be contacted – if at all?
7   Under what circumstances should contact be made?
8   How soon should the normal work routine resume after the trip?

Possible solutions to these questions might be as follows:

1   All correspondence will be dealt with by the secretary as seen fit, with the exception of personal mail which will either be forwarded or retained until the executive's return. Such action would normally necessitate answering some, acknowledging some by informing the writer that it will be dealt with on the executive's return, and rerouting some to an assistant. Brief notes would be taken of all correspondence, and copies of outgoing mail would be kept on file for updating on the executive's return.
2   Some decisions may be delegated to the secretary while others may go to an assistant or another executive of equal rank.
3   This would normally be dealt with by someone briefed prior to the departure.
4   It is assumed that this will apply to long term appointments. As soon as the executive's trip is confirmed, contact visitors, either to suggest alternative dates, or to notify them that their appointment will be with another person, whose name and position should be identified.
5   Where the executive should normally have attended the meeting, notification should be

made to the chairperson or where permissible, a substitute identified.

6 This will depend on the location and whether it is fixed for the duration of the absence.

7 This will depend on both business and domestic circumstances existing at the time of departure.

8 This will depend on the duration of the visit and on the type of travel undertaken. However, it is usual to allow for some 'catching-up' time immediately following an executive's return.

Office security
Maintaining confidentiality

An important aspect of the work of many secretaries is that of maintaining confidentiality. This will be more important in certain areas of work, and many secretaries may even find themselves signing the Official Secrets Act if they work for a government department and are likely to come into contact with classified information which could be of value to someone else.

Nowadays industrial espionage is more of a potential hazard than one might imagine. Information can be a valuable commodity, and can include details of contracts, designs, prices, personnel, future policy and so on.

Individuals intent on gaining information will have a wide range of tactics to achieve their objectives. In certain environments secretaries can be particularly vulnerable and must be alert to the possibilities of theft, fraud, information leaks, breaches of confidentiality, weaknesses in security provisions and even perhaps bomb threats and kidnapping, which were virtually unheard of until recently.

Precautions which might be taken at company level

1 The use of security agencies.
2 Close liaison with the local police and their crime prevention section.
3 Regular patrol of buildings by security personnel and perhaps guard dogs.
4 Installation of alarm systems.
5 Strict reception screening procedures.
6 Restricted access to high-security areas.
7 Careful handling and issue of keys.

8 Installation of closed-circuit television (CCTV).
9 Installation of fireproof filing cabinets.
10 Restricted handling of confidential information.
11 Introduction of frequent charges to computer passwords and regular checks of the system.
12 Appointment of an official Press Officer.

Safeguards which a secretary might operate

1 Have all-round alertness.
2 Report any suspicious circumstances or individual.
3 Be tidy – never leave confidential papers lying around.
4 Keep drawers closed and locked if they contain confidential information.
5 Make a note of the serial numbers of all office equipment and mark it with indelible markers.
6 Do not label keys in an obvious manner – use a code.
7 Do not leave visitors unsupervised.
8 Escort visitors off the premises.
9 Be careful during telephone conversations where you can be overheard – offer to call back where necessary.
10 Mark 'confidential', 'private' or 'personal' mail accordingly.
11 Utilise recorded delivery, registered post or special messenger services as appropriate.
12 Take care with carbon paper and carbon ribbons – they can be read!
13 Shred or incinerate all discarded confidential material.
14 Take extra care with material stored in memory typewriters or word processors – remove leads and discs.
15 Always remember to remove the original from the flat bed of the photocopier.
16 Do not indulge in idle gossip.
17 Take care when using an intercom system.
18 Be careful about leaks via switchboard personnel.
19 Do not leave tapes on dictation or transcription machines.
20 Position your desk where visitors to the office cannot read over your shoulder.
21 Where you have an electronic typewriter or a word processor, scroll the text into the machine

or off the screen when people are liable to read confidential material.

22 Do not leave work in the typewriter or on the word processor screen if you have to leave the office.
23 Be careful in delegating work.
24 Be constantly on your guard.

Human relations in the office

An exciting aspect of secretarial work is meeting new people of all kinds. Such meetings will broaden your own horizons, and hopefully other people will derive pleasure from meeting you.

How do you establish good human relations? Start with the assumption that everyone is an individual and deserves to be treated as such. It is important to recognise that people are sometimes ambitious. They may need to have recognition and will appreciate being given the opportunity to express their individuality, so try to meet them half way.

Remember that organisations are made up of individuals, and it is the relationships which exist between these individuals which contribute substantially to the success of an organisation and to the quality of the working environment. Coping effectively with human relationships is a very important aspect of any secretary's work.

Points to remember

1 Greet people warmly.
2 Make introductions meaningful.
3 Remember names.
4 Use titles appropriately, ie judge the degree of formality required.
5 Be polite – even when under stress.
6 Be friendly but not over-familiar or personal.
7 Keep confidences.
8 Avoid office gossip.
9 Show respect for the ideas and viewpoints of others.
10 Try to be a good listener.
11 Be helpful whenever possible.
12 Try not to show favouritism in front of others.
13 Be professional in all aspects.
14 Establish a good working rapport with colleagues.

The secretary/boss relationship – the way to success

1 Each must view the other as a professional and recognise the interdependence of roles.
2 Each must accept that the other has their own objectives regarding work.
3 Each must respect the other as an individual and not as an extension of themselves.
4 There should be a working partnership not a competition.
5 Of necessity one – the secretary – must take the role of junior partner.
6 The junior partner should, however, be 'groomed' as a stand-in and consequently should have the confidence to act in the boss's place where necessary.
7 Involvement in all aspects of the work pays dividends. The secretary may, if given the opportunity, be able to make a contribution to the wider aspects of the job and so relieve a considerable amount of pressure.
8 Define areas and boundaries of responsibility closely so that there is no confusion and consequent time wasting.
9 Allow time for planning and consultation – even if it means building it into the daily schedule.
10 Always bring problems into the open. Don't brood over them and create an atmosphere.
11 Listen to the other's point of view.
12 Maintain a sense of humour.
13 Learn to apologise gracefully.
14 Learn to accept constructive criticism.
15 Accept compliments with pleasure.
16 Try to establish an air of positive cooperation and tolerance.
17 Try to view the other as a valued colleague rather than a superior/subordinate.
18 Always find a little time to engage in small talk, particularly at the beginning of the day.
19 Try to discover what makes the other tick.

Working with superiors

Within any organisation a secretary is likely to come into frequent contact with the boss's colleagues and superiors. It is your responsibility to cooperate with superiors at all times, but also to ensure that there is no conflict of loyalty. This can arise, for example, where a superior attempts to exercise authority in relation to the use of your time. Always seek the permission of your own immediate superior before undertaking work for someone else. Technically the superior concerned should seek the boss's agreement personally before approaching the secretary.

Working with colleagues

In all working situations you can expect to get on better with some colleagues than with others. This is only human nature, and it would be unrealistic to suggest that it will be otherwise. Individuals will be of different ages, will come from different backgrounds, will have different types of experience and will differ in temperament. It is worthwhile remembering that good relations with individuals at your own level can be worth their weight in gold. You will be in a position to call on one another for advice and assistance and share what are likely to be common problems at work. Always try to avoid conflict. The maxim for successful relationships is 'treat others as you would like them to treat you'.

Working with subordinates

Subordinates are likely to fall into two categories:

- those who are junior to you in terms of age
- those who occupy lower status roles.

Try to treat the former as you would like your boss to treat you, and you will not go far wrong. When delegating work, be sure that you have given precise instructions. Offer constructive criticism where appropriate, but also give credit where it is due. Above all, be human. Juniors like to feel that you too can make mistakes, but try to maintain standards which are worthy of emulation.

With the latter it is important to establish a good working rapport, as it is likely that you will need to call upon their services from time to time. Where you have managed to establish good relationships it is likely that they will soon pay dividends, eg a good relationship with the mailing department or reprographic section will make it much easier for you to ask a favour when the time comes. Similarly, good links with catering, cleaning and maintenance staff are likely to ensure that you will be able to rely on their service and support more readily than if you are approaching them for the first time.

Working for more than one executive

Much attention is given to the obvious impacts of new equipment and systems, but less to their considerable implications for the employer/employee relationship. The growth of sophisticated office equipment has brought with it quite dramatic changes in staffing and consequent changes in relationships. Perhaps the most significant change as far as secretaries are concerned is the emergence of what might be called the 'time-sharing secretary'. Many practising secretaries would certainly endorse this point of view, and feel that whereas they have adapted to new equipment like word processors relatively quickly, it took longer and was more demanding to become accustomed to working for more than one boss! It will often take every ounce of a secretary's energy, imagination and human relations skills to meet the requirements set by different executives and to treat each fairly.

There is justification for organisations adopting time-sharing secretarial services on the grounds of economy alone. Improved equipment and systems relieve much of the repetitive routine work, so releasing secretaries to perform more managerial support functions. One-to-one secretary/boss situations are becoming much less common, and they will tend to become the exception rather than the rule. It is, therefore, important that trainee secretaries should develop the sort of flexible approach which will lead them to success in terms of securing employment in a changing business world.

Hints for handling time sharing

1   Treat executives as individuals and try to establish a working rapport with each.
2   Develop an interest in the activities of each executive.
3   Develop your own secretarial role and skills where necessary.
4   Modify your style to fit in with each executive. This necessitates an extremely flexible approach but should add to the challenge of your job, while enabling each executive to retain a unique style.
5   Establish an informal relationship with each executive so that you may iron out any problems and plan in an atmosphere of cooperation.
6   Be sure to treat each executive's work as confidential.
7   Show no favouritism.

8 Do not play one executive off against another.
9 Ignore their own superior/subordinate relationships. This can result in conflicting loyalties.
10 Discourage any jealousy or attempts at priority claims on your secretarial services.
11 Take care in coordinating the diaries (a composite forward planner may prove more efficient, or you may be fortunate enough to have access to electronic diary facilities).
12 Try to be one jump ahead at all times.

Managing time

The majority of secretaries will often have more to do than they can accomplish in any given time. The successful secretary will accomplish the 'single most important thing' in that given time, and as much more as is feasible. Sound judgement as to what is the 'single most important thing' separates the effective secretary from the ineffective one. Another important point is to stay with a task until it is complete. You have accomplished nothing if you have four tasks three-quarters of the way towards completion! It is better to have two projects completed and out of the way.

Things that eat into your time

- performing unnecessary work
- failing to complete a task
- failing to plan and budget your time
- slow reading
- inability to make decisions
- failure to consult printed instructions, eg staff handbooks, instruction manuals
- inability to listen attentively to instructions
- frittering away time on personal activities, eg reading papers and magazines, making personal phone calls
- an untidy desk
- making unnecessary drafts of routine correspondence

Twenty hints for better management of time

1 Set yourself targets.
2 Set aside some time every day for planning.
3 Keep checklists.
4 Make a 'things to do today' list.
5 Note the *priority* items and attend to them first.

6 Keep frequently consulted materials to hand, eg telephone numbers.
7 Keep wall charts and visual control boards up to date.
8 File every day.
9 Discard unwanted paper – do not hoard.
10 Keep drawers tidy and label containers.
11 Put things away when you have finished with them.
12 Set aside regular times each day for certain tasks – develop a routine.
13 Group tasks together, eg try to do all photocopying together.
14 See every task through – do not leave things half done.
15 Break up a large task into manageable units.
16 Be systematic and tidy – do not crumble under pressure.
17 If you are busy, learn to say 'no' pleasantly but assertively.
18 Improve your reading speed and accuracy.
19 Be confident – avoid checking and rechecking (better proofreading can save time in the long run!).
20 Take your time – do not panic – stop to think. Remember that correcting errors is time-consuming!

The team approach

If a secretary and boss operate as a team it is essential that the secretary knows what the boss's objectives are at all times. A secretary and boss should discuss together at regular intervals what each can do to enhance the overall performance of 'the team'.

Conclusion

If we accept that the skills, qualities and attitudes outlined in this unit are the characteristics which go towards making a secretary in the true sense of the word, we must necessarily accept that a secretary's role and function is in the managerial/executive support capacity and not purely in the provision of traditional secretarial skills. A secretary is becoming viewed increasingly as part of a management team, and thus requires a far wider knowledge and appreciation of business, people and their management. No longer will good skills be sufficient in themselves to ensure a good secretarial position. People skills and business skills will also be required.

1 How would you distinguish between a shorthand typist and a secretary?
2 What would be a secretary's likely preparations prior to taking dictation?
3 Why do discrepancies arise in diary keeping?
4 When making appointments, what *four* points should you always bear in mind?
5 When receiving visitors on behalf of your employer, what should you remember?
6 How would you deal with a sales representative who has not made an appointment?
7 What sort of *aide-memoires* might a competent secretary make?
8 Apart from travel, what sort of arrangements might a secretary make?
9 When making foreign travel arrangements, what points must be clarified in advance?
10 Why is maintaining confidentiality an important aspect of a secretary's role?
11 How can a secretary help maintain confidentiality in the daily routine?
12 What do you think are important aspects in a secretary's relationship with junior staff?
13 Why is it becoming increasingly common for a secretary to work for more than one executive?
14 What factors contribute to poor management of a secretary's time?
15 When an organisation is about to appoint secretarial staff, what sort of additional qualities are they likely to look for in applicants?

Personal activities

1 Keep *two* diaries, one for personal use (appointments, birthdays and special events), the other for school or college events (homework, examination dates, meetings, term dates).

2 When you go on a holiday with your family or friends, devise a travel itinerary and prepare a countdown calendar as you near the departure date. Take a particular interest in all the travel arrangements and necessary bookings as well as insurance cover and the arrangements for currency if applicable.

3 Be prepared to volunteer to help with the organisation of any social event the family is arranging. Much of the organisation is the same for major business events!

Group activity

Choose some sort of informal event which you and your fellow students might like to arrange and consider the organisation involved. Prepare a checklist and assess how much time it would take to arrange such an event. Examples might be:

- a buffet lunch
- a visit to the theatre
- a day trip to a place of interest.

Situation-based activities

1 You work for Jonathan Taylor, the Sales Manager of a large wholesale builders' merchants in Leeds. Mr Taylor has worked with the company for over forty years, having progressed from a minor position as a school leaver to his current post. He is due to retire in two months' time and is anxious to call on all his old customers and generally leave things organised for his successor. This means that he will be out of the office a lot as customers come from various distant locations. Business is extremely good at present and the general work of the office must be kept going. Mr Taylor's successor has still to be appointed.

a Study Mr Taylor's diary (*see* Fig 38) for next week and decide which evening would be best for him to have dinner with a business colleague in Scarborough. He would stay overnight. Please book him into a four-star hotel and supply the details. Plan his return route to Leeds to take in a call to York, where we would like you to book a table for four for luncheon at a convenient hotel. Use suitable reference books to provide the information you require.

b It has come to your notice that the staff are planning a very elaborate farewell for Mr Taylor, and you know that he would prefer something less ostentatious as he has talked with you about it quite often. How will you attempt to influence this situation to the satisfaction of everyone?

In addition, you have been asked to try to find out what sort of farewell gift Mr Taylor would like. How would you try to do this?

c Today, while Mr Taylor is out of the office, a sales representative with whom he has had frequent dealings in the past has arrived without an appointment. How would you deal with this?

d You have received an invitation to address a group of secretarial students at the local college of further education on secretarial work and the type of qualifications, skills and qualities which employers are looking for. Prepare notes for your talk.

Monday 21	Thursday 24
0930 Progress Meeting 1230 Lunch - Metropole Hotel - TJ 1530 Mr Spencer - Hargreaves + Co	1400 — Interview Panel
Tuesday 22 1000 University - Works Dept 11·30 Phil Jackson - Fairbrothers with MD	**Friday 25** 1000 Bradford City Council 1430 Works Council Meeting
Wednesday 23 1500 - Bill Giles, Personnel re next weeks interviews (15 mins. only)	**Saturday 26**
NOTES	Sunday 27

Fig 38

2 Imagine that you work as Secretary/PA to a Member of Parliament. Conditions are somewhat cramped in the House of Commons and you share an office with another MP's Secretary, Sylvia, who is much less experienced than you. Several problems have arisen over the past few weeks and you need to resolve them as quickly as possible. How would you handle them tactfully? You like Sylvia as a person and know you will have to continue to work together.

a Sylvia is extremely untidy, and her papers are continually spilling over into your work area.
b When you have been out of the office and Sylvia has answered your telephone, she has often left an insufficient message; you have had the problem of attempting to interpret it on your return, by which time she may not be there to clarify.
c Yesterday when you came back from lunch a friend of Sylvia's was seated at your desk reading an internal memo that was directed to your MP.
d Sylvia frequently interrupts your work with queries about hers.
e Sylvia is always discussing her MP's work

with you over coffee and lunch breaks and enjoys endulging in the general gossip and rumours which circulate in a place like the House.

3 You work in the Housing Department of a local authority and your immediate superior is Mrs Jones, the Housing Manager.

a When you arrive at the office this morning at 0845 the following items/tasks/messages are in your in-tray. Explain how you would deal with each one and state the one to which you would give priority, giving reasons for your selection.

  i minutes from last week's meeting of the Social Services Committee on which Mrs Jones sits
  ii a letter addressed to Mrs Jones and marked 'Personal'
  iii a note from Mr Dickson from Environmental Health saying that he cannot keep the luncheon appointment he has with Mrs Jones today
  iv a note written by Mrs Jones to you last evening at 1930 asking you to check that

an overhead projector is in the committee room for the meeting which she is scheduled to chair at 0930 hours

v a message from the switchboard taken at 0835 hours to say that Mrs Jones will not be in the office until after 1000 hours as her mother has been taken ill suddenly and she has gone to the hospital

vi this month's copy of the local authority calendar of events

vii apologies for absence from Robert Mayer for this morning's meeting

viii the copy of a monthly journal which Mrs Jones always circulates to her assistants in the first instance

b Much of the work of the Housing Department is centred around the outcomes of meetings and much of the correspondence received cannot be dealt with until after such meetings.

Explain the sort of bring-forward system you might devise, and how you would deal with the correspondence in the meantime.

c Prepare notes of guidance for a junior member of staff who will stand in for you while you are on holiday:

i in preparing correspondence for signature
ii in making appointments
iii in taking dictation
iv in maintaining confidentiality

4 You work for a busy public relations firm in the centre of London. Life is extremely hectic and you need to coordinate the daily activities of three executives.

a What sort of problems are you likely to encounter?

b What sort of diary(ies) would you keep for them?

c Give *ten* 'pearls of wisdom' on the effective management of time to a new secretary who has just joined the company and is working for two executives for the first time.

d Outline the arrangements you would make to organise an informal buffet luncheon in the committee room in two days' time.

e Knowing that you work for a public relations firm, a girl friend who is also a secretary has asked your advice about getting on with her boss. She has just started a new job and feels that her new boss is constantly comparing her, sometimes unfavourably, with his previous secretary who has just retired. What advice would you give her?

f Your company is involved in the launch of a new product which is attracting considerable interest in the media. You have had three persistent telephone calls from a reporter already this week and now he has arrived in your office. What will you do?

5 You are required to undertake the travel arrangements for three of the staff within your organisation. One is going to the USA on a three-week coast-to-coast lecture tour. The second is visiting two of the organisation's subsidiary companies – one in Lyons, the other in Barcelona – and is travelling by car as his wife is going to join him later in Spain for a two-week holiday. The third is attending a four-day sales convention at Gleneagles Hotel in Scotland, where he is scheduled to give a presentation on the third day of the company's latest promotional item.

Describe the preparations and arrangements you would make on behalf of each, clearly indicating the unique aspects of each trip and the reference books and other sources you would use to help you.

State the special items (eg passports, tickets, maps) each will require, and how you will arrange to contact each in his absence.

6 Your work for Mr Reginald Lamont, the Export Manager of an electronics company which has substantial commitments overseas, particularly in Europe. Mr Lamont is the President of the Staff Association within the company. From the assorted information given below, enter the material as it would appear (a) in your executive's diary and (b) in your own diary for the month of February. Design suitable diary layouts for this activity.

14 February	Staff Association Valentine's Day Dance – 8 pm Sports Centre
22 February	Mr L is due to travel to Brussels on business. He will stay for three nights at the Europa Hotel and will fly British Airways as usual. He needs currency to be organised.
8 February	Mr L's daughter's 21st birthday. You are invited to her party on the following Saturday at the Lamont's home (6.30 pm)
3 February	R & D Committee Meeting – committee room 1430
5 February	Lunch with Neville Mariner of Lexitron Fibres – 1230 Britannia Hotel, Carlton Room
19 February	Tentative arrangement to see Herr Winckl from Hamburg
21 February	Finalise agenda for Export Directors' Meeting in one week's time.

6

Understanding record management

Aim of the unit

The unit emphasises the importance of efficient record management and provides the essential foundations for devising appropriate filing and indexing systems.

Specific objectives

At the end of this unit you should be able to:

1　Define filing.
2　Suggest reasons for inefficient filing.
3　Identify the essential ingredients of a good system.
4　Set up an appropriate system from a given set of circumstances.
5　Compare and contrast different methods of classification.
6　State the advantages and disadvantages of different methods of classification.
7　Provide simple rules for filing.
8　Explain cross-referencing.
9　Select appropriate filing equipment.
10　Explain the operation of a central filing department.
11　State the advantages and disadvantages of central filing.
12　Select suitable filing accessories.
13　Set up and maintain an indexing system.
14　Compare and contrast various indexing methods.
15　Explain the need for a retention policy.
16　Describe possible uses of microphotography.
17　State the advantages and disadvantages of microfilm.
18　Suggest ways of storing microfilm/fiche.
19　Indicate the points to be borne in mind when selecting equipment.
20　Explain electronic filing.

As a topic, 'filing and indexing' is frequently greeted by groans and sighs. However, its importance cannot be over-stressed and all aspiring secretaries should aim to master the art of effective record management. Successful record-keeping of any kind is a question of exercising logical thought in devising the system and then operating it methodically and with respect.

A word about systems

Much confusion arises out of the use of the word 'system', which is interpreted differently by different people. Basically the word 'system' can be used when referring to filing in any of the following ways:

- to describe the method of classification, eg alphabetical, numerical
- to describe the sort of equipment used, eg vertical filing, lateral filing, electronic filing
- to distinguish between departmental and centralised filing
- to indicate the actual procedure adopted by staff in physically filing the papers
- in relation to the methods used when referring to or borrowing records.

Obviously as a student of secretarial practice and procedures you will be concerned with all five aspects, but you must exercise care when interpreting usage in an examination question.

Some definitions of filing

The study of general reference books and textbooks an office procedures will suggest a selection of definitions. The following are common ones:

Filing is the action of placing papers in consecutive order for preservation and reference (*Oxford English Dictionary*).

Filing is the basis of record-keeping; it entails the processing, arranging and storing of records so that they can be located when required.

Filing is the storing of letters, records, carbon copies and documents in folders, binders, drawers and cabinets especially designed for the purpose.

Filing is the storing of correspondence in a retrieval system whence it may be obtained for reference.

A filing system is a device whereby documents can be safely preserved in a methodical manner so that they can be referred to quickly and easily.

Filing is the storing of letters and documents in a systematic way so that they may be retrieved at a latter date for reference purposes.

It can be seen from the variety of definitions given above that filing and filing systems mean different things to different people. The point which all the definitions have in common is the reference to 'papers', 'records', 'documents' and 'correspondence', although even here different terminology is adopted for the same thing!

What makes filing a problematic area of office work?

The simple answer to this question is that many managers are constantly complaining that their filing system does not work. No one can ever find anything and the time taken to locate information is ridiculous – or so the story goes! Perhaps then it would make sense to begin by considering some of the reasons for inefficiency in filing.

Common causes of inefficient filing

1 **Lack of proper training** – too often it is mistakenly imagined that everybody knows how to file. Consequently little formal training is given within organisations, and chaos inevitably results where people learn by default.
2 **No one is given the ultimate responsibility for filing** – with the exception of centralised systems, which are usually operated by highly skilled filing clerks, the average organisation often leaves the responsibility for the filing

open ended. Very often it is left to juniors and even temporary staff.
3 **The system of classification is inappropriate** – the simple maxim in selecting a classification system is to consider how we think about documents, ie by name of customer or client, by subject, by geographical location, by date or by number. The adoption of the obvious is often the best method.
4 **Absence of a retention policy** – management must decide when documents are to be destroyed or transferred to long-term storage. Often documents are kept too long (cluttering up a system and making it difficult to operate) or alternatively they are destroyed too quickly. Note that this is also true for electronic systems.
5 **Inappropriate location** – sometimes documents are stored too far away from those who need them. This leads to loss of documents and failure to return them.
6 **Inadequate tracer/follow-up systems** – documents are often removed from a file by an unknown person or department and either not returned or lost altogether. Where there is no tracer or follow-up system there is no obvious starting place when searching to retrieve the missing files.
7 **No system of cross-referencing is included to speed up retrieval** – many systems are extremely cumbersome and slow to use unless they are adequately cross-referenced (*see* later section).
8 **Too many people may have access to the system** – the more people who use a system – particularly if they are untrained – the more likely it is that documents will go astray or be misfiled when returned.
9 **Lack of regular filing** – the failure to file on a regular (ideally daily) basis can result in inefficiency. Staff will often spend time looking for documents which have still to be filed!
10 **Failure to adapt to changing circumstances** – many systems are permitted to remain static despite the changing needs of business and irrespective of rapid expansion.

Setting up a system

Before anyone can set up a workable system it will be necessary to carry out a very careful analysis of requirements. Such analysis should ideally be carried out impartially over a realistic period, and should be aimed at answering the following questions:

1 How many documents are to be filed initially?
2 How many additional documents will be filed each week?
3 How often are these documents likely to be referred to?
4 How long must documents be kept available for immediate access?
5 Do they need to be retained indefinitely, and if so how accessible must they be?
6 In what form do they need to be retained? Must they be in their original state, or might microfilm or computer storage be a realistic possibility?
7 How quickly do documents need to be produced?
8 Who normally makes use of them?
9 Who will physically access the documents?
10 How are the documents described or referred to when required?
11 How much space can realistically be devoted to filing?
12 How important is security?

Once you have established answers to such questions you will be in a much better position to estimate the essential requirements of a new system or perhaps more than one system. One point that you should always bear in mind is that there is no best system. Any filing system must be devised to fit the particular needs of the individual, department or organisation.

Suggested essentials of a good system

When devising a system it is desirable to bear in mind certain factors that you would try to incorporate into a system in order to make it a good one. The following is a selection of the sorts of criteria you might consider:

- simplicity
- appropriate classification
- accessibility
- selection of suitable equipment
- safety in terms of minimising loss
- safety in terms of avoiding damage by fire, water, dust.

- safety in terms of maintaining confidentiality
- compactness – not taking up too much valuable floor space
- elasticity – capable of expansion as required
- speed of retrieval
- trained staff
- economical – in terms of time, cost of equipment and accessories
- sufficient cross-referencing
- an 'out guide' or 'tracer' system should be incorporated
- 'thinning out' should be performed on a regular basis
- daily filing

Methods of classification

Different methods will prove suitable in different circumstances. The following are the methods most commonly used in offices today, together with their relative advantages and disadvantages.

Alphabetical

The alphabet is the basis of most systems. This method refers to the filing of documents according to the first letter of the name. When the first letters of files are the same you simply progress through the name until you reach a different letter (suggested basic rules for alphabetical filing are given later in this unit). Alphabetical filing is the most common method of classification and is particularly successful when applied to the filing of correspondence, which is frequently thought of according to the name of the correspondent. Another natural application would be the maintenance of staff records.

Advantages

- convenience of grouping related documents
- simple to understand and operate
- a direct method, requiring no index
- useful for incorporating miscellaneous papers

Disadvantages

- cumbersome in a large system
- confusion may arise with common names
- difficult to estimate space requirements, eg how many Hs, how many Ps

- possibility of material being filed under more than one letter, so necessitating cross-referencing

Numerical

In numerical classification documents are arranged in number order. Each document or folder is given a number and filed in serial number order. Examples of documents filed in this way would be sales invoices, orders and committee minutes, but any documents may be allocated numbers where it is considered appropriate.

Advantages

- unlimited expansion is possible
- possible to give each document a unique number
- encourages greater accuracy
- the file number can be used as a reference
- the index can be used in its own right for other purposes, eg addresses and telephone numbers
- secrecy is easy to maintain

Disadvantages

- no direct access: need to consult an index
- involves more work, both to set up and to operate
- possibility of transposing figures

Note: Sometimes block allocations are given departmentally, eg

1–999   housing
1000–1999   finance
This does facilitate recognition, at least to a limited extent, and can be helpful where reference numbers are used in the sorting of incoming mail.

Subject

In subject classification documents are arranged, usually in alphabetical order, according to the subject matter, eg electricity, gas, income tax, rates, telephone, water. This should not be confused with pure alphabetical filing, which normally refers to individual or firm names. Subject filing is often used in education establishments where subjects have a special significance.

Advantages

- easy to understand, being based on the alphabet

- convenient for grouping related materials
- direct access: no index required
- allows for unlimited expansion
- can be more confidential than using individuals' names
- useful where only the subject is known

Disadvantages

- people may not think in the same way: hence the likelihood of individuals opening new files unnecessarily
- can become cumbersome owing to there being too many files
- difficult to estimate space requirements
- an index may be needed in certain instances

Geographical

Here documents are arranged, once again probably in alphabetical order, according to their geographical location. This is useful, for example, where sales areas are of relevance and where information may be required on a country or regional basis. Another common example would be the files of offices of local authorities, where properties may have a greater significance than the occupants.

Advantages

- convenient where the location is known.
- an element of direct filing is possible
- useful where regional information may be required
- useful for gathering statistics for comparative purposes

Disadvantages

- weak knowledge of geography on the part of filing personnel can cause chaos
- there may be a need for occasional index
- regional boundaries may be altered

Chronological

In chronological classification documents are arranged according to the date. This system will rarely be used as a complete method, as it is only practical where all the documents are of one type and where the date is a distinguishing feature. Travel organisations may use this method, operating on departure dates. At a more personal level a 'tickler file' would operate from a chronological file (*see* Unit 5). It is important to note that it is usual to arrange papers in chronological order within folders which are filed in some other method of classification.

Advantages

- where a date has some special significance over all else
- an essential aspect of most other systems

Disadvantages

- meaningless without an index
- likelihood of cramming under certain dates

Terminal digit

The terminal digit system is a variation of the numerical system. The efficiency of a system using consecutive numbers diminishes when a system becomes very big. Therefore, large organisations dealing with thousands of files opt for a terminal digit method of classification. Typical examples of organisations using this system would be insurance companies, hospitals and building societies. Whereas numbers are read from left to right in a basic numerical system, they are broken into pairs in a terminal digit system and read from right to left. For example, in 259843, 43 would be the terminal digit and would indicate something to the filing clerk. For instance, 43 may represent the drawer number, 98 the file number and 25 the position of the document within the file.

Advantages

- speeds up location in a large system
- distributes the filing through several drawers, so overcoming crowding
- capable of varied interpretation in different circumstances, eg the number groupings could be different from one system to another
- high degree of accuracy possible

Disadvantages

- more complex to learn and operate
- requires special training
- still needs an alphabetical index

Rules for alphabetical filing

1 Take the name to be filed, eg Charles D Blake, and transpose the unit comprising the name so that the surname Blake is your first filing unit. Then take the first Christian name as your second unit, and so on. Thus Blake, Charles D is the order for filing.

2 File according to the initial letter of the surname and each subsequent letter, eg
Black, John
Blake, Charles D
Blakis, Anna
Blenkinsop, Arthur
Bloom, Leopold

2 If the surnames are the same, file according to the initials, eg
Blake, Charles D
Blake, Charles K
Blake, Diane P

4 The 'nothing before something' rule. This is where filing convention differs basically from the most common alphabetical index of them all, namely a telephone directory. In the telephone directory first names and initials only are intermingled but in true filing it is customary to begin with the least information, perhaps purely a surname, to follow with all initials and then full first names, eg
Jones,
Jones, J
Jones, John
Jones, Johnathan

5 Treat surname prefixes as part of the name, and all names beginning with M', Mc and Mac as if they were spelt with Mac prior to the next syllable, eg
De Havilland, George
De La Motte, Catherine
Di Napli, Roberto
Le Mesurier, John
McAdam, John
MacAdam, William
McAlpine, Cyril

6 File all names with the prefix St or Saint under Saint, eg
St John, Ian
St John-Stevas, John
St Stephen's Hospital

7 Ignore the hyphen in hyphenated names and

treat the surname as one unit, eg:
Hamilton-Forbes, Jason
Kingsley-White, Jane
MacMichael-Philips, Adrian

8 Where commonly abbreviated names are filed they should be treated as if written out in full, eg
British Broadcasting Corporation
British Oxygen Company
Imperial Chemical Industries
Independent Television Authority

but cross references should be inserted as:
BBC
BOC
IBA
ICI

9 Where the name of an organisation consists of separate letters that are not actual abbreviations, treat each letter as a separate indexing unit. It is usual to file names consisting of initials before whole words, eg
ABC Cinema
ABC Cleaners
ABC Valet Service
Abbey Lodge Hotel

10 Ignore 'the' in company names when filing. Similarly, ignore conjunctions and prepositions when preparing your indexing units, eg
(The) Metal Box Company Ltd
Metal Containers Ltd
(The) Metal Corporation (of) America
Miller (and) Jones

11 Ignore titles and degrees as indexing units, eg
(Dr) Sandra Carter
John Davidson (PhD, MSc, MBIM)
(Rev) Simon Harvey
(Prof) Angela Marini
(Maj) David Simpson
(Sir) William Trent

12 Treat any number as if it were written in full, eg
21 Club – Twenty-one Club
Over 40s Society – Over Forties Society
(The) 9th Street Theatre – (The) Ninth Street Theatre

13 File government departments and ministries under the *key* word, eg
Defence, Ministry of
Education and Science, Department of (cross-referenced under DES)

Track and Industry, Department of (cross referenced under DTI)

14 Subdivide files for council bodies into departments, eg
Manchester City Council:
Education Department
Housing Department
Social Services Department

Note: An important point to remember in relation to alphabetical filing is to file under the name of the firm, company or institution and *not* under the name of your individual contact within the organisation.

A word about cross-referencing

Cross-referencing is a process designed to help locate records which could conceivably have been filed or requested under more than one title or caption. A cross-reference card is prepared for insertion at the alternative location. In some organisations it will not be uncommon to find actual material in more than one place in the system, such is the advantage of inexpensive photocopying!

An example of a cross-reference is:
Inserted under ICI. ICI *see* Imperial Chemical Industries.

The process of filing

There are *seven* basic steps in a typical filing routine.

1 *Collecting* – papers which are to be filed should be collected together in a filing tray or basket. Where a centralised system of filing is in operation, the contents of this basket will be collected periodically by the interoffice messenger service which will deliver to the Central Filing Department. Care must always be taken that papers are inserted in the correct basket or tray.

2 *Inspecting* – prior to actual filing each paper or document should be inspected for some sort of release symbol or mark which will indicate that it is ready for filing. Papers should not be filed if there is no such indication. The release symbol may be the initials of the person sending the material for filing; the word 'file' or a letter F and the date; a line through the text; or any other previously agreed mark.

3 *Indexing* – indexing is the process of selecting

the appropriate caption or name under which to file and of determining the order of the units which follow. Much will, of course, be dependent upon the system of classification and it is difficult to provide precise rules. Judgment is required in terms of deciding how the article ought to be filed, taking into account how it is likely to be requested at a later date.

4   *Cross-referencing* (*see* previous section) – once the indexing has been determined it will be appropriate to consider the need for a cross-reference. If one is thought to be necessary it should be prepared at this point in the procedure.

5   *Coding* – once an item has been indexed it is coded. This is the process of marking every item to indicate how it has been indexed. Normally the relevant word is underlined. If, however, the name does not appear in the text, or a numerical system is used, the name or number would be written in the top right-hand corner of the document.

6   *Sorting* – where a considerable amount of filing is being done it is advisable to undertake some preliminary sorting first. Many different sorting aids are available (*see* Fig 39). The benefit of sorting in advance of actual filing is that it minimises the need to re-enter drawers and folders.

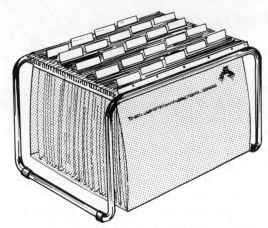

Fig 40 Filing dividers

may form linked units or be separate, and the labelling will correspond with the dividers.

Methods of filing

In general files are likely to be stored in *four* principal ways, and it is important that you are able to distinguish clearly between them. At the beginning of this unit the problem of the definition of 'system' was pointed out; the actual physical method of storage is one 'system'. Another problem may arise from the fact that individual manufacturers of filing equipment may vary the terminology they use to describe virtually the same thing, so exercise particular care in this area.

1   *Vertical filing* – this is where the document folders are placed one behind the other, usually in a traditional filing cabinet drawer which will often be fitted with suspension pockets.

2   *Lateral filing* – this is where document folders or rigid files are lined up side by side as in a library arrangement and are read from left to right. Here again suspension files may be set up in this formation.

3   *Horizontal filing* – this is where documents, usually large-scale items like maps or plans, are laid flat, one on top of the other, in narrow drawers.

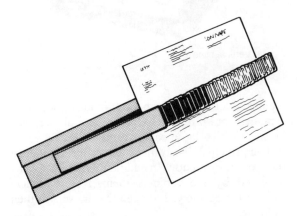

Fig 39 Sorting aids

7   *Filing* – the final step is the actual storing of the papers in file folders of different sizes and design. These folders are used in conjunction with dividers called **guides** which are tabbed or labelled for easy reading (*see* Fig 40). Dividers

4   *Circular filing* – this is where papers are placed in book-type folders and placed in a circular arrangement on layers of shelves which rotate for ease of location. These units are often referred to as carousels.

Filing equipment

A wide range of filing equipment is available and the sort selected will be largely determined by:

- the nature of the material to be filed, eg is it general correspondence, orders, plans, drawings, minutes, confidential information etc?
- the quantity to be filed
- the space available
- the money available
- the speed with which it is necessary to access information.
- the personnel using the system – who are they and how many of them are there?
- the length of time which the material needs to be kept
- whether or not duplicate copies exist elsewhere
- the degree of safety required – how vulnerable are the contents, and what level of security and confidentiality is attached to them?
- the importance of its physical appearance – where will the equipment be sited – in public view or in a basement?

What is essential is that you have the right equipment. Any job requires the right tools and the right supplies, and filing is no exception. Just as you would take time and care in selecting furniture for your home, so too would you give careful thought to the selection of filing equipment. It is after all an investment, something which will be used for many years and which may need to stand up to a lot of handling, so quality is very important as well as ease of operating and the ability to expand the system later.

Vertical cabinets

Vertical cabinets (*see* Fig 41) are still commonly found in many offices. They come in various sizes with between one and six drawers, and are available in a range of colours as well as in different materials. Two-drawer cabinets are useful in the region of one's immediate work area, and can even be used as pedestals for a desk top. Three-drawer cabinets are useful in forming a counter arrangement. The most common size is, of course, the four-drawer cabinet which is the traditional size found in the majority of offices. Vertical cabinets are easy to use and the drawers can be fitted with suspension pockets which

Fig 41 Vertical filing

are linked together to form a continuous 'concertina' arrangement into which folders are placed, and between which loose papers cannot slip.

The principal disadvantage of vertical cabinets is the space they occupy. In addition to the floor space occupied by the cabinets themselves, sufficient space must be allowed to open the drawers to their full extent.

Note: It is extremely dangerous to open more than one drawer of a vertical cabinet at a time, as the weight of papers can cause the cabinet to tip forward with the possibility of a serious accident. However, most modern cabinets have a built-in safety feature preventing more than one drawer being opened at the same time.

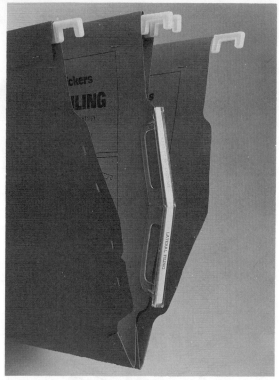

Fig 42 Lateral suspension pocket

Fig 43 Lateral filing – multi-purpose cabinets

Lateral cabinets

Where space saving is a significant factor, many firms have opted for lateral cabinets. These are popular in that they take up much less valuable and expensive (in terms of city centre rental charges, for instance) floor space, and it is possible to store records virtually from floor to ceiling. Files are still laid on their spines, usually in suspended pockets, but they are laid side by side so maximising the use of space. Here again different tabbing is available and it will usually be possible to angle the tabs to enable simple reading: for example, on high shelves the tabs will be angled downwards, whereas on low levels they will be angled upwards. It is also usual for tabs to be protected by a plastic cover, and the plastic often has magnifying properties to facilitate reading (*see* Fig 42).

Lateral, multi-purpose cabinets

A popular variation of the basic lateral cabinet is the multi-purpose file (*see* Fig 43). This allows the storage of a variety of different items together in the one cabinet, eg general office files (both laterally and vertically – on a pull-out frame); computer printout; loose items like print wheels, cartridges and diskettes; folders; and record cards. There is a pull-out shelf for use by filing personnel. These cabinets come in different heights and have various options in fitments and doors, eg

- two-door
- quarter folding doors
- retractable door
- roller blind door

Horizontal files

It would be remiss not to mention horizontal files, although they are often replaced now by chest plan files which are usually mobile and take up less space. Traditional horizontal filing takes up a lot of floor space; the plans, drawings or whatever are not very

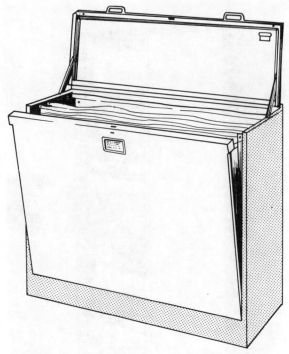

Fig 44 Chest plan file

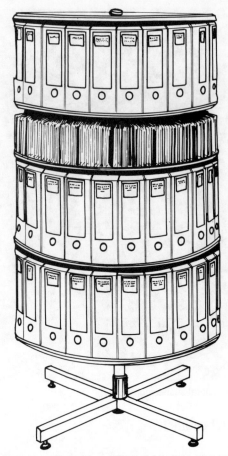

Fig 45 Rotary file

easily accessible and tend to become damaged on the edges from frequent handling. Also the cabinets cannot be used for any other purpose, eg as a desk top, since there is nowhere to put one's knees.

Chest plan files (Fig 44) operate like chest freezers. The index is in the lid and the plans are either suspended from clips or stand on their ends between some form of divider. It is even possible, in order to save more space, to have the dividers made of a sort of wavy plastic so that the documents are curved round the dividers, so taking up less space than they would if kept absolutely flat.

Rotary files or carousel units

As the name suggests, rotary files or carousel units rotate for ease of reference. The files (often of the lever arch variety) or folders are arranged on tiers of circular shelves which rotate independently on an axis, so enabling the clerk to turn the tier until the required file is to hand (*see* Fig 45).

Mobile files

In many open-plan or landscaped offices it is common to see many mobile files. These will usually be of desk height and may either be open topped or have a lid which can be locked in place. Mobile units come in a wide range of styles with many drawer options. They combine orderly storage with flexible and space-saving use, and systems are easily designed and built to individual specifications. An example of a mobile file is given in Fig 46.

Automated mobile filing

In a large organisation (eg where a central filing library is operated) elaborate, highly automated systems can be found. Here files can run freely on tracks and can be pushed together to save space or separated for ease of access. This enables a very dense concentration of filing to be placed in a limited space. It is also very secure when closed and has the advantage of being dustproof.

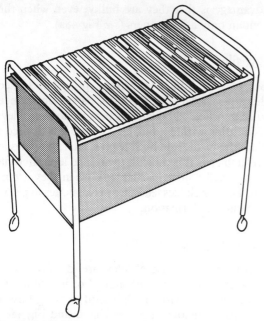

Fig 46 Mobile file

Fig 47 Powered filing

Powered filing

Alternatively files can be stored laterally on a conveyor belt arrangement which can rotate in either direction, so enabling the clerk to retrieve files automatically and with virtually no physical effort. An example of a power-driven lateral filing system is given in Fig 47.

Central filing

With central filing all (or some) of the records of a business are filed in one location rather than in separate departments and offices throughout the building. Central filing means that all papers about the same subject, but originating from different departments, will be stored in common files within the central filing department. Individuals wishing to consult these files borrow them or consult them within this department.

It is worth noting that it is not always possible to make a straight choice between central or departmental filing. In many organisations half-way measures are adopted, whereby active or current files are stored departmentally while 'dead' files or reserve files are stored centrally. Also, certain types of documentation may not be suitable for storage in a central file, eg personnel records or documents which are the exclusive concern of one department. Similarly, where an organisation is very spread out, perhaps occupying several buildings or different sites, central filing would be inappropriate.

In view of the space required to set up a central filing department, this facility would be considered by an organisation when choosing new premises or (more likely still) when planning purpose-built accommodation. At the building stages electronic aids can easily be incorporated in the design or tracks can be built into the floor to utilise mobile files.

Another factor in relation to the bulk storage of files is weight. Paper is an extremely heavy commodity, and care must be taken not to overload cabinets and place excessive pressure on floors, particularly those above ground level. Office floors are usually constructed to carry a lower loading than factory floors, and may need to be strengthened where filing is concentrated other than on the ground floor.

Advantages of central filing

- uniform filing procedures
- development of specialist filing personnel

- improved supervision of records
- fixed responsibility for filing
- convenient in terms of location of correspondence on one subject
- eliminates unnecessary duplication of files
- management has better control over records
- discourages hoarding on the part of individuals
- safety and security measures are more easily incorporated
- staff become educated to the idea that files are the property of the organisation rather than the individual
- becomes feasible to consider expensive filing techniques, eg microfilming or electronic filing (*see* later in this unit).

Disadvantages of central filing

- central filing staff may possess little departmental knowledge
- bureaucratic procedures may cause delays
- the more files stored the longer it is likely to take to find files, unless sophisticated electronic retrieval procedures are used
- problematic where filing staff may be ill or away at the same time
- restricts the opportunity for junior staff to learn about filing
- location may be distant from certain departments
- a bit like a library in terms of the required file already in the possession of another department

Note: As with the majority of centralised services, the advantages can often be seen more readily from the management point of view, whereas the disadvantages would tend to be considered from an individual viewpoint. Put another way, the advantages of central filing could be seen as the disadvantages of departmental filing and vice versa.

Filing accessories (*see* Fig. 48)

Lever arch files

With lever arch files papers need to be punched, and then the documents are secured on two arch-shaped metal rods which are opened and closed via a lever – hence the name. The principal advantage of such file is the ability to remove a single paper at any position in the file. Also the inclusion of A–Z guide cards speeds up the search process. The dis-

advantage is that they are bulky, even when they contain only a few papers (*see* Fig 48a).

Box files

Box files are firm boxes with a spring clip to keep the papers secure (*see* Fig 48b). Papers do not need to be punched, although it is possible to have a lever arch fitting within a box file. Where it is desired to place the boxes side by side on a shelf, box files are preferable, as it is difficult to arrange lever arch files on a straight shelf, particularly when they are not full. Lever arch files lend themselves better to placing in a circular formation.

Expanding files

Expanding 'concertina' files are divided into a number of pockets – either A–Z or in a numerical split. They are particularly useful as bring-forward systems or 'tickler' files (*see* Unit 5 and Fig 48c.)

Multipart files

Multipart files consist of a few (usually seven or nine) manila dividers fastened together to form one comprehensive file for unpunched papers. The dividers are tabbed for quick reference and are held together by elastic across the corners.

Other files

A wide range of files and folders is available offering different types of clips and fastenings, as well as the flat files and envelope/document wallets commonly used in filing systems (*see* Fig 48e).

Indexing equipment (*see* Fig 49)

Many systems of filing depend on an index, and indexes are also useful in their own right. Most frequently they come in card or book form, although the methods of storage can vary considerably. The following are some common examples.

Small drawers or boxes

In boxed indexes cards are arranged one behind the other with guide cards to facilitate selection (*see* Fig 49a). Cards are available in many different sizes,

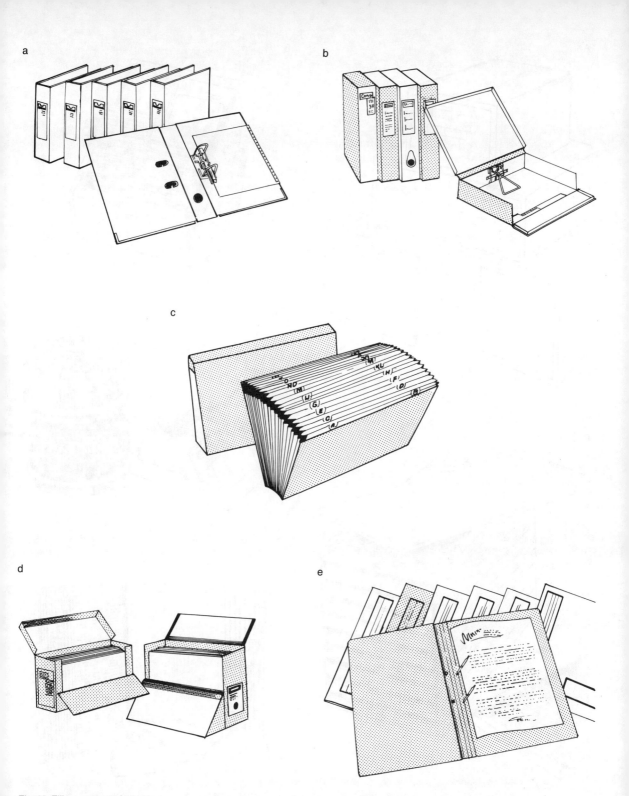

Fig 48 Filing accessories

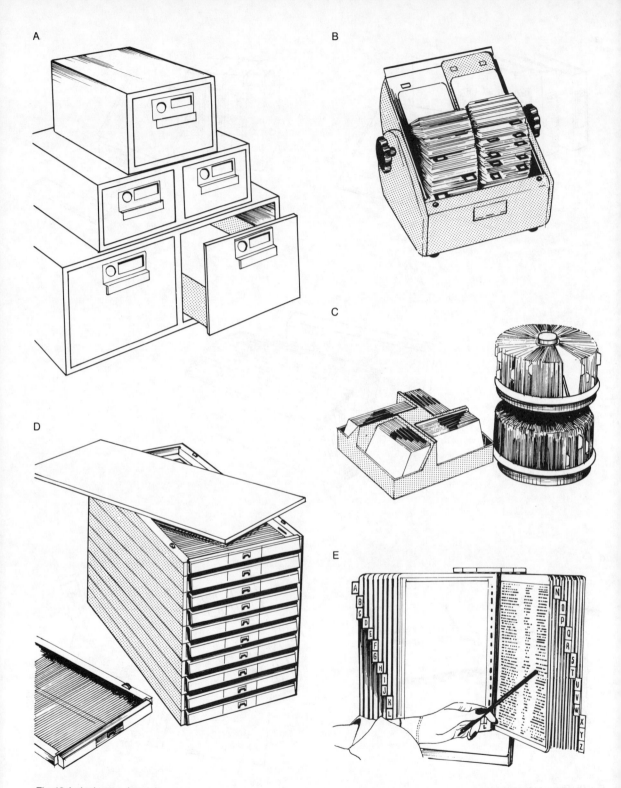

Fig 49 Indexing equipment

line rulings and colours. This method has the advantage of simplicity in terms of preparation and usage, but cards can easily become lost or misplaced within the index. You should note that where libraries use this system they have a hole punched through the cards and then have them 'threaded' on rods within the drawers. Selections of index cards can also be stored in rotatable desk-top units capable of storing up to 1000 cards (*see* Fig 49b).

Rotary card index

The rotary card index is a variation of the previous method where the cards are fixed to the wheel. These indexing systems (Fig 49c) may be large scale involving several large carousel tiers incorporating thousands of cards, or they may be small desk-top wheels consisting of small cards displaying brief information like name, address and telephone number.

Visible card indexing

With visible card indexing cards are placed on shallow trays (Fig 49d), several of which may be slotted into an indexing unit and locked for safe keeping. The cards overlap one another so that only the edges are visible. Cards may be drawn up for a variety of purposes from personnel records to stock control to customer information. The visible edges display only key details which will aid the searching process. Variations of this method of indexing are used in portable books or panel forms.

Visible strip indexing

Where a limited amount of non-confidential information is required, the visible strip is a useful method (Fig 49e). It is easily prepared and may be updated instantly by the removal or insertion of the appropriate strip. Also the strips are available in a range of colours which can be useful in terms of distinguishing between different entries and so speeding up the location. Examples of this might include an internal telephone directory, names, departments and works numbers of staff (for personnel department use).

A word about signalling

Signals are eye-catching markers placed on file titles or on index cards. They are used for coding purposes and are available in bright colours to attract the attention. An example of the use of signalling might be in the maintenance of personnel records where junior staff are awarded birthday increments of salary. Their record cards could be signalled so that the Personnel Clerk would not forget to process the increment in time for the appropriate salary payment.

Retention policy

As mentioned previously, one of the reasons for inefficiency in filing systems can be the absence of a retention policy. The decision on what must be kept, where and for how long ought to be a decision made at a high level. Where no such decisions are made the tendency will be to retain everything indefinitely. During their lifespan, documents will usually spend time in *four* principal locations:

1 At a desk – when they are being actively used.
2 In localised storage when they may be called upon for quick reference.
3 In a centralised file when they are required only for occasional reference.
4 In some form of long-term storage where it may, for instance, be a statutory requirement to keep certain records for a lengthy period of time and perhaps even indefinitely.

At the end of any of these stages it is likely that documents may be destroyed or transferred, either to an alternative location or perhaps on to an alternative means of storage, eg microfilm or computer.

What is vital is that due consideration is given to each item rather than simply relegating every paper to a tray for filing, when in fact many papers may not need to be retained at all and should, therefore, be directed to the waste paper basket!

Questions to be asked in relation to a retention policy

1 How valuable is the document?
2 Are there copies elsewhere?
3 How often are they needed?
4 How quickly would they be required?
5 Is their retention in hard copy form a statutory obligation?
6 Is it possible to have them retained in some other format?

7 How much space is available for storage?
8 How much money is available?

Shredding machines

One very useful piece of equipment in relation to record management is the shredding machine (*see* Fig 50). These are available in a range of sizes from the small executive model for individual office use to large industrial shredders for dealing with bulk paper supplies like computer printouts. The benefit of shredding, which reduces the paper to very fine strands which are impossible to piece together and read, is that the waste paper can be collected and sold for recycling purposes. In an age where environmental considerations are important, saving of a valuable material like paper is a worthwhile exercise. Previously much reusable paper was burned in order to avoid security leaks and any breach of confidentiality.

Microfilming

A popular and convenient way of storing information for later retrieval is to photograph office records in miniature via microphotography. The film is then processed on to small rolls of film or sheets of microfiche and stored instead of the original records. By this method, savings of over 90 per cent are estimated over paper storage.

Film is available in various widths and lengths. The holding capacity of the film depends on the reduction ratio used in filming. The most common size of roll film for filming general business documents is 16 mm in 100 foot lengths, while for microfiche 15 × 10 cm transparency sheets accommodating 98 frames are normal.

Possible ways of changing to microfilm/fiche

Depending on the circumstances, the volume of documents to be transferred to film/fiche and the finance available, various options are open to an organisation.

1 The least expensive way, and that probably favoured by smaller firms, will be to call in a specialist firm to do the filming and developing and simply to install readers.

Fig 50 Shredding machine; *Reproduced by kind permission of Rexel Business Machines*

2 The inbetween step would be to invest in a camera and reader, but send away the film for processing.
3 The most expensive way, but economical in the long term where many documents need to be handled and processed and where microfilming is adopted as an integral aspect of a business system, would be to install all the microfilm requirements including the processing unit, and so have the capacity to see the task through from start to finish. However, whichever method is selected the transference on to film/fiche means that the original documents can either be destroyed altogether (where hard copy originals would never be called upon) or alternatively transferred to low-cost reserve storage.

What are the advantages of microfilming?

1 There is a saving in terms of filing and floor space.
2 There is a saving in terms of filing and indexing equipment.

3 Safety can be ensured by storing original documents in a bank, for example, and using film for daily reference.

4 Faster copying can be done on to film than by any other method.

5 There is a saving in terms of 'weeding out'. Everything will be on film and only really important things need be maintained in their original format.

6 Film, most of which is fireproof, has better lasting qualities than paper.

7 It can improve the overall efficiency of office systems.

8 Film and fiche can be easily sent through the post as they are less bulky and it will be safe and economical compared with sending originals.

9 Images are accepted as legal evidence.

Are these disadvantages?

1 You cannot refer to the film or fiche without setting up a reader.

2 It can be inconvenient to use a reader when you are tired or you wish to refer to documents frequently or in a hurry.

3 Sometimes it can be difficult to locate the precise frame (ie the document you wish to consult) on the film.

4 Processing can be inferior and cause problems due to illegibility.

5 Records on coloured paper can be difficult to reproduce.

6 The preparation of papers for filming can be time consuming.

7 Difficult and costly to update.

What is jacket microfilm?

Jacket microfilm is a combination of the traditional film strip and microfiche. Here short lengths of film strip are slotted into carriers for quicker reference and ease of handling. These have the advantage of being more easily updated.

Storage and general handling

Microfilm rolls are stored in cylindrical containers and then placed in labelled boxes or drawers. Microfiche can be stored in indexing sequence, similar to a card index, in panels or drawers.

Where carefully indexed, film and fiche can be retrieved automatically for reading by push-button selection of the file number, which will bring the desired frame on to the reader screen. No document handling is therefore required.

Link-up with computer

Microfilm or microfiche can be used to transfer data direct from computer without printing. This is known as computer output on microfilm/fiche (COM). The translation speed can be up to 120 000 characters per second. The advantages to be gained are considerable in that in addition to the saving of staff time, stationery costs are substantially reduced and the increased reduction ratio and the speed with which COM fiche is produced enables greater quantities of data to be handled, stored and moved around.

Reading film and fiche

With the latest microfilm reader/printers (*see* Fig 51) it is possible to have a clearly readable full-size

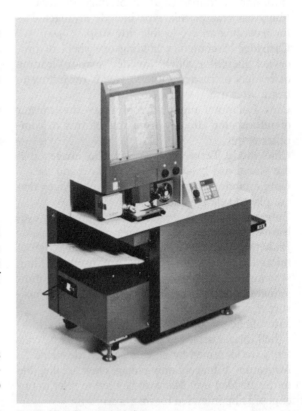

Fig 51 Microfilm reader/printer

hard copy of any selected film frame simply by pressing the PRINT button when the appropriate frame appears on the screen.

Glossary of microfilming terms

Aperture card A card which is normally an 80-column punch card containing a rectangular hole in which a frame of 35 mm microfilm can be mounted. The aperture card is used mainly for drawing office applications and for patents.

Camera, flow (rotary) A camera in which both the film and the document being filmed move during exposure. The film transport is linked to the document transport so there is no relative movement. Flow cameras are widely used in office microfilm systems.

Camera, planetary A camera in which during exposure both the film and the document being filmed remain stationary.

Camera, step and repeat A camera which is able to expose a number of separate images on a piece of film; normally images are arranged in a series of rows and columns. Used to produce microfiche. Many cameras of this type include arrangements for recording an eye-legible title strip.

Cartridge A container holding one spool of processed microfilm which provides 'snap-in' loading of readers or reader/printers. Needs rewinding to begin after use.

CIM Computer input microfilming – the transfer of information directly from microforms to computer stores.

Cine mode Term used to describe images that are placed one below the other, ie heel and toe.

Comic mode Terms used to describe images that are placed side by side.

Enlarger printer A device which reproduces eye-legible prints from microimages.

Jackets A channelled plastic carrier for strips of microfilm. Microfilm jackets are used in filing systems such as personnel records, where the individual files have to be updated. Usually they measure 6 × 4 in or 104 × 148 mm.

Microfiche A sheet of microfilm containing individual images arranged in a grid pattern. The contents are identified by an eye-legible title strip.

Microfilm Film containing images that are illegible to the unaided eye. May also be used to refer to unexposed film intended for microrecording.

Microform A generic term for any media, either paper or film, which contain images too small to be read by the unaided eye.

Processor Any device for processing the various microfilm materials. Most modern silver processors for microfilm are designed for non-darkroom use.

Reader A device for projecting microimages that are eye-legible on to a front or rear projection screen.

Reader printer A device which incorporates the functions of a reader and an enlarger printer in a single unit.

Electronic filing

Despite the fact that physically handling paper is what people are familiar with, many arguments are put forward for introducing alternative filing methods and taking another step towards the so-called 'paperless office'. The environmental lobby to reduce paper and save trees is strong, while the increasing cost of office rental space, which can be as high as £80 per square foot per year in certain locations, is also an incentive, given the amount of space which traditional filing storage can take up.

Apart from cost, one of the barriers to 'going electronic' which means transferring paper records to computer, has been the time taken to key in the data in the first place. However with optical character recognition (OCR) the process can be speeded up immensely while the human error factor of mis-keying is, of course, eliminated. OCR systems can convert text and graphics into images which can then be held on computer disk.

Magnetic media storage can be on floppy and hard disks or on magnetic tape and access to the information stored can be via a variety of different types of terminal.

Advantages of electronic filing

- space saving
- paper saving
- enables vast quantities of information to be stored for future retrieval
- enables speedy location of information with no physical movement needed by the user who can search for data from the workstation
- records can be stored on screen or printouts taken

- links with other computer application are possible, eg word processing
- more than one person can consult data held on file at the same time
- the system performs many filing routines automatically, eg arranging in alphabetical order, searching for data requested
- where information is centralised, tight access controls can be built into the system via passwords, thereby enhancing security and improving overall management control

Disadvantages of electronic filing

- the time involved inputting data where there is no OCR facility
- the expense of establishing the system
- the likelihood of losing data, although this is thought to be minimal and certainly no more (probably considerably less) than with a manual, hard copy system
- the need to take back-up copies
- the tendency to overload a system with information that is not strictly necessary (should be avoided by strict housekeeping and systems management)
- system breakdowns denying access to data held
- computer fraud (minimised by constant security monitoring)

Optical storage (*see* Fig 52)

While optical storage has not yet replaced magnetic storage, it is worth noting its place in the move towards increased office automation (OA).

A 12 inch optical or laser disk is capable of storing vast quantities (somewhere in the region of 500 000 pages) of information. Apart from high volume storage capacity, such disks are unaffected by dust and finger marks and so highly suitable for typical office conditions.

However, at present writing data to optical disks and reading from them is slower than using magnetic media systems and the majority of disks are of the Write Once, Read Many (WORM) variety, which means that they cannot be erased and so would really only be suitable for archiving purposes where permanent records are sought.

Self-test

1 Why is filing important to an organisation?

2 What are the reasons for filing?
3 What is the basis of most filing classifications?
4 What could be meant by the word 'system' in connection with filing?
5 What sort of numerical classification system is often adopted by large organisations?
6 When would a geographical classification be useful?
7 What are the drawbacks of geographical filing?
8 What factors would you bear in mind when selecting a method of classification?
9 What advice would you give to a junior who is filing for the first time?
10 What sorts of documents have statutory requirements for the length of time they are filed?
11 Why might an organisation consider microphotography?
12 What do you understand by the term 'COM'?
13 What are the advantages of electronic filing?

Personal Activities

Filing and indexing is an area of secretarial work which you as a student can put into practice every day. You will have many things you could and possibly should file, so why not devise your own system?

Examples of things you might file will include:

- your school or college notes for all your different subjects
- press cuttings you collect
- records and cassettes
- personal bills, receipts and bank statements.

In a personal system you have the freedom to exercise any kind of method you like. It can be as simple or as complex as you care to make it, and you can incorporate any cross-referencing techniques, codes, follow-up systems and guides you would find useful.

What types of systems might you find it convenient to set up? Ask yourself these questions:

1 What do I need to file?
2 How do I keep things at the moment?
3 Is it efficient? Can I always find things when I want them?
4 If not, why not?
5 How many different categories of information do I need to file?
6 How do I think of them or refer to them?
7 Which sort of order makes best sense?
8 Do I need everything with me all the time?
9 What can I do to make things stand out?
10 At what point, if any, can I discard things?
11 Will the system I have in mind cost much?
12 Would a separate index prove useful?

Answering these few simple questions in relation to your personal record management should help indicate the possibilities open to you in relation to setting up your own filing and indexing system.

Group Activity

If you are fortunate enough to have a model/training office in which you undertake practical activities, it should be possible for you to devise and set up filing and indexing systems for a variety of matters. The following are some examples:

1 File personal files, colour coded for all different classes. These could be prepared aphabetically, or a personal number could be allocated to each student making use of the facilities. (Where the latter method is selected, it will, of course, be necessary to prepare a separate index.)
2 File all past examination papers.
3 File all handout materials.
4 File all practice exercises and solutions.
5 File all details on equipment and supplies.
6 File back copies of magazines and periodicals and cross-reference accordingly.
7 File all audio material used in practical activity sessions.
8 File all blank forms, headed paper and materials.

These suggestions should provide you with some initial ideas and you should be able to utilise a wide range of equipment and a variety of systems of classifications.

Situation-based activities

1 Your organisation is moving to new premises in the city centre. The new offices are largely open plan in design and the public has ready access to the office area. At present records are kept in a variety of locations, a range of different systems

Fig 52 Optical storage

are used, and the equipment and methods are far from standardised. It is important that the company presents a well-organised image to its clientele, and new multipurpose equipment is envisaged.

a What sort of equipment might be considered?
b In what ways could the company attempt to standardise?
c What factors must be borne in mind in selecting new systems and equipment?

2 Imagine that you have just been appointed Secretary/Personal Assistant to the Managing Director of a new company and that at present very few files exist. The work of the company is internationally based and very technical in nature, and covers four main areas of interest. Some of the documentation will have a legal nature, and much will be confidential.

The company is expected to expand rapidly in the next few months. Your boss is a stickler for detail and expects efficiency in record management and follow-up procedures.

a What sorts of systems would you set up initially?
b What equipment and materials would you require?
c Which systems of classification would you select for different aspects of the work, and why?
d What follow-up techniques might you initiate?
e How would you attempt to ensure strict confidentiality in your systems?

3 Your company is about to have its records transferred on to microfilm/fiche. Identify any problems which might arise and state what preparatory steps would need to be taken to facilitate the transition. Also, describe the sort of equipment that the company will need initially to become operational in the minimum time, and the additional equipment that might be needed in due course.

4 Your boss is constantly complaining that files are being removed from the cabinets without any indication of their whereabouts. This can result in lengthy delays and considerable inconvenience. She asks you to devise a system to improve matters. What would you do, and how would you attempt to ensure that staff adhere to your system?

5 You have been asked to look at the question of the disposal of confidential records in the office.

Write a note to your chief giving your recommendations.

6 Assume that you are employed as a secretary by an employment agency which supplies permanent and temporary office, sales and domestic staff to firms in the area. The manager has asked you to look at the filing cabinets in the office as these are very full, and to:

a suggest which files should be removed
b say how they should be disposed of, bearing in mind that some are very confidential
c suggest other types of storage cabinets which would save space; the ones at present being used are four-drawer and two-drawer ones
d suggest a method whereby anyone looking for a file would know where to find it even if it had been taken out temporarily.

7 Up to this time all your department's records have been kept using traditional filing equipment and procedures. It is proposed that you will, in the next six months, transfer all records on to electronic media with a view to increasing the effectiveness of information retrieval and updating and improving security of confidential records.

a What initial problems will you be likely to experience with such a changeover?
b Indicate how you would tackle implementation.
c What differences would there be in indexing?
d What are the advantages of operating a database management system?

Additional exercise on practical filing and indexing

1 Rearranging lists of names, topics, places, numbers etc on paper is all very well, but is no substitute for physically handling cards, papers and folders. Filing and indexing is to some extent like shuffling cards – one becomes better with practice. Sometimes it is difficult to gain realistic filing practice in the classroom, but the following activity can prove a worthwhile preparation in providing the sort of materials which you can usefully use later to practise your actual filing skills.

What will you need?
• a telephone directory
• an atlas or AA/RAC book
• an examining board's syllabus
• the birthdays of your fellow students
• blank cards (ideally coloured), or if unavailable, coloured sheets of paper

This is what you do
If using cards, maximise the space by drawing them up as Fig 52a.

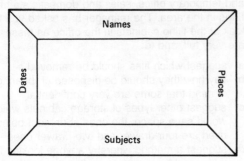

Names

Dates

Places

Subjects

Fig 52a

a At random select as many names as you like – for example twenty per set of cards – and write or type them neatly in the same space on each card.
b Using an atlas or AA/RAC book select place names – again at random – and complete the cards accordingly.
c Similarly, complete the areas with subjects and dates.
d You should now have several sets of cards of sheets with four categories of information recorded.

e Shuffle the cards or papers and make sure that you have the categories all the same way up.
You now have the basis for a practical filing activity.
Using a stopwatch, time each other in sorting the cards/papers into correct filling order.

It will be useful to devise solutions to check the accuracy of your filing. To save still more time you can code all your names/dates/places/ subjects, and then you simply need to call out the codes for checking purposes.

2 Where you have your own word processing disk, access the index and look at it critically. Without going into the named files/documents, can you recall what they are about? If not, why not? Might you have named them better? Remember that indexing and coding is just as important when using an electronic method of storage as it is with a paper based system.

If you experience difficulties in locating your documents through poor titling of files, rename them in more appropriate ways. It will also be useful to make a printout of your index for easy reference purposes, when you are not using the system. This becomes even more useful where you begin to have several disks.

At the same time it will be useful to undertake some basic 'housekeeping'. Are there any items which could be deleted altogether to save disk space?

7

Understanding financial and control systems

Aim of the unit

This unit considers the principal areas concerned with business facts and figures which are likely to be encountered in the course of secretarial work. It examines their role in controlling business operations, together with the relevant documentation, calculation and presentation involved.

Specific objectives

At the end of this unit you should be able to:

1   Devise a simple procedure for issuing office stationery.
2   Devise a system for keeping accurate stock records.
3   Complete a stationery requisition.
4   Trace the documentation involved in the completion of a business transaction.
5   Identify and explain the purposes of basic business documents.
6   Calculate VAT and calculate and distinguish between cash and trade discounts.
7   Identify the various services offered by commercial banks.
8   Complete essential banking documentation.
9   Compare and contrast standing orders and direct debits.
10 Explain the operation of the credit transfer system.
11 Differentiate between a cheque guarantee card and a credit card.
12 Prepare a bank reconciliation statement.
13 Keep an accurate petty cash book.
14 Explain the advantages of flexible working hours.
15 Calculate flexitime.
16 Briefly explain the process for calculation and make-up of wages.
17 Analyse a salary slip.
18 Explain the functions of the principal income tax forms.
19 Explain the uses and operation of basic accounting packages.

Stationery issue and stock control

All organisations need ample supplies of stationery and general office consumables if they are to function efficiently and effectively. The larger the organisation the more stock that will be required and consequently the larger the financial outlay and the greater the need to arrange suitable and secure storage facilities and to establish sound procedures for its control and issue.

Office stationery and supplies will most likely be purchased centrally for an organisation in order to gain the advantages of bulk buying and quantity discounts. There are also considerable benefits to be obtained from using the expertise of specialist purchasing staff who know the markets and the suppliers.

Once the goods are on the organisation's premises they may be issued either centrally or on a departmental basis. Whichever method is adopted the issue and control of stock will be monitored closely. Stationery and office supplies can represent a considerable capital sum, so storage must be carefully organised and supervised.

Storage procedure

1   Select and fit appropriate storage facilities which must be dry, well ventilated and adequately lit.

2 Keep these storage areas (they may be rooms or cupboards within a room) locked. Materials are often portable and liable to indiscriminate usage and pilfering.
3 Materials should be stored with due consideration to fire hazard.
4 Shelves should be clearly labelled.
5 Maximum and minimum stock levels should be determined (possibly via initial estimates taken from staff on annual usage). Maximum levels will largely be dependent upon space, financial outlay available and shelf life, whereas minimum levels will depend on the speed with which stocks can be replenished.
6 New supplies should go to the back; old stock should be brought forward. This is known as the FIFO principle (first in, first out).
7 All stock should be accounted for by some form of stocktaking (eg an annual stock check or a perpetual inventory—the latter being particularly appropriate for stationery and office supplies where it is usual to maintain accurate stock lists).
8 Stock record cards should be drawn up for each item of stock.
9 Heavy items should be stored near ground level for ease of handling, and items infrequently requested could be stored higher up on the shelves.
10 Any items affected by light or heat should be stored accordingly.

Issue procedure

1 No stock is issued without an authorised requisition.
2 Materials should be issued in predetermined units of issue, eg reams of paper, packets of envelopes or individual rolls of tape.
3 All goods should be signed for on receipt.
4 Issues should be made at specified times only.
5 All staff should have a copy of the stock list available to them.
6 All staff should be notified of the issue procedures and times.
7 Stock record cards should be updated after each issue period.

The business transaction

In any business where there is a transfer of goods or services from one party to another there will be documentation involved in the transaction. A diagrammatical representation of this is given in Fig 53. Transactions may be cash or credit, and in order to keep a record of them every transaction will have an original document which can be recorded in books of account. The following is a selection of the steps in a typical business transaction together with a brief explanation, where appropriate, of the likely documents involved.

The enquiry

Where someone is interested in the product or service of an organisation they are likely to place an initial enquiry. This could be made over the telephone, in person, by letter or even in printed form. Enquiries may be general in nature or they may take the form of very specific requests for infor-

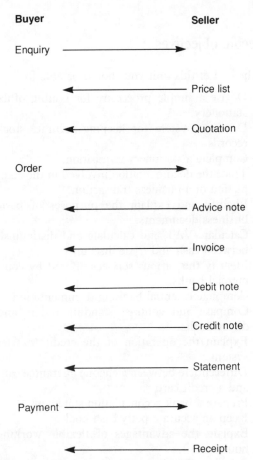

Fig 53 Documents in a business transaction

mation and prices. An enquiry is not recorded in books of account.

The price list

Many organisations maintain stocks of preprinted price lists together with leaflets providing details of their products or services, which can be sent out to the prospective customer in response to an enquiry. It is worth mentioning the use of catalogues at this point. Most catalogues are printed without prices; they are expensive to produce, and with the fluctuations in price of many articles, costly reprints would constantly be required. Price lists are, therefore, prepared to accompany many catalogues and glossy brochures so that when any change is instigated, only the price list need be updated, possibly with the aid of a word processing machine.

The price list is not relevant to books of account.

Quotation

Where more than a standard enquiry or a service is required, customers may ask for a quotation. This will often be a form letter, where only the essential variables need to be inserted (another useful application of word processing). It should contain not only the quantities that can be supplied or full details of the services offered, but also information about delivery and completion dates, methods of delivery and payment terms.

Order

It is possible to place an order in a standard business letter or perhaps even by telephone, but it is more likely to be made out on a specially printed form. Order forms may be issued in a standard format by the suppliers to ease the preparation by their stores department and general processing by the accounts department. Alternatively organisations placing a number or orders to different companies may use their own standard form sent out in numerical sequence, probably from a central purchasing department.

Invoice

An invoice is a document which is made out whenever one person sells goods to another, and it can be used in courts of law as evidence of a contract for the sale of goods. It is made out by the supplier and may have as many as five copies, usually printed on different colours of paper for ease of recognition and handling. Invoices contain the following information:

a names and addresses of both parties to the sale
b date of the sale
c description of goods, quantity, unit price and details of any trade discount
d terms of sale, ie discount which may be taken and credit period allowed
e many firms include the letters E & O E (errors and omissions excepted) at the bottom of their invoices as a safeguard so that they are in a position to rectify any errors and omissions later if necessary.

What about the copy invoices?

The *top* copy is the customer's copy of the contract of sale. It will be processed through the purchases journal.

The *second* copy is the seller's copy of the contract of sale. The sale will be recorded in the sales journal.

The *third* copy, usually referred to as the advice note, may either be sent in advance of the goods to announce their arrival or may be parcelled with the actual goods before they leave the stores. This document notifies the buyer of what goods to expect and will also indicate any goods 'to follow'.

At this point the buyer will be able to check the contents of the parcel and enter them in the appropriate record book.

The *fourth* copy is an exact replica of the advice note but is referred to as the **despatch note**, and enables the seller's despatch department to keep a check of the progress of the order.

The *fifth* copy, often called the **delivery note**, goes to the stores or despatch department and is issued with the goods to the delivery agent (perhaps a van driver) who will ultimately present it for signature when the goods are delivered. This delivery note will be returned to the stores or despatch department for entry in the appropriate record book.

In addition to these copies, there may be the following:

- a representative's copy
- a transport department copy
- a head office copy

• a costing department copy

Where an invoice is a multiple copy document it will normally take the form of continuous stationery to ease the task of preparation. These continuous stationery packs will be specially prepared to a company's specification of design and copy colour, and will either be interleaved with one-run carbons or prepared on NCR (no carbon required) paper. It is worth noting that not all copies will contain all information on costs and VAT – only the top copy, second copy and perhaps those destined for head office or a representative need have that information. Despatch/delivery/advice/transport copies will only require details of goods and quantities.

Value added tax (VAT)

Introduced in the UK in 1973, VAT is applied to certain goods and services and is currently levied at at 15 per cent. Some of what are termed 'essential commodities' are not subject to VAT in this country at present and certain undertakings, eg educational institutions, are exempt from the tax.

Where it is charged, suppliers are required to include VAT on all invoices which are likely to be used as 'tax invoices'. It should be noted that VAT is added to the **net** value of goods or services after deducting discounts.

While invoices received will include VAT, so too will invoices sent out to customers (provided that the level of business transacted annually necessitates VAT registration). Periodically (about once every three months) VAT returns are made to HM Customs and Excise and the difference between the tax charged by suppliers and the tax charged to customers is adjusted by means of a payment or refund.

Cash discount

A cash discount is given to debtors for prompt settlement of debts, and is offered as an inducement to the buyer to settle quickly and gain the discount.

Trade discount

Trade discount is quite different from a cash discount, being a reduction on the stated price of the article as advertised in the catalogue or price list. It is given by manufacturer or wholesaler to the retailer to enable the latter to make a profit on the catalogue price.

Debit note

This is a document very like an invoice and is made out by the supplier when the purchaser has been undercharged in some way on the invoice. For example, carriage may have been omitted or a typographical error may have been made against an item on the invoice, thereby necessitating an additional charge. In terms of bookkeeping a debit note is treated in the same way as an invoice.

Credit note

This operates in a reverse manner to a debit note and is again issued by the supplier to the purchaser, but this time to reduce the amount of the invoice. It might be issued where goods are returned, where they may have been damaged in transit or where there has been an overcharge of some kind. To distinguish it from the invoice or debit note, a credit note is printed in red and there will normally be two copies. The top copy will go to the purchaser who has either returned goods or claimed for an overcharge and will then be entered in his purchases returns book, whereas the duplicate is kept by the seller and entered in his sales returns book.

Statement

This is normally sent by the seller to all debtors at the end of the month as a reminder of the amounts which they currently owe for goods or services acquired from the seller during the month. The statement will not list all the details which have appeared in the invoices, debit or credit notes sent during the month but will simply provide a summary and give the appropriate reference numbers. Some firms prepare invoices and statements simultaneously by using some form of mechanised bookkeeping system and so reducing labour; others prepare statements by photocopying the ledger accounts on a high-speed copier. Where a second statement is sent out it is customary to print it in red and simply use the words 'to account rendered' followed by the amount rather than go to the trouble of relisting all the details in the original statement.

When a debtor receives a statement he should

check it against his invoices and/or bookkeeping records. If correct and if entitled to deduct a discount he would most likely return it with any discount shown as a covering document for his settlement cheque. Some suppliers will automatically receipt the statement and return it whereas others, unless specially requested to do so, will simply accept that the cheque will operate as a receipt. (The Cheques Act 1957 made receipts no longer necessary in Great Britain. However, they may, of course, be demanded as although a cheque cleared by a paying bank does act as a receipt it does not acknowledge the payment of a *specific* debt.)

Banking

The English banking system is a tripartite one:

1 The Bank of England
2 Specialised institutions like discount houses and merchant banks, which deal with special customers and provide funds for special purposes
3 The commercial or joint stock banks which deal with the general public

It is the third level with which we will be directly concerned. Commercial banks are very important for the British economy because they play a central part in business activity.

What services do they provide?

1 Current account services such as:

- the cheque system
- standing orders
- direct debit facilities
- the credit transfer system
- cash dispenser facilities
- overdrafts
- bank loans
- night-safe facilities
- banker's draft facilities

2 Deposit account services
3 Savings account services
4 Budget account services
5 Other services, such as:

- foreign exchange facilities
- advice on stocks and shares
- executorship and trustee services

- custodians of valuables
- insurance
- mortgage facilities
- income tax advice
- services in the export field
- credit ratings and creditworthiness
- economic information
- banker's credit cards
- Eurocheque cards
- debit cards
- discounting of bills of exchange
- investment management services

Obviously certain aspects of banking will have more relevance to practising secretaries than others, and some of the services mentioned here are now elaborated on.

Standing orders

Where fixed payments need to be made at regular intervals for items such as insurance premiums, rent and rates, mortgage repayments and equipment rental you can instruct your bank to make the payment of a stated sum to a stated organisation on a given day of the month, quarter or whatever, on your behalf. The request must be made to the bank in writing to initiate the service, and similarly a written request must be made to instruct the bank to cease making the payments.

Direct debit

As with a standing order, you give your bank a written instruction to meet payments as they fall due; but in this case the organisation named in your instruction presents a demand for the payment which the bank deducts from your account. There are two methods of direct debit, one providing for payment of fixed amounts, the other for unspecified amounts, ie where the amounts due may be variable.

How does direct debiting work?

1 An organisation invites you to complete a form authorising direct debits to be made.
2 You return the form to the organisation which passes it on to your bank, and in due course your account is debited in accordance with these instructions.

Advantages

1 It is simpler than paying bills by cheque.
2 It is flexible – the amount and/or intervals between payments can vary (unlike with a standing order).
3 It saves time.
4 Only organisations approved by the banks are allowed to operate the system.
5 The organisation concerned must always tell you *in advance* the amount and date of the payment where your instruction permits payments of unspecified amounts.
6 You have the right to cancel your direct debit instruction simply by writing to your bank.

The credit transfer system

This system can be used for the payment of several creditors without the drawer having to prepare separate cheques for each amount. Instead the drawer writes one cheque for the total sum involved, completes the necessary summary list and fills in the appropriate credit transfer slips. This method is increasingly used in the payment of wages. The bank arranges for the credit slips to be sent out to the creditors through their banks. The creditor must, in the first place, have given his written authority for payments to be made in this way. Obviously this is a very safe and simple way of paying wages as pay packets do not need to be made up and security guards are not needed to collect the money from the bank.

Note: The credit transfer system can also be used to settle accounts at the end of the month, and many firms encourage this practice by incorporating tear-off forms on the statements they send out.

Overdrafts

These are a convenient way of borrowing money from the bank without going through the formal procedure of completing documentation for a loan. Such an arrangement simply permits a customer to overdraw on his account up to a predetermined amount (by consultation with the Bank Manager), ie he can withdraw more than he has on deposit. A special method of repayment need not necessarily be stipulated but it will be usual to set a time limit on the overdraft. Interest will be charged, at the rate of about 2% above MLR (minimum lending rate). The amount of interest charged on an overdraft is calculated only on the amount overdrawn and not necessarily, therefore, on the upper limit of the overdraft as granted. It is the cheapest form of borrowing because interest is charged only on the actual amount owing on a daily basis. With the exception of very small overdrafts it will be usual for the bank to request some form of security. During a credit squeeze or at times of economic recession, bank overdrafts are more difficult to secure.

Loans

Loans are usually for larger sums of money and the repayment period is likely to be longer. The arrangements are more formal with documents being signed and exchanged. Interest will be paid either by regular instalments or in a lump sum at the end of a year.

Factors influencing banks in respect of granting overdrafts or loans

• the creditworthiness of the applicant and his previous financial record
• for what purpose the money is required
• the nature of the collateral offered as security
• the length of time involved and the rate of repayment

Banker's draft facilities

A banker's draft is like a cheque drawn by the bank on itself. It enables a customer to offer persons or firms to whom he is in debt a document in payment with the absolute authority of a bank to back it. Such drafts are often used where a trader is dealing with a wholesaler or manufacturer for the first time or when he offers payment abroad. Where a personal cheque may not be acceptable to a foreigner, a draft backed by one of the major banks would most likely be taken.

Cheque cards

These are issued by most banks to approved customers and guarantee that a cheque up to £50 will be met by the bank. Cheque guarantee cards of £100 and even £250 are now available to certain customers on application. Most shopkeepers and other business agencies will be unlikely to accept a cheque unless it is supported by a cheque card. The practice is to present the card together with the cheque, and the business will compare the signatures and endorse your cheque with the number on your cheque card. Cheque cards are also accepted as proof of identity when a person wishes to cash a cheque at a branch other than his own.

Credit cards

These are now issued by most banks to customers with sound credit ratings. They may be used to withdraw cash at other branches and to obtain credit at a large number of establishments (shops, garages, hotels, restaurants, theatres, transport undertakings) in both this country and abroad. An embossed card is used to record the customer's code on a special multicopy invoice. The customer signs the copy and the signature will be checked against that on the card. The customer pays no extra but the trader pays a charge towards processing. However, by joining such a scheme organisations are likely to substantially increase their customer numbers and the extra takings will offset the charge. The customer receives a monthly statement from the credit company which has in the interim paid the seller (less a commission). All uses of the card will be listed on the statement and the customer should check his statement against the counterfoils he gets back from the trader. He will be required to either pay the amount in full within the next few weeks, and so incur no interest, or make a part payment (a minimum amount is always quoted on the statement) in which case interest will be charged on the balance left owing. It should be noted that interest rates are high!

Access and Barclaycard

The two largest schemes operating in Britain are Visa and Access, both of which are operated by the banks. Often these may be combined with a cheque card for customers with current accounts at the relevant banks.

American Express and Diners

In addition to the systems operated by the bank there are also credit systems operated by private companies, the best known of which are American Express and Diners. With these, prospective customers must complete an application form and pay an enrolment fee plus an annual subscription for the service. However, the American Express card carries no interest charges. Holders are simply required to pay promptly in full on receiving each monthly statement. Obviously these services can be more expensive than those operated by the banks, but they mean that business people can travel all over the world and yet carry the minimum amount of cash.

Debit cards

Linked to current or savings accounts, debit cards serve as cheque substitutes. They can be used to pay for goods immediately or to draw cash from automated teller machines (ATMs) situated outside banks. The difference from a credit card is that when the retailer seeks bank authorisation for a transaction the amount is **automatically** deducted from the account there and then, rather than billed by the credit card company for later settlement.

Bank statements

All individuals operating bank accounts should take care to check all statements received for accuracy. Statements are issued periodically – monthly, quarterly, half-yearly or on request, and provide a detailed account of the transactions which have gone through the account. An example of a bank statement for the operation of a current account is given in Fig 54.

Banking technology and outside competition

Towards the end of the 1980s banking harnessed the benefits of technology allowing procedures to become increasingly automated in an attempt to provide a more efficient service. In addition they were forced to respond to competition from building societies following the latter's right to diversify its operations as a result of the **Building Societies Act 1986**. What were traditionally strictly banking territories are now open to aggressive competition from the building societies, particularly in respect of areas like interest-paying current accounts, Saturday opening and home banking facilities,

Customer's name and full postal address			Bank's name, branch and address			
11503904 Account number						5 Page

DATE	PARTICULARS		DEBITS	CREDITS	BALANCE	
23 May 19	BALANCE FORWARD				112.67	
24 May	Abbey Life	DD	25.50		87.17	
26 May	587668		6.00		81.17	
31 May	Deposit account	TR		200.00	281.17	
3 June	587667		50.00			
	587669		6.00		225.17	
6 June	London Bond Street	CD	30.00		195.17	
7 June	587670		20.00		175.17	
8 June	587672		23.98		151.19	
9 June	587673		17.40			
	587671		84.03		49.76	
13 June	587674		100.00		51.24	DR
15 June	City of Westminster	*		641.24	590.00	
	587675		50.00		540.00	
18 June	Halifax Bdg Soc	SO	143.70		396.30	
20 June	Deposit account	SO	25.00		371.30	
24 June	587677		42.50			
	587676		12.50			
	587678		19.80		286.50	
30 June	Bank charges	CH	7.20		279.30	
2 July	ICI	DV		37.40	316.70	
3 July	587679		11.50			
	587680		19.20		286.00	
4 July	London Oxford Street	CD	50.00		236.00	
5 July					236.00	

ABBREVIATIONS:

CD	Cash dispenser	SO	Standing order	
DD	Direct debit	TR	Transfer	
DV	Dividend	CH	Charges	
DR	Indicates a BALANCE DUE to the bank			

* Beside an entry denotes a transfer by computer for which no voucher has been produced

Fig 54 Bank statement

initially offered exclusively by the building societies but now on offer from many banks as well.

Bank reconciliation statements

Where financial records are handled and processed by different agencies, eg you and the bank, it will be more than likely that the figures you arrive at will not agree with those produced by the bank when they present a statement. Hence the need for 'reconciliation'. In business it is common for figures to be apparently in disagreement with one another but reasonable explanations for the difference will reconcile the two sets of figures and show that both sets are in fact *correct* from their own information.

What makes the figures disagree?

There are two main reasons (excluding basic mathematical error) which cause this to happen.

1 Where one party lacks knowledge of the actions performed by the other, eg where you may have written a cheque in payment of a debt but the creditor has yet to present the cheque for payment. In this instance the balance you have will be less than the balance shown by the bank. Alternatively, the bank may have deducted bank charges of which you are unaware, in which case your balance will appear to be greater than that at the bank.

2 Delays occur. You may have received payment from debtors in the form of cheques and consequently boosted your bank balance, but your statement will not show this until the cheques have been presented to your bank and subsequently cleared, which may take several days. Other examples of delays could be in the use of a night safe or a cash dispenser's facilities. Similarly it is perfectly feasible to miscalculate the timing of payment of direct debits.

Such instances tend to be handled on a relatively *ad hoc* basis by private individuals when calculating apparent discrepancies in their current account balances. However, in a business context, any individual responsible for recording cash/bank transactions will need to reconcile cash book figures with those shown on a bank statement. This will involve working carefully through the bank statement, marking off each item against that recorded in the cash book. On so doing it will be possible to take any discrepancies into account, deducting unpresented cheques from the bank balance together with any bank charges deducted or direct debits due but not shown as being paid in the bank statement, and adding any sums of money lodged with the bank but awaiting clearance. By following this procedure it should be possible to reconcile the figures in the bank statement and the cash book.

Other control systems

Organisations also need to set up a variety of other control procedures to monitor and improve day-to-day working practices. One such procedure concerns petty cash provision while two other common

ones are the operation of flexible working hours and claiming for expenses incurred on company business. All three are considered briefly here.

Petty cash

As a secretary it is likely that you may be required to operate a system for petty cash. The availability of small sums of money is essential to the smooth operation of any office. Every sort of expense cannot be settled satisfactorily by cheque, nor is it reasonable that staff should not have provision for the instant reimbursement of expenses incurred by them on company business. Similarly it is possible that the organisation will not carry every conceivable item of stock which might occasionally be required, and in such circumstances special items will be financed from petty cash.

The imprest system

The most usual system for the maintenance of petty cash is known as the 'imprest system'. This system enables the cashier to check petty cash expenditure very simply while limiting total outlay to a fixed sum of money – the imprest. This operates like a float in a shop till. It is determined at the outset and issued by the Cashier. During the term of the petty cash book, which could be weekly, monthly or even quarterly (according to individual requirements), monies are subtracted from (and occasionally added to) the float and noted usually in a general total column and in separate analysis columns (see Fig 55).

These analysis columns, which can be headed according to requirement, enable petty expenditure on any class of item to be determined at a glance. At the end of the period the columns are totalled (analysis columns should always add up to the sum of the total column), and when added to the sum of money remaining in the cash box should represent the starting sum. Once checked the expenses should be reimbursed by the Chief Cashier, so re-establishing the initial 'imprest'.

Petty cash vouchers

Payments are authorised on petty cash vouchers (see Fig 56). These are normally issued prior to

Dr   PETTY CASH ACCOUNT   Cr

Received	Date	Fo	Details	V No	Total paid out							

Fig 55 Petty cash book

Petty Cash Voucher

Folio _____

Date _____

For what required	Amount	
	£	p

Signature _____

Passed by _____

Ivy series

Fig 56 Petty cash voucher

expenditure in numerical order and are entered for checking purposes in a special column in the petty cash book (see Fig 55). Alternatively staff may produce receipts for goods or services and be reimbursed on the strength of such receipts for expenditure incurred by them in the course and interest of their work.

Flexitime

Flexitime is a simple idea which enables employees, within certain limits, to control the starting and finishing times of their working day. It is used extensively in government offices and also in industry generally, where it is gaining in popularity and is sometimes even offered as an incentive in advertisements.

How does flexitime work?

The period of the day during which the office is open is divided into two types of time: **coretime** (between something like 1000 and 1200 hours in the morning and 1400 and 1600 hours in the afternoon) when everybody must be present, and **flexitime** at either end of the day and at lunchtime when people can choose to be present or not, provided the demands of the department are met and due consideration is given to all those concerned in the operation of the system. (It is usual to stipulate a minimum of half an hour and a maximum of two hours for lunch.) In any case, sufficient hours of flexitime must be worked to bring the total working hours up to the contract total within a week or month.

The advantages of flexitime

1 It enables staff to exercise choice on when they start and finish for the day.
2 It reduces the need for overtime, thereby saving money for the employer.
3 It extends the working day at little cost to the employer other than basic overheads.
4 It helps avoid peak travel times.
5 It helps staff accommodate personal arrangements, eg shopping, luncheon appointments, hairdresser, doctor, dentist, domestic arrangements.
6 It enables extra hours worked to be credited towards half-days off or even full days, which can be taken to make a long weekend. (Normally there will be a limit to the number of hours an individual can have credited, over and above the contracted hours, during a particular accounting period of, for example, four weeks.)
7 It eliminates the problem of bad timekeeping.

The disadvantages of flexitime

1 Rules can be somewhat complex and must be adhered to by all if the system is to operate effectively.
2 Requires the installation of a special time recorder and the issue of individual keys to all staff in the system.
3 Adds to the complexity of wage calculations.
4 Certain jobs do not lend themselves to the operation of this sort of system.

Claiming for expenses

Where company personnel have expense accounts or are entitled to claim back certain types of expenses incurred, there will be procedures to be followed.

Executives who operate expense accounts will be given an indication of their budget for a certain period, and it will be their responsibility to see that they keep their business expenses within that predetermined budget. It is likely that they will also be issued with a credit card which they may use in connection with company business. They will need to keep receipts for all items which they pay for by credit card and may be required to account for such expenditure.

Where an individual does not have an expenses budget to work from it is still possible that he or she may have occasion to claim expenses, and this would normally be done by completing the necessary form at the appropriate time in the accounting period. There will usually be a final date for submission of expenses claims for payment with the next month's salary.

The types of item which expenses are usually claimed for would be as follows:

- travel (fares or mileage where no company car)
- company car expenses (fuel, repair bills, car parking)
- meals
- entertaining clients on company business

The procedure for claiming back such expenses is often outlined in a staff handbook and special claim forms would be used. The steps for completion would then be something along the following lines:

1 Complete the necessary details, attaching receipts and tickets as required.
2 Sign the form.
3 Pass to superior for checking and authorisation.
4 Pass on to appropriate personnel for coding and calculation of payment for inclusion with next salary.

Wages and salaries

While this book is not intended to go into great detail about the payment of wages and salaries, which is complex and frequently changing, it is essential that any prospective secretary should be in possession of basic facts in relation to employee remuneration, whether it be on a wage or salary basis. Also it is important for all employees to have an appreciation of the calculation of their wages or salaries and to know how and why certain deductions are made.

Wages

Wages will normally be paid weekly and are likely to be calculated in the following ways:

- *hourly* on a flat (or basic rate) for a certain

number of hours, with extra payment for hours worked over and above the basic rate
- *piece work rates* paid for the completion of a given amount of work

How are the calculations made?

Most hourly paid workers operate a **clock card** system whereby their arrival and departure times are recorded by inserting their personal clock card into a time recording machine which will normally be located, together with the racks of clock cards, near the entrance.

At the end of the week the clock cards will be checked and processed by the wages clerks and the rate of pay calculated according to the hours worked. including any overtime. It is of interest to note that some modern recording systems are linked to a computer which automatically calculates wages. With such a system each employee has a small personalised plastic key which, when inserted into the timing mechanism, registers the arrival or departure and feeds the information to the computer. A visual display unit on the time recorder enables employees to make their own time checks on hours worked.

The initial calculation of hours worked leads to the *gross pay* which is the total amount due to an employee before deductions – statutory and voluntary – are made.

Most workers will be paid their wages in cash, although there is an increasing tendency to make payment into a bank, post office or building society account to lessen the risks incurred when handling large sums of money. Where payment is made in cash, strict security precautions will be undertaken during the transfer of money from the bank to the wages department, often using specialist security services.

In the wages department the wage packets will then be made up from the information processed, probably with the help of a computer or at least an electronic accounting machine. It is important to recognise that a cash analysis will have been carried out, again probably by machine, to find out the different coin and note denominations required to actually make up the packets. Wage packets come in many different styles and often are either made of an opaque paper or contain a window so that the cash contents may be checked before the envelope is opened. This is to prevent fraud. It is normal practice to require employees to check their envelopes on receipt so that any discrepancy can be acknowledged with the minimum of query. It will be usual for employees to receive details of what deductions have been made, ending up with a *net pay* figure. The envelope will also contain details of the employee's name and department and/or works number.

Salaries

Salaries are normally paid monthly and are calculated as one-twelfth of the annual salary figure. It will be unlikely for salaries to be paid in cash, although technically an employee could insist on payment in this way. The most usual method will be by direct payment into a bank, post office or building society account (particularly a bank) by means of credit transfer. Here the employee will receive only a salary advice slip containing details of name, department and/or employee number, annual salary figure, tax code number, National Insurance number and gross salary figure. Additions will be made for any overtime pay or additional expenses claimed or tax refund, and deductions for income tax, super-annuation, National Insurance and any other voluntary deductions, resulting in a net salary figure for the month. A specimen salary slip is shown as Fig 57.

Other possible means of remuneration

Commission Sometimes sales personnel are paid on a commission basis, ie they receive a percentage based on the total sales. This may be on a strict commission basis or could operate on a flat rate salary plus commission.

Fees Certain professional people operate on a fee basis, eg medical consultants or solicitors. However there is usually a fee scale to assist and protect the individual availing himself of the service.

Incentive schemes Some organisations operate incentive schemes which are designed to encourage workers to work harder and perhaps produce more goods. They are also intended as an encouragement for an individual to remain with an organisation. Profit-sharing is a popular form of incentive. Here employees may be given either a share of the firm's profits or perhaps shares in the company itself.

Bonus schemes Many organisations operate bonus schemes whereby employees are rewarded for their

Salary advice

Dept	Employee No	Employee name	NI number	NIC type	Tax code	Tax year	Tax month	Month ending	Annual salary
05	0297	WALLS J	TP 241900D	D	0 260 L	1989/90	03	30.06.89	8525.00

Pay and allowances

Overtime hours	Overtime pay	Basic pay	NI benefit adjustment	Code	Amount	Code	Amount	Code	Amount	Code	Amount	Gross pay
		710.42										710.42

Deductions (R = refund)

Superann	Income tax	NIC	Union sub Code	Union sub Amount	Code	Amount	Code	Amount	Code	Amount	Code	Amount	Total deductions
42.65	123.34	132.10	79	3.00	56	1.00							169.99

TOTALS TO DATE IN THIS EMPLOYMENT					PREVIOUS EMPLOYMENT		Net pay
Pay less superann	Tax deducted	NI deducted	Superann (Net pay scheme)	Stat sick pay	Pay	Tax deducted	
2003.31	370.02	96.80	127.95				540.43

Examples of codes

Allowances

01 Car allowance
02 Laundry allowance
03 Rent allowance
04 Travel expenses
05 Materials allowance

Deductions

52 Court orders
53 Housing rent
54 Hospital contributions
55 SAYE
56 Charity

Fig 57

hard work and effort. This bonus may come in the form of double wages at peak times like Christmas or holiday periods or may be offered in recognition of a particular effort which has brought about positive results for the company.

Expenses These are not strictly forms of remuneration but are viewed as 'perks' by many employees and would certainly feature in their personal calculations of earning capacity. Typical expenses are a car allowance or mileage for using a car on company business.

Income tax

Employees will all be liable to pay income tax on their income earned during a fiscal year, ie from 6 April one year to 5 April the following year. This tax is collected by employers via the system known as **PAYE** (pay as you earn) and paid on behalf of employees to the Inland Revenue. An employer knows how much tax to deduct from using **tax tables** in association with an employee's **code number**. A code number is allocated to an individual on the basis of details furnished by him to the Inland Revenue in completing a *tax claims form*. Individuals may claim tax allowance against the following:

- personal allowance
- married person's allowance
- dependent relatives
- certain expenses incurred in the nature of your employment and not reimbursed by the employer

The list of allowances is liable to change and up-to-date information should always be sought from a local tax office.

Once the allowances are claimed via the tax claims form, the Inland Revenue will issue the tax payer with a code number which will indicate the amount of money which may be earned before income tax needs to be paid. This number should be given to the employer who will then know how much tax-free pay to allow (note that the employer does not know how the code number is arrived at, and so is unaware of the personal details and circumstances of employees). All income over and above the tax-free allowance will be liable to tax. The rate of tax applied will vary according to an individual's gross income. After a certain amount at the standard rate of tax prevailing at any given time a taxpayer is taxed at the next tax level. Full details of the PAYE

system are given in the *Employer's Guide to PAYE* issued by the Inland Revenue.

National insurance

The other statutory deduction which affects employees' wages or salaries is National Insurance. Contributions are related to earnings and are collected together with income tax under the PAYE procedure.

National Insurance numbers are allocated to all contributors by the DSS (Department of Social Security), normally on commencement of the first job, and the number remains the same for life. An employee must give his number to his employer on request.

Contributions are payable by both employees and employers and are subject to lower and upper earnings limits, expressed in weekly terms, irrespective of the fact that salaries may be paid monthly. The lower and upper limits are reviewed annually and students should obtain the current National Insurance leaflet from the Post Office for up-to-date amounts. Another useful leaflet obtainable from the DSS is the *Employer's Guide to National Insurance Contributions*.

What does National Insurance cover?

National Insurance helps pay for a number of cash benefits, including the following:

- unemployment benefits
- sickness benefits
- payments for injuries sustained at work
- maternity allowances
- widow's pension should a husband die before the wife reaches the relevant age
- retirement pension
- death grant

Documentation involved in the calculation and payment of wages and salaries

A vast number of forms are issued both by the Inland Revenue and the DSS, but the most common ones are detailed briefly in the following:

P11

This is a tax deduction card held by the wages

department in respect of each employee and detailing the following:

- gross pay due each week or month
- total amount earned so far in the fiscal year
- the amount of tax-free pay to which the employee is entitled

- the total taxable pay
- the total tax due to date — obtainable from the tax tables
- the tax deducted (or refunded) in the week or month

WEEK 2
Apr 13 to Apr 19

TABLE A–FREE PAY

Code	Total free pay to date	Code	Total free pay to date	Code	Total free pay to date	Code	Total free pay to date	Code	Total free pay to date	Code	Total free pay to date	Code	Total free pay to date	Code	Total free pay to date
	£		£		£		£		£		£		£		£
0	NIL														
1	0·74	61	23·82	121	46·90	181	69·98	241	93·04	301	116·12	361	139·20	421	162·28
2	1·12	62	24·20	122	47·28	182	70·36	242	93·44	302	116·50	362	139·58	422	162·66
3	1·50	63	24·58	123	47·66	183	70·74	243	93·82	303	116·90	363	139·98	423	163·04
4	1·90	64	24·98	124	48·04	184	71·12	244	94·20	304	117·28	364	140·36	424	163·44
5	2·28	65	25·36	125	48·44	185	71·50	245	94·58	305	117·66	365	140·74	425	163·82
6	2·66	66	25·74	126	48·82	186	71·90	246	94·98	306	118·04	366	141·12	426	164·20
7	3·04	67	26·12	127	49·20	187	72·28	247	95·36	307	118·44	367	141·50	427	164·58
8	3·44	68	26·50	128	49·58	188	72·66	248	95·74	308	118·82	368	141·90	428	164·98
9	3·82	69	26·90	129	49·98	189	73·04	249	96·12	309	119·20	369	142·28	429	165·36
10	4·20	70	27·28	130	50·36	190	73·44	250	96·50	310	119·58	370	142·66	430	165·74
11	4·58	71	27·66	131	50·74	191	73·82	251	96·90	311	119·98	371	143·04	431	166·12
12	4·98	72	28·04	132	51·12	192	74·20	252	97·28	312	120·36	372	143·44	432	166·50
13	5·36	73	28·44	133	51·50	193	74·58	253	97·66	313	120·74	373	143·82	433	166·90
14	5·74	74	28·82	134	51·90	194	74·98	254	98·04	314	121·12	374	144·20	434	167·28
15	6·12	75	29·20	135	52·28	195	75·36	255	98·44	315	121·50	375	144·58	435	167·66
16	6·50	76	29·58	136	52·66	196	75·74	256	98·82	316	121·90	376	144·98	436	168·04
17	6·90	77	29·98	137	53·04	197	76·12	257	99·20	317	122·28	377	145·36	437	168·44
18	7·28	78	30·36	138	53·44	198	76·50	258	99·58	318	122·66	378	145·74	438	168·82
19	7·66	79	30·74	139	53·82	199	76·90	259	99·98	319	123·04	379	146·12	439	169·20
20	8·04	80	31·12	140	54·20	200	77·28	260	100·36	320	123·44	380	146·50	440	169·58
21	8·44	81	31·50	141	54·58	201	77·66	261	100·74	321	123·82	381	146·90	441	169·98
22	8·82	82	31·90	142	54·98	202	78·04	262	101·12	322	124·20	382	147·28	442	170·36
23	9·20	83	32·28	143	55·36	203	78·44	263	101·50	323	124·58	383	147·66	443	170·74
24	9·58	84	32·66	144	55·74	204	78·82	264	101·90	324	124·98	384	148·04	444	171·12
25	9·98	85	33·04	145	56·12	205	79·20	265	102·28	325	125·36	385	148·44	445	171·50
26	10·36	86	33·44	146	56·50	206	79·58	266	102·66	326	125·74	386	148·82	446	171·90
27	10·74	87	33·82	147	56·90	207	79·98	267	103·04	327	126·12	387	149·20	447	172·28
28	11·12	88	34·20	148	57·28	208	80·36	268	103·44	328	126·50	388	149·58	448	172·66
29	11·50	89	34·58	149	57·66	209	80·74	269	103·82	329	126·90	389	149·98	449	173·04
30	11·90	90	34·98	150	58·04	210	81·12	270	104·20	330	127·28	390	150·36	450	173·44
31	12·28	91	35·36	151	58·44	211	81·50	271	104·58	331	127·66	391	150·74	451	173·82
32	12·66	92	35·74	152	58·82	212	81·90	272	104·98	332	128·04	392	151·12	452	174·20
33	13·04	93	36·12	153	59·20	213	82·28	273	105·36	333	128·44	393	151·50	453	174·58
34	13·44	94	36·50	154	59·58	214	82·66	274	105·74	334	128·82	394	151·90	454	174·98
35	13·82	95	36·90	155	59·98	215	83·04	275	106·12	335	129·20	395	152·28	455	175·36
36	14·20	96	37·28	156	60·36	216	83·44	276	106·50	336	129·58	396	152·66	456	175·74
37	14·58	97	37·66	157	60·74	217	83·82	277	106·90	337	129·98	397	153·04	457	176·12
38	14·98	98	38·04	158	61·12	218	84·20	278	107·28	338	130·36	398	153·44	458	176·50
39	15·36	99	38·44	159	61·50	219	84·58	279	107·66	339	130·74	399	153·82	459	176·90
40	15·74	100	38·82	160	61·90	220	84·98	280	108·04	340	131·12	400	154·20	460	177·28
41	16·12	101	39·20	161	62·28	221	85·36	281	108·44	341	131·50	401	154·58	461	177·66
42	16·50	102	39·58	162	62·66	222	85·74	282	108·82	342	131·90	402	154·98	462	178·04
43	16·90	103	39·98	163	63·04	223	86·12	283	109·20	343	132·28	403	155·36	463	178·44
44	17·28	104	40·36	164	63·44	224	86·50	284	109·58	344	132·66	404	155·74	464	178·82
45	17·66	105	40·74	165	63·82	225	86·90	285	109·98	345	133·04	405	156·12	465	179·20
46	18·04	106	41·12	166	64·20	226	87·28	286	110·36	346	133·44	406	156·50	466	179·58
47	18·44	107	41·50	167	64·58	227	87·66	287	110·74	347	133·82	407	156·90	467	179·98
48	18·82	108	41·90	168	64·98	228	88·04	288	111·12	348	134·20	408	157·28	468	180·36
49	19·20	109	42·28	169	65·36	229	88·44	289	111·50	349	134·58	409	157·66	469	180·74
50	19·58	110	42·66	170	65·74	230	88·82	290	111·90	350	134·98	410	158·04	470	181·12
51	19·98	111	43·04	171	66·12	231	89·20	291	112·28	351	135·36	411	158·44	471	181·50
52	20·36	112	43·44	172	66·50	232	89·58	292	112·66	352	135·74	412	158·82	472	181·90
53	20·74	113	43·82	173	66·90	233	89·98	293	113·04	353	136·12	413	159·20	473	182·28
54	21·12	114	44·20	174	67·28	234	90·36	294	113·44	354	136·50	414	159·58	474	182·66
55	21·50	115	44·58	175	67·66	235	90·74	295	113·82	355	136·90	415	159·98	475	183·04
56	21·90	116	44·98	176	68·04	236	91·12	296	114·20	356	137·28	416	160·36	476	183·44
57	22·28	117	45·36	177	68·44	237	91·50	297	114·58	357	137·66	417	160·74	477	183·82
58	22·66	118	45·74	178	68·82	238	91·90	298	114·98	358	138·04	418	161·12	478	184·20
59	23·04	119	46·12	179	69·20	239	92·28	299	115·36	359	138·44	419	161·50	479	184·58
60	23·44	120	46·50	180	69·58	240	92·66	300	115·74	360	138·82	420	161·90	480	184·98

see page 2

SPECIMEN

Fig 58 Tax Table A extract SPECIMEN

Tax tables

These consist of two books. Table A is a book indicating the free pay tables for each week or month of the financial year. The amount of tax-free pay to date is shown opposite each code number (see Fig 58). Table B refers to tax due on taxable pay to date up to weekly and monthly limits. (There are also Tables C and D which exceed the figures given in Table B.)

P45

This is a three-part form issued by an employer

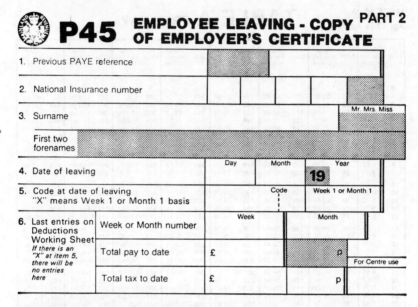

P45 EMPLOYEE LEAVING - COPY OF EMPLOYER'S CERTIFICATE
PART 2

		Day	Month	Year
1. Previous PAYE reference				
2. National Insurance number				
3. Surname				Mr. Mrs. Miss
First two forenames				
4. Date of leaving		Day	Month	Year 19
5. Code at date of leaving "X" means Week 1 or Month 1 basis			Code	Week 1 or Month 1

6. Last entries on Deductions Working Sheet *If there is an "X" at item 5, there will be no entries here*	Week or Month number	Week		Month
	Total pay to date	£		p
	Total tax to date	£	p	For Centre use

EMPLOYEE - THIS FORM IS IMPORTANT. *DO NOT LOSE IT.* You cannot get a duplicate. *Do not separate the two parts.*

- **GOING TO A NEW JOB?**
  Give this form to your new employer, otherwise he will have to tax you under the emergency code.

- **CLAIMING UNEMPLOYMENT BENEFIT?**
  Take this form to the benefit office.

- **CLAIMING A TAX REFUND?**
  If you are not working and not claiming unemployment benefit, get form P50 from any Tax Office or PAYE Enquiry Office. The form tells you what to do.

PLEASE NOTE: If for some special reason you do not want your new employer to know the details entered on this form send it to your Tax Office BEFORE you start your new job, and give the name and address of your new employer. The Tax Office can make special arrangements, but you may pay too much tax for a time as a result.

INSTRUCTIONS TO NEW EMPLOYER

- Check and complete this form and prepare a Deductions Working Sheet according to the "New Employee" instructions on the P8 (BLUE CARD).

- Detach Part 3 and send it to your Tax Office **IMMEDIATELY.** *Keep Part 2.*

P45

Fig 59 P45 form

when an employee changes job. It must be completed by the current employer, ie the person holding the P11. On completion it must be sent to the tax office dealing with the employee's affairs as soon as the employment is terminated. Parts 2 and 3 which are joined together and contain the same information as part 1 – transferred via NCR paper – must not be separated by the employee, who must present them to his new employer. The new employer then retains part 2 and sends part 3 to *his* local tax office. The two tax offices (assuming they may be different) will then confer and transfer the employee's tax file if necessary. The form shows how much income tax has been deducted up to the date of leaving one employment, together with the current code number of the employee. Should an employee for some reason fail to hand over his P45 at his new employment tax will be deducted on an emergency coding and may well be more than is usually paid. An example of a P45 is given in Fig 59.

P60

After 5 April each year the employer must by law give all employees from whose pay tax has been deducted a certificate of pay and tax deductions. This form should show the total amount paid to the employee during the year ended 5 April and the total tax deducted less any refunds. An example of a P60 is given in Fig 60.

P2

This is the notice of coding sent to all taxpayers each year, and will be updated on receipt of information from the taxpayer that his personal circumstances have altered in some way, so affecting his allowances.

P1

This is the tax return form itself, which should be completed as necessary by the taxpayer.

P60 Certificate of pay and tax deducted   **Do not destroy**

| Employer's full name and address | | Tax District and reference | Year to 5 April |
| | | Employee's works/payroll no. etc. | 19 |

| Employee's National Insurance number | | Employee's surname *(in BLOCK CAPITALS)* | First two forenames | Final tax code |

Total for year		Previous employment		This employment	Tax deducted or refunded *"R" indicates refund*
Pay	Tax deducted	Pay	Tax deducted	Pay	
£	£	£	£	£	£

National Insurance contributions in this employment				Employee's Widows and Orphans/life insurance contributions in this employment		
Contribution Table letter	Total of Employee's and Employer's Contributions payable 1a	Employee's Contributions payable 1b	Employee's Contributions at Contracted-out rate included in column 1b 1c			Week 53 payment indicator
	£	£	£			
	£	£	£			
	£	£	£	£		
	£	£	£			

I/We certify that the particulars given above include the total amount of pay for income tax purposes (including overtime, bonus, commission etc.) paid to you by me/us in the year shown above and the total tax deducted by me/us (less any refunds) in that year.

TO THE EMPLOYEE
Keep this certificate. It will help you to check any Notice of Assessment which the Tax Office may send you in due course. A duplicate form P60 cannot be supplied.

P60

Fig 60 P60 form

Accounting software

Any procedures involving numerical calculations are ideally suited to the logic of a computer and accounting applications were among the first to be handled by large mainframe computers. Such systems were, of course, costly and restricted to large organisations, but in recent years accounting programs have been developed for microcomputers and are now well within the reach and expertise of smaller users.

Vast ranges of programs are now commercially available, varying in capability from those with limited features for very routine applications to those made up of several modules, each dealing with a specific accounting function. Typical modules in an **integrated accounting package** would be as follows:

- Sales ledger
- Purchases ledger
- Nominal ledger
- Payroll
- Stock control
- Automatic invoicing
- Order processing

The idea behind such integrated packages is that unlike with manual accounting and bookkeeping procedures, the data need only be entered once, even though it may affect several procedures. Therefore, whereas in a manual system the processing of an order would necessitate adjusting stock levels, generating an invoice and updating sales and nominal ledgers, all entries in a computerised system will be made automatically. Consequently accounting programs are used by many different personnel within an organisation, according to the nature and content of their jobs. For example, a manager may use one to obtain an overview of business activities while a clerk may use it to update data or prepare invoices and statements.

5 When might a company send out a debit note?
6 Suggest six services which a current account customer of a bank may use.
7 Give an example of one occasion when you might use a standing order and another when you might use a direct debit.
8 When would a bank overdraft be preferable to a personal loan, and why?
9 What is meant by petty cash?
10 How does the imprest system work?
11 How does flexitime work?
12 Identify two ways in which wages might be calculated.
13 Name four items which National Insurance covers.
14 What is a P45?
15 When do employees receive a P60 and what does it show?
16 Identify five modules you would expect to find in a typical integrated accounting package.

Personal activities

1 Visit your local bank and building society and collect their literature outlining the various services and facilities they offer. Study it carefully, comparing and contrasting the services they provide.

2 If you use a credit card consider how best to maximise the credit facility it provides. Also calculate the interest you can expect to pay if you pay only the minimum amount requested on your statement. Interest rates are very high when considered on an annual basis!

3 Given that it is advisable to have current literature on all matters which are subject to amendment because of changes in legislation following, for example, the Budget, write to or call in at your local Inland Revenue and DHSS offices and secure the relevant leaflets.

Self-test

1 Why is it necessary to have a system of stock control?
2 What points would you consider when setting up a stationery store?
3 What information is contained on an invoice?
4 Where an organisation adopts multiple-copy invoices where might the additional copies go?

Group activity

Imagine that you have had a windfall of £1000. Either individually or in groups of two or three pretend to invest the money in a variety of different ways for a period of six months. Examples would be different types of interest paying accounts, National Savings Certificates or in stocks and shares. Compare your results at the end of the six month period.

1 Imagine that your boss has asked you to be responsible for the issue of stationery within your department, as the present system (or lack of one!) is resulting in chaos. Staff are helping themselves from the stationery store, and when they have used up supplies items are frequently out of stock for long periods; there is also a high level of wastage. Eventually the intention is that this duty should be delegated to a more junior member of staff, but you have been given authority to ensure that a new system is organised and running smoothly in the first instance.

   a Explain, in detail, the steps you would take to reorganise the stationery store.
   b How would you determine what stock should be carried?
   c How would you record the stock?
   d Design a form for staff to requisition supplies.
   e Outline the procedure you have devised in a memo to all staff.

2 Imagine that one of your duties is the maintenance of the petty cash for your office. You work in a firm of solicitors. You are given a monthly sum of £30 to use in this connection. From the vouchers shown in Fig 61, complete a suitable petty cash book with appropriate analysis columns and balance it at the end of the month, ready for checking by the Chief Accountant. The month in question is June. Take into account the following additional details:

   a a receipt for £4.50 for a bar lunch which one of the accounting assistants was asked to take with a representative
   b a receipt for 68p for biscuits which the Office Junior bought on the Senior Partner's instructions
   c £1.70 in cash which was given to you by a client for a long-distance telephone call made from your office

3 Your organisation has started a scheme of flexitime based on the daily splits given in Fig 62. The following apply:

   a In any week you must work a minimum of thirty-five hours.
   b The accounting period for flexitime is four weeks.
   c The maximum working day is nine hours on Monday to Thursday, and eight hours on Friday.
   d The maximum carry-forwards at end of an

accounting period are plus ten hours and minus seven hours.
   e Flexileave is one day or two half-days per accounting period.

You plan to have a long weekend during the next accounting period. You hope to leave at midday on the Friday and return to work at 1400 the following Monday. You also hope to visit the hairdresser in a two-hour lunch break on the Thursday before the weekend.

To achieve your minimum of thirty-five hours per week you usually work the set hours 0830–1230 and 1330–1630 each week, ie seven hours per day.

   a On the week prior to the weekend in question, how much time do you have to make up to ensure you work thirty-five hours, and how might you arrange this?
   b On the week following the weekend, how much time do you have to compensate for the hours lost on the Monday morning, and how might you do this?

4 Your employer is soon to travel to Italy on important company business. He will be in Rome and Naples for between eight and twelve days and will be travelling extensively during that time. He wants to be sure that he will always have sufficient funds to meet all expenses incurred. However, he has had money stolen on a previous business trip and is somewhat apprehensive, knowing the colourful reputation that Italy has for pickpockets.

   Also, he is hoping to secure a large business deal on behalf of the company and will need substantial funds to ensure that he can secure the business on the spot.

   a What advice would you give in relation to the day-to-day money matters involved? Give full details in support of your suggestions.
   b How can he arrange for acceptable financial backing to support any business deal he may be successful in setting up?
   c How would you secure additional advice on both these matters, and what sort of questions would you need to ask?

5 During your coffee break this morning you were engaged in conversation with someone from the sales force of your company. He was talking about a friend of his who works for a rival firm, and how that firm pays their sales representatives on a strict commission basis, in contrast to your company which operates a flat rate plus commission. Your office junior was also at the coffee table, and afterwards asks you to explain

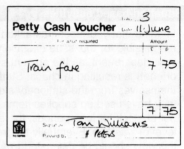

Petty Cash Voucher	Folio 1 Date 3 June		
For what required	Amount	£	p
Bus fares		2	40
		2	40
Signature g Wild			
Passed by V P Jones			

Petty Cash Voucher	Folio 2 Date 6 June		
For what required	Amount	£	p
Recorded delivery packet		–	52
		–	52
Signature Susan Bryden			
Passed by V P Jones			

Petty Cash Voucher	Folio 3 Date 11 June		
For what required	Amount	£	p
Train fare		7	75
		7	75
Signature Tom Williams			
Passed by H Peters			

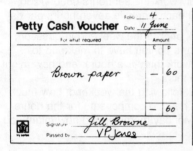

Petty Cash Voucher	Folio 4 Date 11 June		
For what required	Amount	£	p
Brown paper		–	60
		–	60
Signature Jill Browne			
Passed by V P Jones			

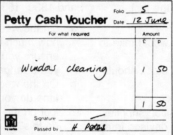

Petty Cash Voucher	Folio 5 Date 12 June		
For what required	Amount	£	p
Window cleaning		1	50
		1	50
Signature			
Passed by H Peters			

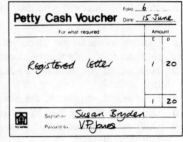

Petty Cash Voucher	Folio 6 Date 15 June		
For what required	Amount	£	p
Registered letter		1	20
		1	20
Signature Susan Bryden			
Passed by V P Jones			

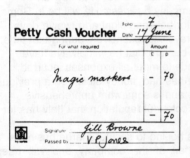

Petty Cash Voucher	Folio 7 Date 17 June		
For what required	Amount	£	p
Magic markers		–	70
		–	70
Signature Jill Browne			
Passed by V P Jones			

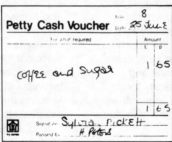

Petty Cash Voucher	Folio 8 Date 25 June		
For what required	Amount	£	p
Coffee and sugar		1	65
		1	65
Signature Sylvia Pickett			
Passed by H Peters			

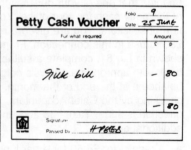

Petty Cash Voucher	Folio 9 Date 25 June		
For what required	Amount	£	p
Milk bill		–	80
		–	80
Signature			
Passed by H Peters			

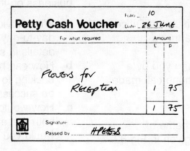

Petty Cash Voucher	Folio 10 Date 26 June		
For what required	Amount	£	p
Flowers for Reception		1	75
		1	75
Signature			
Passed by H Peters			

Fig 61

what he was talking about as she didn't understand a word of it.

Explain in simple terms, and also tell her about the bonus and incentive schemes operated by your organisation.

6 Assume that you work for a company which pays its salaried staff on a monthly basis directly into their bank accounts so that all that is received by staff on 'pay day' is a salary slip.

A new member of staff, Josie Walls, has just joined your section and is receiving a salary for the first time in her working career (she has previously worked only on a part-time basis and was always paid in cash). When she opens her

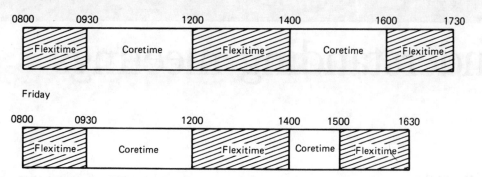

Monday-Thursday

| 0800 | 0930 | 1200 | 1400 | 1600 | 1730 |

Flexitime | Coretime | Flexitime | Coretime | Flexitime

Friday

| 0800 | 0930 | 1200 | 1400 | 1500 | 1630 |

Flexitime | Coretime | Flexitime | Coretime | Flexitime

Fig 62

first salary slip (*see* Fig 57) page 141 she asks you to go through it with her and explain what each item means.

7 You work in the Personnel Department of your company and have just been approached by a newly appointed junior member of staff with the following questions:

   a Why have I been asked to open a bank account?

   b What do I need to do, and where should I open it?

   c Which sort of account should I open?

   d Will I get one of these cards for getting money from the wall?

   e How does the system work from the point of view of the firm?

   f How will I know where I am with my money?

What will you tell her, and what extra advice might you offer?

8

Understanding meetings

Aim of the unit

The unit sets out the purposes of holding meetings, defines the different types, identifies the personnel involved, details their duties and responsibilities, outlines the arrangements required in organising meetings, and explains the possible systems, procedures, documentation and terminology involved.

Specific objectives

At the end of this unit you should be able to:

1   Provide reasons for holding meetings.
2   State the advantages and disadvantages of this means of communication.
3   Identify different types of meeting.
4   Distinguish between formal and informal meetings.
5   Explain the duties and responsibilities of the chairperson and secretary.
6   Compare and contrast the duties of a committee secretary with those of a minute secretary.
7   Recognise the essential ingredients of effective chairing of meetings.
8   Define meeting terminology.
9   Explain the essential preparations in arranging meetings.
10 Draw up agendas and notices.
11 Compile suitable minutes.
12 Explain the operation of electronic meetings.

Introduction

Meetings form a major part of communications within modern business, and all secretaries should be familiar with the procedures involved. The secretary's involvement will vary with the nature of the work and the type of organisation. Nevertheless it is essential to have a sound appreciation of what may be required and to be able to adapt the general knowledge acquired to fit differing circumstances.

Why have meetings at all?

Meetings provide an arena for oral communication on all manner of topics, and are used in business for a variety-of purposes:

- to provide information
- to 'float' ideas or proposals
- to generate interest and involvement
- to seek assistance
- to report back on some exercise or activity
- to coordinate activities
- to dispel rumour or anxiety.

The principal advantages of calling meetings are that they enable face-to-face contact by a number of individuals at one time, while providing the opportunity of gauging instantaneous reaction and feedback. There is opportunity for gaining a wide cross-section of opinion where two-way dialogue is encouraged via the asking and answering of questions. Communications can also be both vertical (between those calling the meeting and those in attendance) and horizontal (among those in attendance).

What is important for a successful and effective meeting is that the right people are invited and that they are sufficiently briefed in advance to be in a position to make a worthwhile contribution. This will rest on the adequacy of the period of notice and of the agenda and accompanying briefing documents (detailed later in this unit). In addition it will be dependent to a great extent upon the quality of the chairperson and on the environment in which the meeting takes place.

The disadvantage of meetings is that they can become too numerous, resulting in a great deal of frustration and boredom, owing to much lengthy and often irrelevant discussion, and achieving little or nothing. Also it can be difficult to arrange dates and times convenient for all those who ought to be represented, especially where executives have heavy commitments and tight schedules to keep.

Many of these drawbacks can, of course, be diminished by careful advance planning and preparation, and a secretary will have a significant part to play here. A good chairperson is also vital. Both will be discussed later in the unit.

What sort of meetings are there?

The range of meetings with which a secretary may have involvement is vast and will differ largely in terms of the degree of formality and the numbers in attendance. For example, procedure at statutory meetings is determined by law, whereas other formal meetings are governed by the rules and regulations or the constitution of the organisation. In such instances a secretary will need to have a sound knowledge of the principles of meeting procedure.

Many of the meetings attended may, on the other hand, be very informal. Examples are working party meetings, intradepartmental meetings, brainstorming sessions, encounter groups and even some managerial meetings. There will be no formal rules of procedure, and possibly simply a group leader initiating the action rather than a chairperson. Indeed some such meetings may take place over a lunchtime drink and a sandwich. Likewise such meetings will be informally documented and will rely on verbal post-meeting résumés rather than formal minutes.

Obviously, therefore, a secretary's duties will be much less complex for informal meetings, although even here it will be desirable to exercise organisational ability and to take a healthy interest in what goes on. It is also more likely that a secretary may be called upon to participate actively and express a personal opinion during an informal session than in a formal meeting. It is also possible that a secretary may be required to deputise for the boss at informal meetings if an executive has a busy schedule to fulfil

and finds personal attendance impossible. The lack of tight procedural rules and regulations will readily allow for such a substitution, and it will provide worthwhile experience for any career-minded secretary.

Types of meeting

Formal

Annual general meetings

Annual General Meetings are required by statute, and provide a means by which a company, organisation or society can reappraise its affairs for the past year in the form of an annual report, elect or reinstate office holders for the coming year, and generally declare its future intentions. For a company, the regulations for calling and holding such meetings are laid down in the Companies Acts and must be adhered to precisely. For example, such meetings are open to all shareholders and 14 days' *clear* notice must be given, ie excluding the day of posting the notice and the meeting day itself, otherwise the meeting would be improperly constituted and therefore invalid.

Extraordinary general meetings

Extraordinary general meetings are also open to all shareholders. They are called at the request of representatives of 10 per cent of the total voting shares when it is considered desirable to discuss any special business, possibly abnormal in nature, of concern to the shareholders.

Statutory meetings

Statutory meetings are required by law to ensure proper communication between the directors of a company and its shareholders. Such a meeting must be held not earlier than one month or later than three months after a company commences trading. It is the duty of such a meeting to consider a statutory report which has been circulated previously to all members.

Board meetings

Management meetings of the board of a company are attended by directors and chaired by the chairman of the board or the deputy chairman. In reality these meetings may be relatively informal in nature, depending on the size and composition of the board and the business to be discussed.

Committee meetings

See later in this unit.

Informal

Departmental meetings

Departmental meetings will usually be held either to pass information down the organisation (briefing sessions) or to receive progress reports (perhaps from section heads).

Managerial briefing/progress meetings

Briefing or progress meetings will occur frequently between a manager and subordinates and will form a vital part of the decision-making process. Sometimes the manager will need to brief staff; at other times to learn of their progress, their opinions and ideas. To be effective such meetings will depend on good interpersonal relationships.

Working parties

The setting up of a working party is a popular approach to solving problems by gathering together a group of individuals from different areas of work, with different levels of responsibility and with different degrees of expertise. Such a group can often bring to a problem a fresh approach, and the structure of such a meeting permits great flexibility and encourages individuality and ideas.

What about committees?

In Unit 1, reference was made to committee organisation. Obviously where this type of organisational structure prevails it will be essential that a secretary is well versed in committee procedure. The increasing complexity of modern industry, together with the emergence of greater worker participation in certain areas of management decisions (eg welfare, pay), has led to an increase in the use of committee organisation in both the public and private sectors.

A good example is local government, which has of course always operated on a committee structure, with standing committees for all areas for which it is responsible (eg housing, finance, social services, education).

Committee members will either be appointed or elected according to the circumstances. It is even possible to have a combination of both. For example, in a committee set up for some negotiating purpose, members of management may have been appointed because of their expertise and position in the organisation, whereas workers' representatives may have been elected by the workforce as a whole. Another facet of committees which will vary from one committee to another is the authority each has. Some may have executive power, particularly in local government, although it is more likely that their authority will be restricted to giving advice and making recommendations to management.

Types of committee

Executive committee

An executive committee carries on the actual management of an organisation and usually has definite powers delegated to it to make decisions and act on its own initiative on behalf of the organisation. The Board of Directors of a limited company is an executive committee.

Standing committee

A standing committee is concerned with detail rather than general policy, and would be permanently established to deal with recurrent matters which have been delegated to it, like finance. Within a local council, much of the day-to-day work is carried out by standing committees such as housing, health, finance and works. Such a committee will act on its own initiative only within the framework of the powers conferred upon it, and will ultimately report back to the executive committee.

Advisory committee

As the term suggests, an advisory committee is concerned with advising the executive committee. In its own right it may then form its own subcommittees which will report back directly to it, and it will in turn co-ordinate the findings and make recommendations which it will present to the executive committee.

Subcommittee

A parent committee may, if it has the necessary power, appoint a subcommittee from within its members to study and discuss certain matters. Such a subcommittee may either form a standing committee, eg where the intention is to relieve the parent committee of some of its routine work, or it may form an *ad hoc* committee to carry out a special investigation. Either way the subcommittee has no power to take action without reporting back regularly to the parent committee, whose approval it must win.

Ad hoc committee

An *ad hoc* committee is set up for one specific purpose only. *Ad hoc* literally means 'to this', 'for this' purpose. An example might be to plan a special event. Such a committee will be relatively short lived and will be disbanded when its business is completed.

Joint consultative committee

Consultative committees tend to be used for a wide variety of purposes, but are broadly aimed at improving communications and keeping the workforce informed on policy and management decisions. They can prove a useful tool for exchanging ideas, solving problems, airing differences, clearing up misunderstandings and future planning. At their best such meetings can be extremely constructive, but where the issue may be a delicate one, with the different factions of the meeting having established their viewpoints in advance, they can result in confrontation and possibly deadlock. This may only be resolved by postponing the meeting until some of the problems can be tackled on an informal basis.

What is the secretary's role in relation to meetings?

As indicated earlier your role as secretary will depend not only on the type of meeting but also on whether you are the secretary to the chairperson of a committee or perhaps even to the secretary of a committee. The roles will differ slightly but either way you are likely to be required to take minutes (*see* later in this unit).

Where a secretary acts as secretary to a chairperson much of the role will be centred around assisting that person in the conduct of the meeting, by having the correct documents to hand should they be required and by ensuring that any follow-up action required is carefully noted during the meeting and subsequently followed through afterwards.

Where a secretary acts as a secretary to a committee secretary the involvements will tend to be even greater, as there will be much more detail and documentation to attend to, and in addition a considerable amount of 'chasing up', contacting individuals and ensuring that the general meeting arrangements are well planned and organised.

It is worth noting that, when acting as official committee secretary, you should not do all the jobs yourself but should make sure that they are done by others and within the necessary time.

Some committees appoint a minute secretary whose sole responsibility is to take minutes. Where this is the case it should be noted, however, that the committee secretary will still be ultimately responsible for the final format of the minutes which are drafted for the chairperson's approval, and, of course, the chairperson will have the final say regarding what is officially minuted. However, the committee itself will still be required to approve the minutes and can ask for amendments to be made before they are signed as a true record. It is only once they have been signed that they become legally binding.

A secretary's duties and responsibilities

These will fall into different time categories, and are likely to include the following.

Prior to the meeting day

1 Book the venue for the meeting or check the booking if it is a fixed one.
2 Send out the notice convening the meeting together with the agenda, previous minutes (where these are duplicated and circulated) and any other supporting papers.
3 Organise refreshments, if required.

4   Book car parking spaces if representatives from other organisations or guests are expected.
5   Book and make arrangements for the setting up of any audiovisual aids which may be required.
6   Carefully note any apologies for absence as they are received.
7   Gather any necessary information and reports which may be required.
8   Start work on the chairperson's agenda in consultation with the chairperson.
9   Prepare name plates where it is a new committee or where a number of guests are expected and representatives may be unknown to one another.

On the day of the meeting

1   Check the meeting room for heating, ventilation, lighting and seating.
2   Confirm the refreshments and ensure that they will be served at a convenient time.
3   Confirm the parking arrangements.
4   Contact reception if guests are expected.
5   Liaise with the switchboard to reroute calls for the duration of the meeting, making arrangements for emergency calls to be routed to the meeting room should this be considered necessary.
6   Prepare the attendance register which all members will sign on arrival.
7   Either arrange the name plates around the table if this is requested by the chairperson, or have them ready for individual collection by members on arrival.
8   Have available spare copies of the agenda and other relevant papers.
9   Place paper, pens and pencils on the table.
10 Arrange ashtrays (if smoking is permitted).
11 Have drinking water and glasses available.
12 Finalise the chairperson's agenda.
13 Collect all necessary files and documents which may be called upon during the meeting.
14 Have the minute book ready for the chairperson's signature.
15 Place a 'meeting in progress' sign outside the room.

During the meeting

The secretary's primary role is to assist the chairperson, and you will normally sit on the chairperson's right. Very occasionally, where minutes have not been circulated prior to a meeting, the secretary will be called upon to read them and this must be done in a clear voice. You will be required to ensure that the chairperson signs the previous minutes and initials any alterations. Often you will be expected to take minutes, which can of course be a nerve-racking task at a complex meeting or where you may have little previous experience. Should the duties in relation to assisting the chairperson be such that you could not adequately take comprehensive notes as well, a minute secretary may also be appointed with the express purpose of recording the events of the meeting. However, as mentioned previously, the responsibility for accuracy will still rest with the committee secretary. Where minutes are being taken it will be necessary to listen very carefully and note selectively the business transacted, taking down all essential points of discussion. The type of minute ultimately prepared will depend on the circumstances (see Unit 4).

Some points of guidance on minute-taking

1   Familiarise yourself with the way in which the minutes have previously been recorded, by studying earlier minutes. This will also provide useful information in relation to the nature of the business discussed and will help clarify the identities and degree of participation usually associated with members attending the meetings.
2   Where the meeting is of a more informal nature, do not hesitate to seek guidance from members and the chairperson on the way the minutes should be taken. In terms of very formal meetings, guidance should be sought from appropriate reference books on the subject.
3   Try to avoid taking too many notes. Subsequent editing is a very time-consuming business. This is more difficult in the early stages of attending meetings for the purposes of taking minutes, as your inexperience and lack of familiarity will make it more difficult to select what is important. This is where doing your homework beforehand should help!
4   Try to cultivate the art of effective listening. It is all too easy to hear and even make notes while not really concentrating on the content of what is being said!
5   Be sure to record *all* essential items verbatim, eg resolutions and amendments.

6 Be sure to get the names of proposers and seconders correct.

7 Where votes are taken, be sure that you have the correct figures for and against together with any abstentions.

8 Where people have been given the responsibility of following something up before the next meeting, make sure that you have their names and details of the matter to be followed up. Not only will this be recorded in the actual minutes but will also be relevant if the chairperson asks you to check on the progress being made in between meetings.

Other duties and responsibilities during a meeting will be likely to include:

- ensuring that members have signed the attendance register
- noting any authorised changes in the order of agenda items
- dealing with any crisis or emergency that arises, eg leaving the room to seek information where requested to do so by the chairperson
- answering the telephone should it ring
- helping to serve refreshments where necessary
- helping the chairperson time discussions, particularly where there may be a lengthy agenda with a number of items to get through.

Immediately after the meeting

1 Remove the notice of meeting.
2 Notify the switchboard that the meeting has finished.
3 Notify catering staff that they may collect the refreshments trolley.
4 Clear away any surplus papers and destroy.
5 Escort guests off the premises, if required.
6 Return minute book, all files and documents to the office for safekeeping until the next meeting.

Other follow-up procedures

1 Draft the minutes as quickly as possible (*see* Unit 4).
2 Give to the chairperson to check.
3 Prepare final copy for duplication or photocopying and circulation.
4 File one copy of agenda, support papers and minutes for future reference should they be called upon.

5 Retain draft minutes until final copy has been adopted at the next meeting.
6 Index minutes where appropriate.
7 Reserve copy for minute book (see later in this unit).
8 Attend to any necessary correspondence and thank you letters.
9 Devise any necessary *aide–mémoires*.
10 Enter any relevant dates, including the next meeting, in your own diary and the chairperson's dairy.
11 Open a file for the next meeting.
12 Start the agenda for the next meeting.
13 Be prepared to remind any members who have agreed to take any action on behalf of the committee of their commitment.
14 Check periodically with the chairperson that they have undertaken any follow-up action promised.

The chairperson's role in relation to meetings

Unless acting in an *ex officio* capacity the chairperson is elected or nominated by the committee. The chairperson's role is to take charge of the meeting. To do this they must first of all be well versed on the function of the committee or organisation and be in no doubt as to its powers and authority and any reporting back procedures it needs to observe.

It will also be the chairperson's responsibility to ensure that a meeting has been properly convened. Additional duties and responsibilities will be as follows:

1 To ensure that the previous minutes are a correct record.
2 To sign them as a correct record.
3 To work consistently through an agenda.
4 To keep order as required.
5 To ensure that discussion is relevant, to the point and within the committee's powers.
6 To prevent over-talkative members holding the floor.
7 To encourage quieter members to have their say.
8 To formulate proposals and amendments as necessary.
9 To guide and limit discussion as appropriate.
10 To sum up conclusions reached in an unbiased manner.

11 To give decisions on points of order or other incidental matters.

12 To put matters to the vote.

13 To declare the results of voting and ensure that clear decisions can be recorded.

14 To close or adjourn a meeting or topic of discussion.

15 To make decisions, usually in consultation with the secretary, between meetings and generally act on behalf of the committee.

16 To agree the draft minutes.

17 To take any appropriate follow-up action required, as promised.

18 To liaise with the secretary in the preparation of the next agenda.

Substituting for the chairperson

In certain circumstances it may not be uncommon for a secretary to be required to chair a meeting on behalf of a boss. Usually such meetings would be relatively informal in nature, the regulations being such that this sort of substitution would be permitted. An example of such an instance might be a progress meeting of a working party which is reporting back regularly. Whatever the circumstance you would need to be suitably briefed in advance, have carefully studied the necessary papers and reports and be fully conversant with the role your boss wishes you to adopt.

Note: It should not be overlooked that it will be perfectly in order for you as a secretary to be appointed chairperson in your own right, and in such circumstances your role will be that of any chairperson.

Requisites of a valid meeting

In order that the business transacted at a meeting may be valid (legal), the following conditions must be met:

It must be properly convened – this means that notice, in a legally acceptable manner, must be given to every person entitled to attend.

It must be properly constituted – this means that the right person or that person's accepted substitute must be in the chair and a proper quorum must be present.

It must be held in accordance with the rules and regulations of the particular organisation – rules and regulations governing the conduct of meetings (among many other matters) are set out in a company's articles of association, a club's constitution or a local authority's standing orders.

The documentation

Notices

The notice of a meeting is any form of communication adopted by the convenor(s) to summon to the meeting all persons entitled to attend. It is, therefore, possible to use any method laid down by the rules and regulations governing the meeting; where it is an informal meeting with no such provision, any reasonable method would be acceptable. Possible methods include the following:

- written or typed advance notice of the appropriate duration
- verbal notice, eg word of mouth or telephone
- press notice
- bill posting
- door-to-door handbills
- a noticeboard
- broadcasting

All forms of notice must contain certain basic information, namely:

- the venue
- the day, date and time
- the details of any special business to be transacted
- the type of meeting, eg public, committee
- the date of the notice
- the convenor's name

Period of notice

In, for example, the case of an annual general meeting of a company the period is stipulated in the Companies Acts, namely 14 clear days. However, in other instances a 'reasonable' period will suffice. 'Reasonable' can be anything from a few hours for an informal meeting of a few individuals to between 7 and 14 days for normal business, with perhaps 21 days if special business has to be discussed.

Agendas

Literally the word 'agenda' means 'things to be done', but in practice it is more commonly applied to the actual paper which programmes the details of the business to be dealt with at a meeting and the order in which it has to be transacted. It is prepared by the secretary in consultation with the chairperson, and items of business dealt with at the previous meeting are taken into consideration.

An agenda is sent to all members of the committee or organisation entitled to attend the meeting in order to give them time to ponder over, research and perhaps come to decisions on items of business to be discussed. The period of notice, as specified above, is laid down and will normally be between 7 and 14 days. Agendas take different forms but usually include the notice convening the meeting. The following are three typical forms of agenda:

Skeleton – this is simply a brief outline or summary consisting of numbered headings. This form is usually used when included as part of the notice circulated to members. An example of a notice incorporating a skeleton agenda is given in Fig 63.

Detailed – here, following a complete heading indentifying the meeting, items will be listed and details, eg proposals to be discussed, will be submitted in draft form together with the proposer's name. This format will be more commonly found where constitutional changes are proposed and voting is to take place, say at an AGM.

Chairperson's agenda – this contains more information than the ordinary agenda, and space is provided on the right-hand side of the paper for the chairperson to make notes. The additional information helps provide the chairperson with all the

---

```
NOTICE OF MEETING


There will be a meeting of the Safety Committee of Oxford
Chemicals PLC in the Committee Room of the Administration Block
on Wednesday 15 June 19.. at 1400 hours. All Committee members
are requested to attend.


A T Phillips
Secretary


AGENDA


1    Apologies for absence

2    Minutes of the previous meeting

3    Matters arising from the minutes

4    Correspondence

5    Monthly safety report

6    First-aid courses

7    Visit of safety inspector

8    Retirement of Company Safety Officer

9    Any other business

10   Date of next meeting
```

Fig 63 Notice of meeting and agenda

```
CHAIRPERSON'S AGENDA

1    Apologies for absence        ) E Hendy
                                  ) K Dawson
2    Minutes of the previous      )
     meeting                      )
                                  )
3    Matters arising from         ) Fire doors
     the minutes                  )
                                  )
4    Correspondence               ) Letter from GLC
                                  )
5    Monthly safety report        ) The best on record - accident figures
                                  ) have dropped by 25%
                                  )
6    First-aid courses            ) 3 courses - 2 beginners
                                  )              1 refreshers programme
7    Visit of Safety Inspector    ) His first visit to B Block
                                  ) Important to endorse the
                                  ) impression gained during last
                                  ) visit
8    Retirement of Company        ) Celebration function - what sort ?
     Safety Officer               ) Collection for a gift
                                  )
9    Any other business           ) Date of function ?
                                  )
10   Date of next meeting         )
```

Fig 64 Chairperson's agenda

relevant details which will assist them in the conduct of an effective meeting. An example of a chairperson's agenda together with their notes is given in Fig 64.

Minutes

Minutes is the term given to the written record of business transacted at a meeting. The usual style and form was referred to in Unit 4. What should be aimed at is the provision of a precise, unambiguous account of what actually took place – no more and no less – and the account should be sufficiently complete to be understandable to someone not present. Obviously it is desirable to be concise, but completeness should not be sacrificed for this.

Minute books

Bound minute books where the minutes are handwritten are still favoured by some secretaries (particularly those who may not be typists) and they do have advantages over looseleaf ones in that the minutes are less liable to falsification and missing sheets are easily detected, so they will require less elaborate precautions in respect of safekeeping.

However, looseleaf books are more usual and in keeping with modern methods, namely the preparation on a typewriter or word processor for subsequent insertion in some form of ring binder which is used as a minute book. Such methods have the advantages of consistency of appearance and ease of preparation and reading. Also at suitable intervals earlier sheets may be extracted and stored for safekeeping until such times as they may be required.

Looseleaf books do, however, necessitate certain precautions to prevent possible falsification, namely:

- a suitable locking device – this may take the form of keys retained by the chairperson and secretary
- the book itself kept in a fireproof safe
- sheets numbered serially throughout
- blank sheets in the charge of a responsible person
- each sheet initialled by the chairperson at the time of signing the minutes.

Note: Many of these suggested precautions would also be taken in respect of bound books.

Recording meetings

Where a verbatim report of a meeting is required this can be taken by shorthand writers or by using recording machines, or sometimes with a combination of the two. Verbatim shorthand writers need very high speeds – certainly in excess of 140 wpm – although a secretary with a speed in excess of 100 wpm would normally be able to fulfil all that is required for minutes of most meetings. Recording machines are less useful than might at first be imagined as they cannot indicate the names of speakers, which can prove troublesome in attempting to transcribe a heated discussion among several parties and present an accurate minute. Also there is the tendency for the equipment to pick up all forms of extraneous noise, eg shuffling of feet and papers, coughing and the like.

Where a machine may prove useful is during the presentation of a lengthy report where a very fast and fluent speech is made. However, it will be customary to seek the speaker's permission first of all. In such an instance it may well be that the speaker is operating from prepared notes of which he or she may be willing to provide a copy after the meeting. Most speakers are more than happy to do this as it can prevent their being misquoted or misinterpreted in any way.

A brief outline of the possible proceedings of a meeting

Before any new business is discussed it will be usual for the chairperson to make a few preliminary remarks or perhaps present a formal welcome and opening address. The format then will be for the chairperson to guide the meeting through the items on the agenda.

The previous meeting's proceedings will always be considered but it is fairly standard practice, where minutes have been circulated in advance to the members, for the chairperson to ask the meeting's permission to **take the minutes as read**. If the members agree that the record is an accurate one **the minutes are adopted** and the chairperson signs and dates the copy in the minute book. If any changes are considered necessary the chairperson will write the alterations in their own hand and initial them.

Members will then be given the opportunity to raise and discuss any **matters arising from the minutes**. These are likely to occur where one item has been inconclusively dealt with at the previous meeting and where someone may perhaps have additional information to present. Some chairpersons tend to view '**matters arising**' with a certain amount of caution as it can provide another opening for a topic previously discussed. However, it will be a chairperson's duty to ensure that any discussion is relevant to the meeting.

Where the next item on the agenda refers to a topic for discussion and ultimate decision, certain stages will have to be gone through before any decision can be reached:

1   The proposal is stated as **a motion** (usually submitted in writing prior to the meeting so that it may be included in the agenda) together with the name of the person suggesting it (**the proposer**) and where required, the person seconding it (**the seconder**).

2   The chairperson will read out the motion and call upon the proposer to **speak to it**. Where a seconder is required he too will speak. Discussion will then follow and usually each member will be allowed to speak once only, should he wish to do so, although the proposer may speak twice as he is allowed **the right of reply** to points raised during discussion. The proposer will in effect have the last word.

3   Should any **amendments** to the motion be proposed the chairperson will deal with them and take a vote on them according to the rules and regulations (where words are simply added to the original motion, perhaps for clarification, this is referred to as an **addendum**).

4   The revised motion then becomes a **substantive motion** and following a **summing up** the chairperson puts the question, ie presents the proposal in its finalised form to the meeting for their vote.

5   Should a member other than the chairperson wish to bring discussion to a close he may move that the **question be now put** (this is known as a **procedural motion**). Where the meeting agrees a vote would be taken at this stage. If there is no agreement the discussion will continue.

6   When the meeting votes, the chairperson is responsible (with the help of the secretary) for taking the vote. Votes may be taken in several different ways, eg

- **show of hands** – one for each member – the most usual at ordinary meetings
- **a poll** where every member would have to sign a paper for or against
- **a division** as in Parliament, where members file into separate lobbies representing for and against
- **secret ballot** as with elections, both local and national, where a cross is marked opposite a name or an alternative and the slip placed folded in a box.

7   In declaring the result there can be two basic results. The motion may be **carried** or **defeated**. However, the nature of the result is relevant and will need to be recorded in the minutes. Once passed a motion becomes a **resolution**, ie, a decision, and its wording is recorded precisely in the minutes. A motion is passed or carried if the greater number of those entitled to vote agrees to it. How big that **majority** must be depends on the organisation's rules. Where everyone agrees the motion will be said to have been carried **unanimously**, ie all members were in favour. Where a motion is passed **nem con** (*nemine contradicente*) or **nem dis** (*nemine dissentiente*) this means that nobody actually opposed it although some members may have **abstained**, ie refrained from voting.

8   Once a motion has become a resolution it is still possible to make an adjustment. This would be in the form of a **rider** which is in addition to a resolution which has already been passed. Such an addition must be proposed, seconded and voted upon in the usual way. A rider cannot negate what has already been decided by the meeting; it may only add or clarify a point.

When all the items on the agenda have been discussed the meeting will be brought to a close by the chairperson. Where for some reason a meeting may be unable to conclude all the business on the agenda, the chairperson may **adjourn** the meeting until a later date. However, in normal circumstances well-conducted meetings should not over-run and it is one of the chairperson's duties to ensure that they do not.

Any other business

One item which appears on most agendas is 'any other business' or sometimes 'any other urgent business'. It is important that this item should not be abused by members or used to air their 'pet subject' or 'hobby horses' or raise contentious points which may not come within the scope of the meeting. The chairperson must be very strict here and ensure that any topic raised is relevant and could not have been put forward in advance as a proper agenda item. Where a chairperson considers that the point raised merits full discussion he or she will normally suggest that it be advanced as an agenda item for the next meeting. The thing that a chairperson must avoid is permitting as much meeting time to be spent on this item as on the rest of the meeting – something not unheard of, but indicative of very poor meeting conduct.

Date of next meeting

Many meetings, particularly of committees, include this item on their agendas so that a suitable date for most members may be determined well in advance.

Teleconferencing

Organisations are under increased pressure to be more productive and managers are anxious to explore ways in which they can improve efficiency and effectiveness and maximise their time management. One of the ways in which much executive time is taken up is in attending meetings. Some studies into the use of executive time go as far as to suggest that managers can spend on average almost 50 per cent of their time either in meetings or in the travel associated with attending meetings.

Developments in electronic communication media have enabled alternatives to actual physical attendance at meetings to be considered seriously. Like traditional methods of communication there are three options – written, audio or visual (or combinations of the three) – and selection is made dependent on the type of meeting, its duration and purpose.

In terms of written teleconferencing we have already considered communication via computers or facsimile. We have also referred to the possibilities of arranging conference calls via the telephone (audioconferencing). Also, audio conferences often include the addition of some medium for transmitting graphics. This might be facsimile equipment or what is known as an 'electronic blackboard'. The latter would be linked to a monitor and to other monitors set up in each distant location. Written material is transmitted over ordinary telephone lines for instant display on the monitors at the distant locations. This is an extremely useful facility where complex ideas or formulae are being discussed. It is perhaps interesting to consider the application of this kind of technique in colleges for lecture purposes, where students may be located in different buildings or where they cannot all be accommodated together in a room.

Videoconferencing involves the transmission of either pre-recorded or 'live' filmed action, to distant locations for viewing on television screens and represents the third form of electronic meeting. In itself it is not a new idea as BT's Confravision service has existed for many years and the technique is, of course, used regularly on television for news and current affairs programmes. However what it does provide is the added dimension of being able to see other representatives or delegates as well as hear them and receive written communication.

BT's service provides a public videoconferencing facility where groups of people can attend one of the regional studios specially set up for the purpose of conducting electronic meetings between other confravision centres, either in this country or abroad (links exist in the USA, Canada, France, Belgium, West Germany and the Netherlands). Charges are based on hourly rates and are in the region of £200 to £300 within the UK, depending on the distance, while an hour's link to the USA would cost about £1500.

Videoconferencing–private links

With developments in BT's private digital networks (Kilostream and Megastream) private teleconferencing facilities can be set up, between private organisations using their own offices, via what is known as the Videostream service. No special studio accommodation is needed, although companies do require to buy or rent the necessary camera and monitoring equipment. An example of videoconferencing in operation is given in Fig 65.

Advantages of videoconferencing
- saving of travel time
- quickly arranged 'live' meetings are possible
- participants can see and hear one another as well as enjoy the benefits of graphics support
- meetings tend to be briefer and more concisely conducted as the cost factor is more evident
- a permanent recording can be made
- there is easier access to essential files or additional staff expertise should it be required
- participants are less tired due to the elimination of travel and so should work more effectively
- easier to retain confidentiality within an organisation as opposed to meeting at an outside venue such as hotel.

Disadvantages
- such meetings can be more difficult to chair
- participants may play up to or be shy of the camera
- face-to-face pre-meeting contact is lost
- technical problems or breakdowns can occur
- inconvenience of going to a confravision centre to utilise the public service
- equipment costs involved in setting up a private service.

A glossary of meeting terminology

ab initio   From the beginning.

abstention   Where a member refrains from casting a vote either in favour of or against a motion.

addendum   An amendment which *adds* words to a motion.

address the chair   Where a member wishes to speak they must first address the chairperson, eg 'Madam Chairperson', 'Mr Chairman', 'Madam Chair'.

ad hoc   From the Latin meaning 'for the purpose of'. For example, an *ad hoc* committee, sometimes referred to as a 'special' committee, is one set up for a special purpose, and when that purpose is fulfilled the committee is disbanded.

adjournment   The chairperson, with the consent of those present, may adjourn a meeting and reconvene it at a later date to complete unfinished items on the agenda. This may be in order to postpone further discussion owing to lack of information or shortage of time. Adequate notice of the new time for an adjourned meeting must be given.

advisory   Offering advice or suggestion and making recommendations, but taking no direct action.

Fig 65 Videoconferencing; *Reproduced by kind permission of British Telecom*

agenda Schedule of items drawn up for discussion at a meeting.

amendment An alteration to a motion by the addition, deletion or modification of words. Any amendment must be proposed, seconded and put to the vote in the usual way.

annual general meeting (AGM) A statutory meeting held once a year which the organisation's entire membership is eligible to attend.

apologies for absence Excuses given in advance for inability to attend a meeting.

articles of association The rules required by law which govern a company's internal organisation and activities.

ballot A written secret vote conducted in accordance with the organisation's constitution.

by-laws Rules governing an organisation's activities.

casting vote In accordance with the rules and regulations of an organisation, a chairperson may be granted a second vote when there is an equal number of votes for and against a motion. This rule would be incorporated simply for business expediency.

chairperson The person given authority to conduct a meeting.

chairperson's agenda An elaborated form of the basic agenda with space left on the right for the chairperson to make notes.

collective responsibility A convention whereby all members agree to abide by a majority decision.

consensus Agreement by general consent without a formal vote being taken.

constitution Document describing the objects of an association or voluntary body and setting out the rules which govern its activities and limit its powers.

convene To call a meeting.

co-opt To invite an individual to serve on a committee as a result of a majority vote. A person is usually co-opted because of some specialist knowledge or expertise they can provide.

ex officio One invited to attend 'by virtue of office'

but without voting rights, eg the official secretary for a committee or the vice president of an organisation.

honorary   Performed without payment, eg honorary secretary.

in attendance   Present on invitation to give expert help, advice or information but with no voting rights.

in camera   In private.

in extenso   In full – without abridgement.

intra vires   Within the legal power or authority of the organisation.

lie on the table   Something – a motion, letter, report – is said to 'lie on the table' when the meeting decides that no action should be taken on it at present.

lobbying   The term given to the practice of seeking members' support before a meeting.

majority vote   One where the greater number of members voting were either for or against a motion. Articles or rules will set out whether a majority is necessary for a motion to be carried or defeated.

memorandum of association   The statutory requirements which govern a company's objects and general relationship with the outside world.

motion   A formal proposal moved by a member that a certain topic be discussed at a meeting and certain action be taken upon it.

nem con   No one contradicting, ie no votes against the motion, but some members may have abstained.

no confidence   A vote of 'no confidence' may be passed by members of a meeting if they are at variance with the chairperson. If a substantial majority of members are in favour of the decision then the chairperson must vacate the chair in favour of the deputy or some other person nominated by the meeting.

opposer   One who speaks against a motion.

out of order   The chairperson can rule a member 'out of order' where the member is not keeping to the point under discussion or is speaking improperly.

point of order   This is a query raised by a member in respect of procedure or a possible infringement of the standing orders or constitution.

postponement   The action taken to transfer the holding of a meeting to a later date.

proposer   The member putting forward a motion for discussion at a meeting.

proxy   A person appointed in the place of another to represent them at a meeting. Provision must be contained in the regulations.

proxy vote   A member may be appointed to vote by proxy, ie on behalf of another member who is unable to attend the meeting.

quorum   The minimum number of persons, as specified by the regulations, that must be present at a meeting to make it valid.

resolution   Once passed, a motion becomes a resolution.

rider   This is an addition to a resolution after it has been passed. It adds to a resolution rather than altering it. It must be proposed, seconded and put to the meeting in the usual way.

right of reply   The proposer of a motion has the right of reply once the motion has been fully discussed but before it is put to the vote.

seconder   One who supports the proposer of a motion.

sine die   For an indefinite period.

standing orders   The rules compiled by an organisation in respect of the way in which business must be transacted.

status quo   As things stand at present.

statutory meeting   A meeting (usually of the shareholders of a public company) which *must* be held in order to comply with the law.

subcommittee   A group of members from the main or parent committee appointed to deal with a specific aspect of the main committee's work. The functions will be delegated by the main committee, to whom reports and recommendations will be submitted.

tabled   The description applied to a document to be presented to a committee 'on the table' – not one which has been included with the agenda and supporting papers.

teller   A person appointed to count votes by a show of hands.

terms of reference   A statement of the work to be carried out by a group or committee, providing guidelines as to how it should be done and expressing any limitations in respect of methods.

ultra vires   Outside the legal power or authority of the organisation.

unanimous   All being in favour.

verbatim   Word for word.

Self-test

1   State *four* differences between formal and informal meetings.
2   Name *three* types of committee.

3 Provide *four* possible reasons for calling a meeting.
4 What is meant by a 'quorum'?
5 Identify and explain *three* types of agenda.
6 Provide *four* acceptable means of giving notice of a meeting.
7 What constitutes a valid meeting?
8 Give *six* duties of a secretary before a meeting.
9 Give *three* duties of a secretary during a meeting.
10 Give *three* duties of a secretary after a meeting.
11 List *four* qualities which would be sought in a chairperson.
12 When might a chairperson exercise a casting vote?
13 What is meant by the term 'rider'?
14 In a limited company, which document stipulates the rules governing the conduct of meetings?
15 What is a proxy?
16 What is meant by '*ex officio*'?
17 Identify *two* types of minutes which might be taken.
18 How should minutes be recorded?
19 As a secretary to a committee, what sort of follow-up action might you be required to take?
20 What are the main advantages of electronic meetings?

Personal activities

1 Collect specimen notices of any public meetings from your local press and try to match these with any reports which follow.

2 Try to obtain copies of company reports from anyone who may have a shareholding in a public company. The formal notice of the AGM, together with the agenda, is usually contained within the document. Proxy cards are also normally included.

3 If you are a member of an organisation or society, attend any meetings to which you are entitled, and gather any documentation which is circulated.

4 Pay particular attention to any meetings – formal or informal – which may form part of a valuable insight into something of which you may currently have little or no personal experience.

5 Consider attending one of the open meetings of your local authority (council meetings).

Group activities

Meetings form the perfect vehicle for putting theory into practice and exercising your role play skills.
Depending upon the size of your class, form suitable groups and enact all the stages of meeting preparation, conduct and follow-up. Obvious principal roles will be taken by a chairman and secretary, but it is simple to add predetermined committee figures with particular roles to play.

You can hold mock meetings where you can decide on any topic you like. You can also prepare a suitable notice and agenda together with any other supporting literature to brief the members scheduled to attend the meeting, and one or more of the group can practise taking minutes.

Some practical suggestions

1 It will be interesting if several of you take minutes; write them *all* up and circulate them *all* afterwards. Will you be able to believe that you have all reported the same event?

2 Why not arrange this activity around a special topic of interest, eg the introduction of office technology, and invite a guest to give a 'presentation' as part of the meeting? This way you will need to organise the following:

a a subject of interest
b a suitable date, time and place
c a possible guest speaker. This will involve an invitation, possibly a briefing discussion in advance, arrangements for the person's arrival (directions, parking, someone to meet him), someone to make a formal introduction and someone to propose a vote of thanks
d any necessary visual aids, eg an overhead projector
e refreshments
f follow-up procedures – minutes, report of the presentation, formal letter of thanks to the speaker

Obviously this can be a demanding exercise but it will prove worthwhile and enjoyable provided you have the time available and the necessary facilities at your disposal.

3 As an alternative to a formal business meeting, why not adopt more of a debating format? Choose, for example, three topics; the following are some possible suggestions:

Women in management
Qualifications versus experience
Does technology dehumanise the workplace?
It is better to support your own country's economy than to holiday abroad
The case for and against zoos
Would a Freedom of Information Act be a curse or a blessing?

(Always select topics which have an argument for and against.)

Then appoint three chairpersons three sets of speakers (two for and two against each motion) and a teller to record votes.

Follow the conventional rules of debate (akin to those adopted in any formal meeting) and apply a strict time allowance. On each occasion the chairperson is required to accept three questions from members of the audience (who should also be making notes of the proceedings), and in conclusion should sum up the case for and against the issue under debate and put the motion to the vote. At this time the teller should count the votes and then pass a paper to the chairperson, who will announce the result.

Situation-based activities

1   Assume that you are Secretary to Sarah Williams, who chairs the monthly meeting of the Finance Committee within your organisation. This is a standing committee of eleven representatives plus Mrs Williams, and you have a regular booking of the board room for the first Tuesday of every month at 1400 hours.

In connection with these meetings, you are required to undertake the following tasks:

a   Prepare a checklist of all the necessary duties and arrangements you will have to undertake between now (the day after this month's meeting) and the actual day of the meeting next month.

b   Prepare a suitable notice and agenda for next month's meeting to be circulated to all committee members. Type this, or use a word processor if possible.

Agendas for these meetings take on a very consistent format, commencing with the three items usual for most agendas and concluding with the usual two items. Next month's meeting has also to discuss a proposed reduction of 3 per cent in revenue allocation to individual departments, the financing of research studies on the part of staff, and the attempt to secure EEC funding in respect of a proposed extension to plant.

c   In two months' time you will be on holiday, and Janette, a junior secretary in your department, is going to stand in for you at the Finance Committee meeting. This will be the first time she has acted as a secretary in this capacity, and she has never taken minutes before.

Provide her with some useful advice on both aspects in the form of notes of guidance to which she can easily refer.

2   Imagine that you are involved in a local action group which is concerned about the possibility of a Motorway development near your village.

You wish to call a public protest meeting to which the press will be invited and you hope to attract substantial interest. How would you publicise this event, and how would the arrangements for this type of meeting differ from those which a secretary would make within a business organisation? Identify specific individuals who, as members of the community affected, might wish to cooperate or take a leading role, and indicate the sort of results you would anticipate from such a meeting, together with the sort of follow-up you would envisage.

3   Your boss is chairperson of the Staff Association within your company. The meeting of the Association, the main point of which is to finalise details for the annual staff dinner and dance, is scheduled for tomorrow. However, your boss has received unexpected instructions to visit head office tomorrow, and it is too late to reschedule the meeting. Unfortunately the vice-chair is on holiday, so you have been asked to stand in for your boss (the constitution permits such a substitution!)

What steps would you take to prepare yourself for this meeting, and what points would you try to remember in terms of chairing effectively, bearing in mind that these meetings are relatively informal and that time is always in short supply?

4   Imagine that a representative from a European subsidiary of your company is spending two weeks in your department as part of an exchange programme. His English is pretty good, but he has just sat in on a very lengthy formal meeting as an observer and is perplexed by some of the terminology he has heard and some of the practices he has observed. He asks you to explain.

a   From the following list, provide written examples (rather than pure definitions) of the usage of the terms, so that he will have something to refer to later in support of the verbal explanations you will offer:

quorum	nem con
motion	rider
point of order	articles of association
status quo	ad hoc
through the chair	on the table

b He also asks you to explain why the chairperson had to sign the minute book *twice* and why it appeared to be typewritten as to his knowledge minutes were always handwritten.

5 The following is the notice of meeting and agenda for the AGM of your local drama society.

Oakland Drama Society

Notice is hereby given that the Annual Meeting of the Oakland Drama Society will be held in the Rehearsal Room of the Little Theatre on Tuesday 8 May 19 – at 1930 hours.

Nominations for office bearers (duly seconded) should be made in writing on the enclosed form and forwarded to the Secretary no later than three days before the meeting. Members are also asked to study the attached list of possible productions for next season as put forward by the present committee. Voting will take place at the AGM for the four productions favoured by the membership

Honorary Secretary

Agenda
1 Chairperson's welcome
2 Apologies for absence
3 Minutes of the previous AGM
4 Matters arising from the minutes
5 Secretary's report
6 Treasurer's report
7 Election of office bearers:
   Vice-chairperson
   Secretary
   Treasurer
8 Appointment of two new committee members to replace those retiring on rotation
9 Reappointment of the Auditors
10 Theatre renovation fund
11 Next season's productions
12 Any other business
13 Date of next meeting

Use your imagination and your knowledge of meeting procedure to prepare a suitably annotated chairperson's agenda and a set of minutes. The nomination form and the list of productions are given as Figs 66 and 67.

```
Oakland Drama Society

Nomination slip

Position.................................................

Name of person proposed.................................

Signature of proposer...................................

Signature of seconder...................................

Date of nomination......................................
```

Fig 66

```
Suggested productions for next season

1   Ring Round the Moon                        Jean Anouilh

2   Shadow of a Gunman                         Sean O'Casey

3   Cat on a Hot Tin Roof                      Tennessee Williams

4   Roots                                      Arnold Wesker

5   Who's Afraid of Virginia Woolf?            Edward Albee

6   The Importance of Being Earnest            Oscar Wilde

7   In Camera                                  Jean-Paul Sartre

8   The Ghost Train                            Arnold Ridley
```

Fig 67

9

Researching and presenting information

Aim of the unit

The unit provides insight into the wide range of sources available to secretaries for securing and applying essential information. It also examines alternative ways of presenting information.

Specific objective

At the end of this unit you should be able to:

1   Indicate sources of information which practising secretaries may call upon in the course of their work.
2   Identify appropriate information resources for given circumstances.
3   Suggest suitable reference books to which a secretary might refer.
4   Recognise the value of good library usage.
5   Consult a library index.
6   Indicate the criteria to be used in selecting any information resource.
7   Construct your own card index information retrieval system.
8   Identify specialist agencies available for securing information.
9   Recognise the need to consult specialists and experts.
10   Compare and contrast information recorded in different newspapers.
11   Use a dictionary more efficiently.
12   Extract information from a telephone directory at greater speed.
13   Provide advice to junior office personnel on the effective use of newspapers and magazines.
14   Explain the operation of a computerised database.
15   Suggest instances when a secretary might set up and/or consult a database.
16   Explain what is meant by a viewdata system.
17   Distinguish between open and closed user groups.
18   Identify different ways of presenting information.
19   Prepare different forms of charts and graphs.
20   Suggest possible uses for visual planning/control boards.

Introduction

Information has never before been available in such quantity and from so many different sources. However, its existence is only worthwhile when it is exploited to the full. Secretaries must be aware of the sort of information which is used and usable within the organisations they work for, and then learn how to find, process, apply and protect it.

Obviously the information used will reflect both the size and the functions of the organisation as considered in Unit 1, and many large organisations will make use of much more sophisticated technology than smaller firms can or need use. However, whatever the scale of enterprise, dependence on information is growing; profitability will often be positively affected by the timely acquisition of certain information, and adversely affected by the lack of it, while its impact will be largely dependent upon its presentation.

What sort of resources are available?

One important point to clarify from the very beginning is that resources certainly encompass much more than reference books! They are best considered in three categories – those available within an organisation, those of a general nature available from outside and those from specialist agencies.

Internal resources

- personal systems
- office files
- reports
- minutes
- central records
- other specialist departments, eg data processing
- staff – the human resource!
- reference books
- office databases

General resources

- newspapers, journals and periodicals
- radio and television
- public libraries
- travel agents
- citizens' advice bureaux
- tax offices
- local council offices
- Post Office
- chambers of commerce
- videotex, eg Prestel

Specialist resources

- specialist libraries
- embassies and trade delegations
- government departments
- the EEC
- Registrar of Companies
- professional and trade associations
- training boards
- specialist agencies, eg accommodation, advertising, conference organisers, debt collecting,
- security systems
- employment bureaux
- British Institute of Management Foundation
- British Standards Institution
- *Daily Telegraph* Information Bureau
- Industrial Society
- stock exchange
- data banks
- private viewdata

Internal resources

Many very useful resources are often neglected. With the exception of reference books, which will be dealt with particularly in this unit, the other suggestions are mentioned elsewhere in this book. For example, conscientious secretaries will all have frequently consulted names, addresses and telephone numbers to hand, and knowledge of the other departments within the company in which they work will make it easier for them to ask for assistance when necessary. Likewise it is important to keep up to date by reading all relevant reports, minutes and in-house circulars and to cultivate a good working rapport with colleagues, who may often turn out to be the richest and most frequently used resource of all! A quick word with a colleague can often save hours of searching.

Reference books

The range of reference books available is vast, and those of use to business people will vary according to the nature of a company's operations and the duties and responsibilities of its staff. The following is a typical selection of reference works likely to be found in the average business office. This list is subdivided into major topic areas and begins with those considered essential to *any* secretary, even one working in a very small office.

A secretary's selection of reference books

A Good English Dictionary There are many excellent dictionaries available, eg the *Oxford English Dictionary* or *Chambers' Twentieth Century Dictionary*.

Note: Where a secretary uses Pitman's shorthand she might do well to select *Pitman English and Shorthand Dictionary*, which provides both the meanings and the shorthand outlines.

Dictionary of typewriting Pitman's Typewriting Dictionary provides the full range of terms and procedures.

Telephone directories All frequently consulted telephone directories should be available, together with the corresponding *Yellow Pages* and the appropriate dialling codes book.

UK Telex Directory This provides names, addresses and telex numbers of all subscribers together with answer-back codes, charges and services. Information about telex subscribers in other countries is available from their own official directory which may be purchased from the local telephone area office.

Whitaker's Almanac or *Pears Cyclopaedia* Both these books are published annually. The former provides worldwide information about public affairs, government, industry, finance, commerce and the arts, and produces a useful variety of facts and figures as well as a valuable selection of useful names and addresses of societies, government offices and other institutions. The latter provides useful background information and reference material for general everyday use and is divided into three sections – the wider world, general and home and social.

AA or *RAC handbooks* These are both published annually and provide useful details of all major towns and cities in Britain, together with road maps and town plans, information on hotel accommodation and garage facilities and other details of use to any motor traveller.

A – Z guides These fully comprehensive street guides to all the major cities will be useful where an executive travels a lot. They will, for example, be indispensable to a representative.

Good Food Guide This is published annually by the Consumers' Association and features eating establishments throughout the United Kingdom and Ireland. It has a large section for London.

In addition it will be useful for the average secretary to have up-to-date details, possibly in leaflet form, of any Post Office services she may regularly use (complete details are, of course, obtainable from the *Royal Mail Guide*, described later), together with train, air and bus timetables as necessary. It is unlikely that occasional rail users would find it worth while subscribing monthly to the *ABC Rail Guide*, and it will be customary in any event to check all train times with British Rail. Free leaflets of regularly used routes will, therefore, normally prove adequate.

Also to keep up to date secretaries may well find it beneficial to subscribe to a monthly periodical such as *Professional Secretary*. Many organisations will automatically appear on the mailing lists of such periodicals as *Business Equipment Digest* or *Office Equipment News* and they too are useful sources of update.

Books on English usage

Many books are available in this area of reference, and the following is a typical selection.

Fowler's Modern English Usage is a guide to the correct form of English usage, concentrating on points of grammar, punctuation and style.

Roget's Thesaurus of English Words and Phrases is a useful book, available in many different editions, including paperback. Words are arranged, not in alphabetical order, but according to similarity of meaning, and the idea is that writers may select the most appropriate word in any given situation to convey the desired shade of meaning.

Webster's New Dictionary of Synonyms is a dictionary of synonyms and antonyms (similar and contrasted words).

Black's Titles and Forms of Address sets out the correct way of addressing people of rank, or holding official positions, both when writing and in formal speech. It also provides a guide to the pronunciation of unusual surnames.

The Complete Plain Words, a publication reprinted by HMSO, was originally designed by Sir Ernest Gower, a distinguished civil servant, to improve official English. However, this is much more than a book on 'official' English, and is a useful addition to any reference section where someone wishes to use language correctly and in a way in which ideas may be adequately conveyed to others.

The Spoken Word – A BBC Guide was published in 1981 following a monitoring exercise of BBC radio. It deals with pronunciation, vocabulary and grammar and is a useful publication to have on any reference shelf.

Current affairs

Annual Abstract of Statistics, published by HMSO, contains statistical surveys of the social and economic life of Britain. It is supplemented on a monthly basis by the publications *Economic Trends, Monthly Digest of Statistics* and *Financial Statistics*.

Hansard, also published by HMSO, provides daily and weekly verbatim reports of the proceedings of both Houses of Parliament.

Britain: An Official Handbook, again published annually by HMSO, gives an up-to-date description of Britain in terms of its government, its legal institutions, and its financial structure against its physical and social background.

Keesing's Contemporary Archives are weekly newssheets which can be bound together to form an international reference source of world news as taken from the world's press and news information services.

Whitaker's Almanac: *see* Reference books.
Pears Cyclopaedia: *see* Reference books.

Books about people

These fall into four broad categories – those dealing with people in general, those detailing the nobility, those outlining people in government and those dealing with people belonging to particular professions or occupational groups.

General

Who's Who is probably the best-known general reference work, containing information in the form of short biographies of prominent people in this country. It deals with people from all walks of life, although it should be noted that specialised editions are also available, eg

Who's Who in the World
Who's Who in the Theatre
Who's Who in the Motor Industry

There is also a *Who Was Who*, which gives information about people who have died.

The *Dictionary of National Biography* outlines details of inhabitants of the British Isles and the colonies who were considered worthy of note. This publication dates back to early times and excludes persons currently living.

The nobility

Burke's Peerage provides a comprehensive guide to peers and their families. There is also a volume entitled *Burke's Genealogical Heraldic History of the Landed Gentry* which records details of those who over the years have amassed considerable inherited territory but are not in fact peers of the realm.
Debrett's Peerage and Baronetage also details peers of the realm, including life peers, and provides a guide to the wearing of orders and correct forms of address.

People in government

The Times Guide to the House of Commons contains biographical details and photographs of present Members of Parliament, as well as listing unsuccessful candidates, texts of party manifestos and statistical analyses of the corresponding general election.
The Diplomatic Service List is published in four parts and contains full details of all high-ranking personnel in the Home, Commonwealth and Foreign Services.
Vacher's Parliamentary Companion is a quarterly publication which provides information about members of both Houses of Parliament, Cabinet and other ministers, government and public officers, national organisations and industries, the judiciary, ambassadors and high commissioners and the Privy Council. There is also a European version.

Professions and occupational groups

Air Force List bi-annual
Army List annual
Navy List annual
These three publications from HMSO contain lists of senior officers in the armed services, together with other relevant services data.

The Bar List provides a complete reference source for all barristers and advocates in the UK and the Isle of Man, as well as having an international section.
The Solicitors Diary provides a complete list of all solicitors in the UK.
Crockford's Clerical Directory is a complete guide to the Anglican Church.
The Medical Register is published by the General Medical Council and is a complete alphabetical register of all medical practitioners in the UK. There is also an overseas list.
The Dentists' Register is published under the direction of the General Dental Council and lists all dentists registered with the Council. It is subdivided into UK, Commonwealth and Foreign.

Trade and industry

Once again a wide selection exists, made up largely of directories and yearbooks, the following of which provides a cross-section:

Kelly's Manufacturers and Merchants Directory comes in three sections and forms a very useful guide. The first section – the *blue* pages – provides an alphabetical list of all manufacturers, merchants, wholesalers and firms offering an industrial service in London and the rest of the UK. The second section – the *white* pages – is a classified trades section in which all companies listed in the alphabetical section appear under appropriate classified headings. The third section – the *yellow* pages – is the international exporters and services section providing classified information relating to products, subdivided by countries within continents.

UK Kompass is produced in association with the CBI (Confederation of British Industry) and is a comprehensive register of British industry and commerce. Volume I lists products and services, whereas volume II provides company information both alphabetically and geographically. European volumes of this reference source are also available.

British Exports is another similarly useful book, again produced in volumes. Volume I lists products, volume II provides technical data and volume III lists British exporters.

The Civil Service Yearbook provides a summary of the functions of government departments and lists ministers and civil servants down to Assistant Secretary level. Information is updated five times a year.

The Stock Exchange Official Year Book includes details of all officially listed securities, a classified list of companies and their registrars, and a section containing general information on various aspects of the stock market.

The Statistical Year Book is an HMSO publication from international statistical data collected by the United Nations Departments of Economic and Social Affairs Statistical Office.

The British Standards Year Book gives detail of the British Standards Institution (*see* later in this unit) and the services it offers.

The Stateman's Year Book comprises two sections. One gives current information on each country of the world, and the other international organisations like FAO (Food and Agricultural Organisation), NATO (North Atlantic Treaty Organisation), UNESCO (United Nations Educational, Scientific and Cultural Organisation) and WHO (World Health Organisation).

The Bankers' Almanac and Year Book is the standard international reference on banking. *The Hospital and Health Services Year Book and Directory of Equipment and Supplies*, published by the Institute of Health Service Administrators, gives a yearly account of the hospitals and health services in Great Britain and Northern Ireland. *The Education Authorities Directory*, published annually, gives details of all educational establishments in the UK and is subdivided into sections for different sectors of education. It also provides details of courses, principal officers and size of institutions.

The Personnel and Training Management Year Book and Directory gives a comprehensive review of developments in these areas as well as providing useful details on courses, conference centres and all services relating to successful conference operation.

Travel books

Books on travel range from general travel material, including those outlining reputable eating establishments, to specific texts on air, rail and road travel and all the accompanying timetables. The following is a list of the more common ones:

General

The Travel Trade Directory is published annually and contains a valuable selection of useful and up-to-date information on all forms of travel, as well as providing details of all travel operators, addresses of passport and visa offices and all other specialist travel services. The publishers of this book (Morgan-Grampian) also produce the *Travel Trade Gazette*, which is a weekly newspaper of travel information.

The World Calendar of Holidays is another useful annual publication which details public holidays both chronologically and in alphabetical order of country. This is very useful as a reference source as it may mean preventing a wasted journey; for example, an executive could arrive at a foreign destination only to discover that he is in the midst of some holiday or religious festival.

Hints to businessmen is a free series of booklets convering many countries of the world and providing useful advice on travel, entry regulations, customs control, consular facilities, hotels etc. It is produced by the Department of Trade and Industry and is obtainable from the Publicity Department of the British and Overseas Trade Board.

Hotels and Restaurants in Great Britain is published annually by the British Tourist Authority and lists hotels and restaurants which conform to certain minimum standards. It also indicates hotels which provide conference facilities and has a gazetteer of many interesting tourist areas, together with additional notes.

The Good Food Guide see Reference books.

Travel Information Manual is a joint monthly publication of IATA member airlines and contains information for all countries in respect of passport and visa requirements, health regulations, airport taxes, customs, currency and other governmental requirements.

Executive Travel, published monthy by Business Magazines International Ltd for regular travellers, company travel managers and IATA travel agents in the UK, is carried by about 20 international airlines and is available to guests at key UK hotels.

Business Traveller is a subscription magazine published monthly by Perry Publications Ltd. It has an independent editorial policy and carries a range of articles of interest to the business traveller.

Air

The ABC World Airways Guide is published monthly and contains complete timetables for the airlines of the world. It gives details of fares, international travel requirements, passports, visas and health regulations in operation.

The ABC Guide to International Travel is published quarterly and contains similar information to the *World Airways Guide*, but includes journey times from country to country as well as more comprehensive information on a country-to-country basis.

ABC Air/Rail Europe, published monthly, provides a fast and easy reference for air and intercity rail timetables throughout Europe as well as through flights to the Middle East and North Africa.

Rail

ABC Rail Guide, published monthly, gives complete services, timetables and fare charges from all London main line stations. It also includes a provincial intercity section and gives all rail services for London and Southern England. *Passenger Timetable Great Britain* is a yearly publication which provides intercity, local and suburban services and includes the Channel Islands and coastal services.

Passenger Timetable International provides details for travellers on the continent of Europe.

Cook's International Timetable, published monthly, is a guide to the principal rail services of Europe, Africa, America, Asia and Australasia and also

supplies local shipping services in the North Sea, the Baltic and the Mediterranean.

Road

AA and RAC Handbooks: see Reference books.

AA and RAC Guides for Motoring in Europe

ABC Coach and Bus Guide contains full information on coach and bus routes and services available throughout the UK.

National Express Service Guide is published twice a year, in winter and summer, and provides a guide to all express coach services.

Michelin Guides are available for many countries and provide information along the lines of the AA and RAC handbook.

Sea

ABC Shipping Guide is published monthly and provides a worldwide guide to passenger shipping services and cruises. Like the *Airways Guide*, it provides comprehensive information on fares, passenger capacity on ferries, and aspects like operators, agents, head offices and branch offices.

Any office which intends to build up a good travel reference section would also be likely to have a good atlas, eg *Times Atlas of the World* and a selection of maps as considered necessary. Ordnance Survey maps are good, as are many produced by the large petroleum companies.

Post Office services

The Post Office produces many reference books which could be useful to a greater or lesser extent depending upon the nature of the work undertaken. The following is a selection of some of them.

The Royal Mail Guide is published annually by HMSO and is supported by supplements issued throughout the year. In three sections it provides information on the letter, parcel and counter services provided by the Post Office.

The British Telecom Guide gives corresponding information on all telecommunications services and facilities.

Post Offices in the UK contains the postal (and telegraphic) address of every Post Office in Great Britain with the exception of London, together with opening times.

Postal Addresses and Index to Postcode Directories is useful where the correct postal address may different from the usual administrative address according to the nearest main sorting office. This book contains the correct postal addresses of approximately 25 000 place names.

Telephone directories
Classified directories (Yellow Pages)
Dialling codes books
UK Telex Directory

Note: the last four items were covered under Reference books.

Office databases

Reference books have always provided a secretary with one of the traditional sources for obtaining essential information. Nevertheless, researching in this way can be time-consuming and is likely to disrupt work flow when it necessitates breaking off from a particular task and perhaps visiting a library or even making a series of telephone calls. Also, certain types of information need to be accurate and up to date and written material, much of which will have been researched and published months, if not years, earlier, will quickly become dated and so will not always be reliable.

In a technological age databases can provide many solutions to such problems. Some of the answers will be available from an organisation's own computer-held files, while others will be available from specialist sources. As far as internal databases are concerned, these will include information which has been gathered, prepared and collated in-house for access by departments and individuals via the organisation's computer network. Such information might include:

- stock details
- price lists
- sales statistics
- budgetary information
- accounting data
- customer information
- internal telephone numbers.

It should be noted, however, that depending upon the sensitivity and confidentiality of data held, access to certain information may be restricted to personnel with the appropriate authorisation. Access will be made by using the necessary password.

The use of such facilities pre-supposes that those needing such information have access to a terminal and that they know how to interrogate the system. While these factors in themselves indicate installation costs and the expense and time involved in training staff, many useful benefits can be secured. The main ones are as follows:

- information can be obtained at great speed (a research activity which might take two weeks to complete manually can be completed by a computer in a matter of hours!)
- physical paper handling is dramatically reduced
- accuracy is more likely to be achived, provided a good system of database management exists whereby data is updated regularly (with modern systems, certain statistical information, eg stock levels in retailing, will be updated automatically as goods pass through the electronic point of sale (EPOS) system. Similarly, global price changes can be made either on a fixed amount or on a percentage basis.)
- the possibility of incorporating data such as tables of figures or graphics into the preparation of a report, so enhancing the presentation of the document and easing the understanding of the reader

Database management systems (DBMS) software also exists for use with PCs and individual users, specialist departments within an organisation or small businesses can set up their own systems covering a range of possible applications according to the nature of work carried out. Typical examples would be mailing lists, customer records and stock records, but the potential for setting up databases is virtually limitless.

General sources

Newspapers

One very valuable source information which is easily obtained and yet can be easily overlooked is newspapers. Not only do they provide up-to-date news but they help build up an overview of the social, political, economic and cultural life of a country as well as detailing important foreign news. Obviously different papers will provide a different slant and favour different political philosophies, styles and trends. Traditionally there are, of course, the authoritative newspapers, which contain a greater proportion of informative reading matter to photographs and other illustrative materials than appears in the popular tabloids, and it is from this sort of paper that reliable information can normally be gleaned.

It is essential that business executives and their secretaries are generally well informed on the prevailing conditions which exist and must necessarily affect business. Such awareness enables sound forward planning to be undertaken and more astute decisions to be made.

How might a secretary select a newspaper?

1 Study several papers over a period.
2 Follow a particular subject from day to day.
3 Compare and contrast the treatment given.
4 Analyse the style.
5 Check the appropriateness of the paper for your line of business.

Why read a newspaper at all?

1 To keep yourself informed.
2 To keep track of your organisation's interests and those of its competitors.
3 To develop political awareness.
4 To increase your general knowledge.
5 To help you formulate your own opinions.
6 To develop some understanding of financial matters.
7 To find out about social, cultural and sporting events.
8 To generally develop your personality.
9 To enable you to converse intelligently and comfortably on current affairs and items of general interest.

Periodicals

Certain business periodicals have already received passing mention under 'Reference books'. However, it is to a secretary's advantage to be methodical in looking through journals and periodicals as they can be a useful source of background information. It can pay dividends to build up a file of relevant articles and items of news, always remembering, of course, to note the source and the date!

Extracting information can often be preferable to maintaining complete copies of all periodicals received in an office, as the latter can be costly both

in terms of space and searching time (unless you devise an index). Also many large organisations will automatically retain copies in their central library/records section. (Many newspapers and periodicals may even be available on microfilm/fiche.)

Magazines and periodicals that a secretary might meet

- *The Economist*
- *British Business*
- *Industrial Society*
- *Management Accounting*
- *Management Services*
- *Management Today*
- *Personnel Management*
- *Supervisory Management*
- *Training*
- *Marketing*
- *Practical Computing*
- *Data Processing*
- *What to Buy for business*
- *Business Equipment Digest*
- *Office Equipment News*
- *New Scientist*
- *New Society*
- *The Spectator*
- *The Listener*
- *Newsweek*
- *Time*
- *Radio Times*
- *Facilities Manager*
- *Career Secretary*
- *Office Secretary*
- *Professional Secretary*
- *Today's PA*
- *Office and Information Management International*
- *TV Times*
- *Business Education Today*

This is only a specimen list of the many publications currently available, and it should be noted that many specialist magazines will be available for trades and professions.

Possible topics/articles worthy of note

- anything relating to own company
- anything relating to own company's line of business
- anything relating to competitors
- articles/TV programmes on business matters

- articles on business systems
- articles/TV programmes on information technology
- articles/programmes on people of interest
- articles/programmes on places of interest
- articles/programmes with a local flavour
- conference reports
- reviews – books, radio and television programmes
- advertising and promotional features
- articles relating to the Single European Market

Where a selection of headings are considered noteworthy, a subdivided lever arch file could make an interesting scrapbook and provide an invaluable resource in the future. Also, where an office has a busy reception area with frequent visitors who may on occasion be kept waiting, a variety of current newspapers and periodicals will be most welcome, together perhaps with back copies of in-house journals and magazines. Where a company has European connections, a variety of foreign magazines would also be welcome and appropriate.

Radio and television

Radio and television are also useful sources of information. An increasing number of special programmes, some appearing on a daily basis, consider a range of business and financial matters. It will be worthwhile to consult the TV papers and note any which may be worth viewing or, more likely, recording, for perusal later.

Professionally prepared video materials are becoming more readily available and are a popular means of presenting information to busy business people. A well-produced ten minute video can often provide essential information with more impact than a lengthy written document. Videos are also used very successfully for a variety of training and staff development purposes.

Advances in telecommunications have brought great developments in recent years and there is the promise of more to come in the facilities available via television. The increased use of satellite stations makes it possible to obtain up-to-the minute news world wide.

Public libraries

The use an organisation makes of public library facilities will very much depend upon its own resources or lack of them. Where internal resources may be limited and where it is necessary to gather information, secretaries would be well advised to visit the local library and make themselves known to the librarian there. The librarian will normally be happy to help out in any way possible and can probably even answer a query from a telephone call. Such a contact can save hours of sometimes fruitless searching, and where a book or reference may not be available locally the librarian will generally manage to obtain a copy quickly from another library.

Travel agents

The use of travel agents was considered in Unit 5.

Citizen's advice bureaux

Once again the smaller organisation would be more likely to make use of these bureaux. They tend to be particularly well informed on matters relating to consumer protection, for example.

Tax offices

Tax offices were referred to in Unit 7 in relation to information they can supply about tax matters in general and the calculation of individual wages and salaries in particular.

Local council offices

These will be useful sources of information on anything of a local nature, eg planning permissions, council minutes, information on the electorate.

Post offices

All information on postal services and telecommunications are available, and secretarial staff should endeavour to keep up to date with the latest developments and the introduction or withdrawal of services and current rates of charge in operation.

Chambers of commerce

These bodies keep vast ranges of information in record and can be extremely helpful where a secretary may be required to gather statistics.

Videotex

Videotex is the generic expression of the International Telecommunication Union (ITU) to describe television equipment used to display computerised data. Where the information reaches the subscriber's television set or monitor via telephone lines it is referred to as **viewdata** (see BT's Prestel below). However when it arrives via a broadcasting channel it is known as **teletext** and refers to Ceefax (the BBC service) and Oracle (the IBA service).

Prestel

The best known viewdata service in the UK is BT's Prestel which is geared towards the home and business user. The data held by the Prestel computer is accessed via a dedicated Prestel terminal, an adapted microcomputer, word processor, or television monitor plus keyboard, using the telephone. It provides a range of information from current news, financial information, travel and accommodation information, entertainment guides and sports updates to general business services. It also carries certain information which is restricted to 'closed user group' access (*see* page 179) while providing links to other facilities such as telex and electronic mail.

Prestel can also be used in an interactive capacity where a subscriber may order goods and book holidays via the system (teleshopping) and contact certain banks and building societies (telebanking).

Charges are based on the rental of the equipment, including the telephone, plus the normal telephone charges for placing calls to Prestel (based on duration and time of day), together with any additional charges levied by information providers for accessing special frames of information.

Specialist resources

Specialist libraries

It is important to realise the existence of the many specialist libraries which carry information of a specialist or technical nature. The Association of Special Libraries and Information Bureaux (ASLIB) handles specialised published information. It produces a two-volume directory which provides the sources for such information. Volume I details information sources on science, technology and commerce while volume II details sources on medicine, social sciences and humanities.

Valuable specialist libraries are to be found in universities, polytechnics, the Houses of Parliament, the BBC and in many other institutions, and The British Library itself is one of the most comprehensive national libraries in the world.

It is standard practice for many public libraries to specialise in certain subject areas while holding details of other libraries' specialisms on microfilm.

Foreign embassies and trade delegations

These bodies will readily supply information about their particular country upon request, in written form or by telephone.

Government departments

These departments hold vast quantities of information, much of which is available on request, either free of charge or for a nominal fee. Examples of such departments include the Department of Employment, the Department of the Environment, the Department of Education and Science, the Department of Health, the Department of Social Security, the Department of Trade and Industry and the Department of Transport. The addresses of all such departments are given in *Whitaker's Almanac*.

EC

The commission of the European Communities produces and circulates to those on its mailing lists a wide range of publications including *The Week in Europe* which is issued every Thursday and is a summary of highlights concerning Community events; *Background Reports* which are surveys of particular Community policies prepared in a readable style with references to source documents should readers require more detailed information and *Press Releases* of immediate EC news as issued to the media.

Specialist publishers

Publishing companies like Croner Publications Ltd and Kluwer Publishing Ltd produce a range of regularly updated specialist material for business use. The idea is that subscribers receive an initial comprehensive loose-leaf reference manual which is then continually updated via a series of replacement and/or additional inserts which are invoiced to subscribers as changes take place.

An example of one such publication which would be of specific use to secretaries is Kluwer's *The Office Companion* which contains almost 600 pages of up-to-date information on such topics as Conferences/Exhibitions, Politics (including details of all MPs and their constituencies), Employment Legislation, Reference Books/Sources of Information, Office Equipment, Services, Transport and Travel.

Another example of such a publishing technique is *Corner's Europe* which should provide businesses with valuable information to enable them to prepare for completion of the single European Market in 1992.

Registrar of Companies

The Department of Trade is responsible in general for the basic legal framework for the regulation of industrial and commercial enterprises and within the Companies Division the Registrar of Companies requires that all limited companies lodge certain documentation on company formation, namely the Memorandum of Association and the Articles of Association (*see* Unit 8). The Registrar's office will, therefore, carry full details on all limited companies.

Professional and trade associations

A large number of such associations exist, eg the Food Manufacturers Federation, the Motor Agents Association, The National Association of Paper Merchants and the British Independent Grocers Federation. The addresses may, once again, be found in *Whitaker's Almanac*. Many of these organisations publish their own journals, and information of a specialist nature can be obtained from these sources.

Training boards

There used to be 28 training boards (established between 1964 and 1970), but they have gradually been whittled down to a few. However, they are still valuable as sources of information for the industries they represent. An Industrial Training Board

(ITB) consists of an independent chairman, members representing employers and employees within the industry, and members from the education service. It has a permanent staff of training advisers and administrators.

Advertising and publicity agencies

Sometimes an organisation will find it worthwhile to employ professionals to advertise or publicise a new venture, a new product, a new subsidiary company or anything that is worthy of promotion. Such specialists will devise anything from a full-scale campaign to an advertisement for the press or an eye-catching poster.

Public relations experts

Closely allied to publicity is public relations, by which information is spread. Any competitive organisation will recognise the value of good publicity in creating and maintaining a good reputation for a company and its products. Large companies will engage their own PROs (Public Relations Officers), but small firms may rely on the expertise of professional PR agencies who are able to supply expert advice on most aspects of publicity – the press, television, radio, trade photography and advertisements. They will have the facilities and equipment necessary to mount a one-off full-scale campaign should this be envisaged. It is also worth noting that they will often undertake to promote personalities as well. This could include advising on appearance, scheduling appearances, providing voice lessons and generally bringing the individual to the attention of the desired audience.

Accommodation agencies

These can also be useful in providing information on hotels and finding out whether there are vacancies available. They can also be found at most main line railway stations, and can prove useful where a business executive may be making an unscheduled visit to an exhibition or trade fair without having arranged accommodation beforehand.

Ticket agencies

Another well-used agency service is the ticket agency where theatre-goers can, once again, save themselves the time and trouble by using this facility to book theatre seats. They also deal with tickets for many exhibitions.

British Standards Institution

This is *the* recognised body in the UK for the preparation and assurance of national standards in the UK. Goods satisfying their criteria carry the familiar Kite mark.

They provide technical help to exporters, produce extensive literature, which is located in the library at British Standards House, and are able to give detailed information on regulations and approval systems via their advisory and consultancy services. They also provide a translation service.

British Institute of Management (BIM)

This foundation operates as a sort of national clearing house for information on all management matters in the UK. The Information Centre in London has one of the world's biggest management libraries. Members of the Institute receive a monthly journal, *Management Today*, as well as the Institute's newspaper, *Management News*. They may also buy, at discount prices, copies of management survey reports and other useful publications as well as attending special management seminars and training programmes at reduced fees. Non-members, who may be interested in management matters, can also make use of the individual subscriber service and attend courses.

Daily Telegraph Information Bureau

This is a useful telephone service which deals with a wide range of queries on current affairs and general matters, but does not offer medical, legal or highly technical advice of any kind.

Industrial Society

This is a leading UK advisory and training body in management and industrial relations. It will arrange in-company courses and conferences and provide advice when requested. It publishes its own magazine on a two-monthly basis.

The Stock Exchange

The Stock Exchange, together with its branches throughout the UK is also a useful source of information on investment matters and anything relating to stocks and shares.

Databanks

Never before has so much information been available: advances in technology have made it possible to store, manipulate and retrieve information with relative ease. As mentioned earlier, organisations hold considerable amounts of information on their own computers but there are many instances where they will need access to a wider range of information. Such information is held on computers situated at various locations throughout the country and specialising in handling particular classes of specialist information.

Access is available via on-line database systems. This means that a user can contact an information provider's computer over telephone lines via his own organisation's terminal, which can be a general purpose PC, a specially adapted word processor or even a portable lap-top computer, to request information which is held on the databank of the information provider's computer. When the information has been located and sent back to the distant workstation it can be stored for future reference, or printed out. A typical reason for accessing an on-line database would be to secure specific industrial and economic information apertaining to an organisation's particular needs, eg to monitor trends throughout an industry when drawing up a business plan.

Many information providers also offer what is termed a 'gateway' facility to other information providers. That way a user company can ask its first contact (the host computer) to act as a 'middle man' and secure information from another database or 'third party'.

Private viewdata services

Information held on computer is often restricted in terms of access to what are termed 'closed user groups'. (**Note:** this can apply within organisations or on a much wider external scale.) This means that information will only be supplied to particular groups of individuals or organisations. Examples would be the databases set up to serve travel agents or motor traders. Such systems ensure the provision of an efficient up-to-date service but are only accessible to specialist users.

Presenting information

Information comes in all forms, eg words, figures and pictures, and can be presented in a variety of ways, either with or without audio back-up, including:

- written reports
- statistical tables
- symbolic presentations
- graphs
- charts
- diagrams
- maps
- models
- overhead projector transparencies
- slides
- films

For a presentation to have impact and be effective, care must be taken in the selection of the most appropriate method to suit particular circumstances, audience and objectives.

Following recent improvements in media presentation, the public is now more critical of and more accustomed to visual presentation of data. We simply need to study advertisements in any magazine or watch television to appreciate the impact which visual presentation has on our everyday lives.

People can more easily grasp complex facts and figures and absorb statistical information when some form of visual presentation accompanies the spoken word.

Visual aids should, in addition to being informative, be attractive to look at and they must be up to date, otherwise they can prove to be totally misleading and do more harm than good. Other advantages include the following:

1 They increase the speed with which people can assimilate information.
2 They increase the speed with which people can deal with enquiries.
3 They enable comparisons to be made more easily.
4 They simplify the performance of certain routine tasks.
5 They help in the decision-making process by making clear, up-to-date, accurate data available at a glance.

Presenting statistics

Statistics can be presented in a variety of ways and the manner selected will depend on the audience, the purposes and the degree of accuracy required. If it is sufficient to provide an impression in round figures, some form of diagrammatical presentation will often suffice. However, where it is important that precise details are given it will be more usual to present actual figures, perhaps in tabular form. Examples of statistical presentation in written form include company accounts, which usually have the previous year's figures included for comparative purposes, and the share pages of the financial papers.

Charts and graphs

The most obvious alternative method of presentation is a chart or graph. Numerous possibilities exist, of which the following is a selection:

Line graphs

Line graphs may be single line or multi-line and are useful where the aim is to show comparisons or indicate a trend. When preparing line graphs it is important to remember the following:

1 The graph should have a title.
2 Each axis should be clearly labelled.
3 The scale selected should be appropriate and adequate for the purpose.
4 Where more than one line is used the coding should be explained in a key.

It is possible to represent graphs in colour or in black and white by using different densities of line and incorporating both solid and broken lines. Fig 68 is an example of a multi-line graph indicating monthly sales figures over three years.

Bar charts

These may be displayed either vertically or horizontally and, like graphs, can be compiled of single bars or multiple bars. They are extremely effective in indicating comparative information. Bar charts can also be broken down to indicate proportions of something, eg a clear bar could represent total turnover throughout an organisation, and the shaded part of the same bar could indicate exports (see Fig 69). A multiple vertical bar chart is shown in Fig 70.

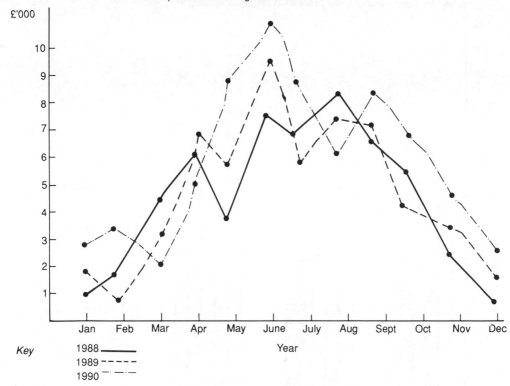

Comparative Sales Figures 1988/89/90

Key
1988 ——
1989 -----
1990 —·—·

Year

Fig 68 Line graph

Details of six months turnover for the current year

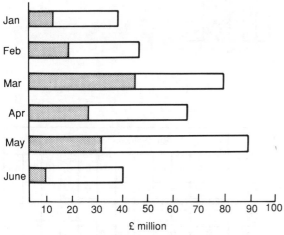

£ million

Key Total bar represents total turnover throughout the organisation.
Shaded portion represents the proportion of exports.

Fig 69 Horizontal bar chart

Histograms

These are specialised bar charts where the vertical bars are permitted to touch one another in graphic representations of frequency distributions. They will often be used where, for example, ages are split into groupings for statiscal purposes, and where the height of the bars may give misleading information concerning frequency, bearing in mind that in preparing bar charts frequency may be represented by the area of a bar *or* by its height. An example, using hypothetical data and unequal age intervals, is given in Fig 71 for house owners in a region. Here it is the overall area of each rectangle which supplies the information.

Gantt charts

These are used where it is desired to compare and contrast estimated figures with actual ones. This could be used where schedules of work are drawn up, eg you could draw your own revision plans for examinations. Fig 72 is an example for revision in

Researching and presenting information **181**

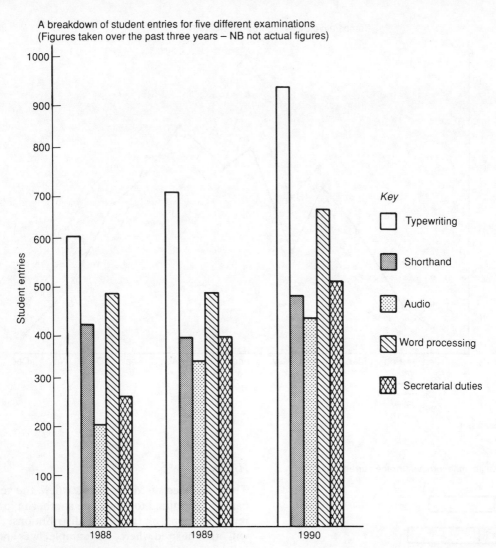

A breakdown of student entries for five different examinations
(Figures taken over the past three years – NB not actual figures)

Key

☐ Typewriting

▨ Shorthand

▨ Audio

▨ Word processing

▨ Secretarial duties

Fig 70 Multiple vertical bar chart

House owners split into age groupings (between 18 and 75)

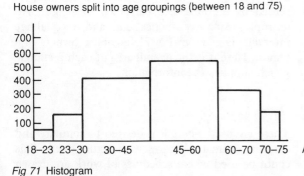

Fig 71 Histogram

Subjects	Breakdown of weeks											
	1	2	3	4	5	6	7	8	9	10	11	12
A												
B												
C												

A is ahead of schedule, B is behind schedule and C is on schedule

Fig 72 Gantt chart

3 subjects over a 12-week period. Subject A is taken in week 9, subject B in week 11 and subject C in week 12 and progress is considered at week 7.

Pie charts

Another simple and popular way of presenting statistics when it is desired to show a part in relation to the whole is to use a pie chart. Here a circle is divided into proportional segments, expressed usually in percentage terms. The circle can also be shaded in different colours to represent different areas. This technique can be most effective in that it is easily interpreted. Fig 73 is an example.

The proportions of time spent on different subjects in the curriculum of a typical secretarial course

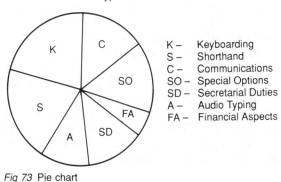

K – Keyboarding
S – Shorthand
C – Communications
SO – Special Options
SD – Secretarial Duties
A – Audio Typing
FA – Financial Aspects

Fig 73 Pie chart

Pictograms

This is a pictorial or symbolic method of producing statistics. An appropriate, easily recognised symbol or picture is selected to represent a certain total number. Fig 74 gives an example for wine imports.

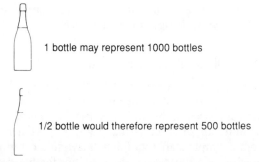

1 bottle may represent 1000 bottles

1/2 bottle would therefore represent 500 bottles

Fig 74 Pictogram

Flow charts

It would be remiss not to mention flow charts, which are increasingly popular as a means of illustrating the progress and process by which a procedure or system is followed through from start to finish. Flow charts are often used in O & M (organisation and methods) investigations, where a team of experts may be scheduled to survey certain working procedures or activities with a view to rationalising or suggesting improvements. The actual 'flow' of documents or information from one person/section/department to another can be neatly and clearly plotted by means of a simple flow chart.

Flow charts are also used in designing computer programs. The procedure is first plotted out diagrammatically and then translated into program steps for feeding into a computer.

Diagrams

Diagrams can be a useful visual aid. They vary from those showing, for example, the floor plan of an individual office or building or the layout for something like stand locations at a large exhibition, to complex circuit diagrams or those involving anatomical structures. Like any other form of chart the important things will be the appropriateness of the scale selected and the clarity of the labelling.

Maps

These are really just sophisticated diagrams and will be essential aids to most executives. They will range from the in-house preparations sent out to delegates about to attend a meeting or conference at say Head Office, to A – Z maps and full-scale road or Ordnance Survey maps. Once again they must be drawn to scale and contain up-to-date information.

Technological support

There have been considerable advances made in the development of graphics software business applications packages and in computer aided design (CAD) programs. Users can now sit at their terminals and create charts, graphs, illustrations, maps, diagrams, designs etc with the minimum of effort. Software specifications now have the degree of sophistication to produce high quality graphics. Even busy managers, with the minimum of creative ability can, with a little training, produce quick charts, while those with more time and interest can explore the capabilities of the software more thoroughly and produce even more spectacular results.

Many different packages are available. Some contain pre-drawn symbols held in picture libraries which can be accessed and integrated into particular applications; others can produce 3D effects and many more applications. Care must be taken in selecting software packages which meet the particular needs of the business concerned, taking into account the need to support the system with the type and quality of printer which can replicate the standard of graphics produced on the screen.

Models

A model can be a diagrammatic presentation of some particular structure or concept, like for example, an organisation chart (*see* Unit 1), which is strictly a model of the structure of a company. However, a model can also be solid and three-dimensional, as for example in the model of a building complex prepared with miniature three-dimensional buildings designed to scale. The added dimension can greatly enhance the impact on an audience and improve the effectiveness of the presentation.

Overhead projector (OHP) transparencies

Many successful presentations or lectures are ably supported by well-prepared and colourful OHP transparencies. It could well be part of a secretary's duties to prepare these which can be done directly on to transparencies, using stencil letters or a typewriter capable of producing large print style. Alternatively a printed mock-up may be prepared which could include researching and preparing suitable photographs or drawings which can be transferred on to transparencies.

This can prove to be interesting work, and the facilities now available for making such transparencies are greatly improved, ranging from desktop copiers capable of transferring printed material on to transparency at the press of a button, to the facilities of an in-house Print Department capable of producing high-quality work. Alternatively reprographic agencies could be used to prepare such materials.

Transparencies can be prepared in a variety of ways and using a variety of materials. They can also be prepared on coloured transparency paper. As with any other visual aid, size and clarity will be of the utmost importance, and the transparencies should always be tested on the overhead projector prior to their use during a lecture or presentation.

Where it is likely that transparencies will be used again it will be worth while having them mounted in cardboard, clearly labelled, indexed and retained in special boxes for future use.

Slides and films

Slides and films are also frequently used to accompany lectures and presentations and can be extremely effective where selected and used with care. They must be appropriate to the purpose and as a general rule short and to the point. Films or slides of any kind can make a welcome break but will lose their impact where they go on too long.

Slides can present a very positive alternative to OHP transparencies, and basically anything which could be shown on an OHP could be prepared for a slide presentation. Such presentations have the advantage that the speaker can, by using a remote control device, move backwards and forwards through the slide sequence at will.

Audio back-up

Whether a presenter wishes to use audio support will be very much a matter of personal preference, and will be determined to some extent by the person's style of presentation and how much they like to ad lib. Where a prepared audio recording is to be used, it is essential that the reproduction is excellent and that it is precisely synchronised with any visual effects it is designed to accompany. A prerecorded commentary can be useful when it is very important to keep within a rigid time allowance.

Visual planning control boards

In dealing with the presentation of data it would be amiss not to mention the use of visual planning control boards in the office (*see* Fig 75). These can be built up to meet virtually any requirements, from a simple staff rota for holidays to a comprehensive plan illustrating the activities for the year ahead and featuring a large number of variables.

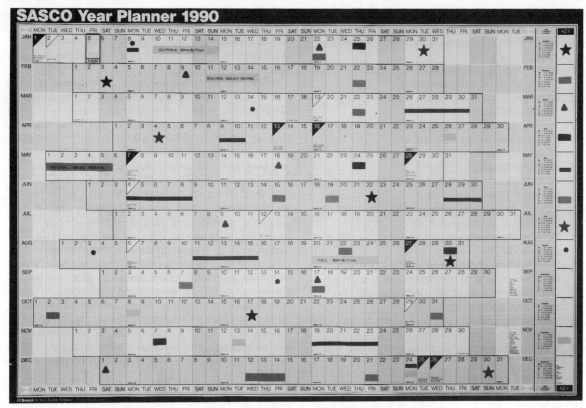

Fig 75 Visual planning control board; *Reproduced by kind permission of Acco Europe Limited*

The overriding aims of such planning boards are the flexibility they offer together with the speed of update which it is possible to achieve. Their ability to enable users to plot future trends, foresee changing circumstances and generally indulge in realistic forward planning should ensure time saving and improved efficiency.

Their use is somewhat a question of habit, and it is essential that they are kept up to date and not treated as a gimmick and a decoration for office walls, otherwise their purpose will be defeated.

They come in various degrees of sophistication, from basic paper charts which can be pinned to a wall or noticeboard and either written on or used with adhesive strips and/or symbols, to the more expensive, reusable magnetic wall-mounted boards used in conjunction with magnetic tape and shapes capable of quick updating and alteration as/when required. Some also come on swivel stands or wall brackets so that two charts can be mounted back to back, saving wall space. In fact, wall brackets are

available which can take several frames on the same fitment.

Whatever type is selected, its siting will be most important. It must be at the correct height and at a distance which is suited to the eyesight of the user, who may, for example, require to refer to it while speaking on the telephone. Like any chart or graph it must be accompanied by a key where necessary to indicate what is meant by the various colours and symbols used.

Self-test

1 Name *five* resources for information which a secretary might use.
2 Indicate *five* criteria which will be likely to influence the selection of an information resource.
3 Name *four* general reference books you would expect to find in an average office.
4 Name *three* reference books associated with *people*.

5 Name *three* reference books associated with *professions*.

6 Name *three* reference books associated with *travel*.

7 Name *three* reference books associated with the supply of *statistical information*.

8 State *six* items of information to be found in *Whitaker's Almanac*.

9 Provide *four* reasons why a secretary should read a good quality daily paper.

10 When might a secretary use the services of a specialist agency?

11 What is the difference between a general and a technical library?

12 What is the popular name for the classified telephone directory in Britain?

13 What is the difference between a dictionary and a thesaurus?

14 What technological innovations might a secretary call upon by way of an information resource?

15 Describe briefly what you understand by the term 'data bank'.

16 What is the principal criteria for information to be worthwhile?

17 What is a histogram, and when might you use one?

18 What is the principal disadvantage of a pictogram?

19 Give *two* examples of situations where it would be appropriate to construct a model.

20 What are the advantages and disadvantages of visual planning and control boards?

Personal activities

If you really think about it, you find and utilise information every day in life. For example:

- you consult bus/train timetables
- you use radio and television papers to establish what programmes are on and when
- you listen to or watch weather forecasts
- you consider menus in restaurants
- you study your school/college timetable
- you read newspapers and magazines
- you read textbooks
- you consult dictionaries and telephone directories
- you enter and retrieve information from your diary

What is important is how effectively you use information and how well you make it work for you. Also, how quick are you? Like anything else, practice makes perfect. If you are hesitant about consulting a dictionary you will never make good use of one. To use any reference book efficiently and effectively you must become familiar with the contents and how they are set out. Always study the notes on how to use the book – even a telephone directory has them! In addition, reference books tend to favour their own abbreviations and symbols and it is necessary to study these first of all.

Reference books are designed for *reference*, not for reading from cover to cover. You need to be aware of the ones which will usefully fit particular circumstances you find yourself in, and to familiarise yourself with their contents and presentation in order that you may dip into them effectively and find what you seek in the minimum time. No one will expect you to memorise the entire contents. Moreover, reference works are constantly changing and most are updated at least annually (hence they are usually very expensive to buy), so there is little point in becoming an expert on *Whitaker's Almanac* for a particular year. Where, on the other hand, you need to refer to information on a regular basis, eg train times, telephone numbers, certain statistical information, conversion tables for weights and measures, temperatures and so on, you will be well advised to devise your own information retrieval system. This may be in the form of a card index, or perhaps a looseleaf book with laminated sheets, suitably 'flagged' as with indexing systems in filing (*see* Unit 6).

Alternatively where you have access to a PC with DBMS software you may be required, or find it helpful, to set up your own database which should be regularly updated.

Using the media as an information resource

The following activities are suggested as simple, easily applied examples of ways in which you can make the media work for you, while providing you with useful practice in the process of selecting what is worthwhile and of interest.

1 Acquire *two* daily newspapers of the same date – one a popular tabloid, the other a more serious broadsheet.

   a Select an item of news covered by both and compare and contrast the coverage in terms of factual information, political bias and general content.

   b Turn to the editorial column. Précis one of the items featured as if you were doing so for your boss.

   c Turn to the classified section. Compare and contrast the contents and calculate the respective charges for inserting an advertisement of your own choosing.

2 Study *two* magazines representative of a particular form of business activity eg *Office Equipment* and *Business Equipment Digest*, both of which specialise in office machinery and equipment.

Objectively compare and contrast the content and layout for one particular month. Decide which one you would favour given the choice, stating the reasons for your preference.

Note: You can adapt this activity to any other subject area where competitive publications are produced.

3 Preview future programmes on radio and television and select an item(s) of interest and relevance to your course of study. As a home exercise, listen to or watch the selected programme(s) with a view to discussion in the following lesson. If your school/college has the facilities, the programme may be taped for playback during actual lesson time.

Using the library as a resource

Libraries form a vital resource for information and it is in your best interests to cultivate their use. Many people are reluctant to use libraries in that they consider them unwelcoming and even hostile environments. This is to a large extent understandable in that walking into many imposing library buildings and finding one's way around the shelves can be a foreboding prospect, and students are often hesitant at approaching library staff for assistance. What you must always remember, however, is that they are the *experts* and are there to help you. In fact, one of the attractions of their job is to be presented with a challenge in the form of a problem to solve, and the problem/query might well be yours!

Using a library is not knowledge we are born with but knowledge we acquire, and we should never be afraid to seek guidance. Libraries will vary greatly in terms of the books they carry and the services they provide. Your local library will obviously differ from that in your school or college, which will in turn differ again from a polytechnic or university library or one of the huge reference libraries to be found in the major cities.

Finding your way around general textbooks
Searching for reference material is a very different matter from selecting a novel. The books on your subject matter will all be located together, and you should find out the appropriate number reference according to the system of classification and cataloguing adopted by the particular library. You should also find the precise location on the shelves. These two simple steps can often save you valuable

time in a library. This will include information from dictionaries, encyclopaedias and yearbooks to specialist directories, abstracts and indexes. Familiarity with the scope and nature of the reference section in your own library will repay you time and time again.

It should be noted that many libraries will carry a special 'reference-only' copy of books which are frequently in demand, so even if the shelf copies are already out on loan you may be able to consult the reference copy in the library.

Newspapers, magazines and journals
Just as the reference section provides a variety of useful texts, so too will the journal section, which is likely to carry a wide range of journals and magazines as well as national and local newspapers. Not only are current copies carried but often back copies, sometimes dating back for many years.

Audiovisual resources
Many libraries are currently establishing video libraries; they already have extensive audio libraries with both cassettes and records to suit all tastes.

Presenting data collected

Using the job advertisement data you started to collect in Unit 2, provide a statistical breakdown under the following headings:

- salary
- qualifications
- type of experience stipulated
- age range
- type of organisation – function and size
- any other frequently occuring information

You will obviously require a substantial number of advertisements (50 or 100) to make this exercise worth while, informative and interesting. If you have not gathered that many, you could pool resources with others in your group and undertake the activity together.

Group activities

Many of the activities you can usefully undertake in groups for the purposes of testing your competence and improving your skill in handling reference materials and obtaining information. They will be dependent upon your ingenuity and the enjoyment you derive from a sense of competition.

For example, if you can form groups and devise questions from the reference books you have in your training office you will derive much more meaning from them and some fun as well. It is important to mention here that useful practice may be gained using out-of-date books, provided the format remains unaltered and the book is still published! Often your school or college library will be happy to pass on last year's editions for use in your training office or workshop. When you devise questions it will always be necessary to provide suitable keys to check the answers later.

You can also put certain aspects of using reference books to the test for speed of retrieval. For example, where several copies of a dictionary are available you can test the speed with which the meaning of a word can be found. The same can be applied to the use of telephone directories; one person selects a name and challenges the others to find it as quickly as possible. A stopwatch can add to the interest of this sort of activity. It is surprising how big a range there will be between the first and the last to locate the information.

Set up your own resource

As has been suggested previously in this book you can, either on an individual basis or in groups, gather much valuable information to support your secretarial studies course. You are living in a rapidly changing world, and the offices of today and tomorrow will certainly be influenced by advances in technology. Textbooks are hard pressed to keep pace with the changes taking place, and you can certainly make a substantial contribution to your knowledge and understanding of office technology and the developments in areas like communications by establishing your own databank of information gleaned from newspapers, magazines and advertising literature. This can be carefully catalogued and made available to all students who utilise the specialist facilities in your school or college. How you choose to set up such a resource will depend on the facilities at your disposal. They may be anything from a range of lever arch or box files, through a card index or visual display boards, to a microcomputer with database management software into which you may enter all the information you collect for later retrieval and easy updating.

Whatever the method, it is capable of providing you with the opportunity of putting theory into practice in a useful and readily updatable way.

Suggested activities associated with your secretarial course

1   Study the hours allocated to the different subjects on your course over a week. Draw up a pie chart which will clearly demonstrate the breakdown of time spent on each subject.
2   Where you have a training office and the opportunity to gain practical experience in the use of a variety of machinery and equipment, it may be possible for you to prepare a visual control board to monitor your progress and that of your group. Simply list your names along one axis and the items of equipment along the other. Select symbols to represent the degrees of proficiency achieved; eg a circle might indicate satisfactory ability, a square might indicate the need for more practice, while a star might signify excellence!
3   Similarly, you can devise a planning board if your course operates on the basis of assignments or phase tests of some kind. Here you can plot those completed, those in the process of completion and those yet to be attempted.

Situation-based activities

1   Assume that you have been newly appointed as a secretary to a busy executive within a medium-sized organisation (the nature of the company's business is for you to select, as is the function of the executive within the company). This is the first secretarial appointment within the particular department, so there are no reference books in the office.

Select *six* books which you would request initially, providing reasons for your selection.

2   Imagine that you work as a secretary for an author of historical novels. Grammar must be accurate, and it is also essential to research information on people and places to provide authenticity to the stories. This is an extremely interesting but time-consuming acitivity.

   a   What reference books would you find directly useful to you?
   b   What specialist sources and expert opinions would you be likely to consult?
   c   What sort of system might you devise to record the information you unearth with a view of being able to refer to it in later novels where appropriate?

3   Your boss is about to spend four days in London. During that time he will attend two business meetings in different parts of the city; one of these will be a business lunch with a client whose business your company wishes to secure, and will have to be at a restaurant of your boss's own choosing. He is also scheduled to visit an exhibition at Olympia, see a play, meet an Italian

business associate who speaks no English, and attend a charity concert at the Barbican. Your boss is an American who has only recently come to Britain and is very unfamiliar with London, having only visited once (as a tourist) several years ago. Also, he has to meet the Italian associate at Heathrow Airport and he does not know what he looks like! All in all it is going to prove a very hectic and somewhat stressful few days, and he is depending upon you to smooth things as far as possible.

You are required to prepare his itinerary for him. What sources of reference would you consult, and what would be your criteria for their selection?

Also, what additional things might you do, and what additional information might you ensure that he has in order to ease the four days?

4   Assume that you work for a research and development team. The executives you work for tend to favour the extensive use of visual planning and control boards for all aspects of the work of the section, including such areas as product development and the results of market research surveys, as well as general administrative matters like holiday rotas and meeting schedules.

You are due to move into new offices. The existing boards were badly damaged when the decorators tried to take them down from the walls in the old offices. As top priority, three new boards have been ordered together with all the necessary symbols and lettering so that you can replace them. Your tasks are as follows:

a   Set up a completely new board to represent the current progress of three products being developed at present. The board should show – at a glance – the progress of internal phase tests 1, 2 and 3, packaging trials and external tests, and the estimated commencement date for full-scale production.

b   Devise a control board to represent the results of market research carried out on two products in three regions of the country.

c   Draw up a four-month planner featuring June, July, August and September. Indicate clearly on the planner the holiday periods of the eight members of staff working in the section, each of whom is due to take up to a maximum of three weeks' holiday over this period.

5   Assume that you act as Secretary to Mary Richmond, the Sales Director for an international company. Much of your work involves statistical presentations and calculations. It is the annual sales convention in four weeks' time, and Mary has to present a report which will require the preparation of appropriate charts and graphs to suitably illustrate a lot of complex statistics.

She gives you the following three sets of information, and asks you to prepare suitable diagrammatical presentations which she can use in conjunction with an overhead projector while submitting her report to the convention.

a   Figures to enable her to show a comparison of the total sales both at home and abroad for the past six years:

	Home	Abroad
5 years' ago	150 000	50 000
4 years' ago	250 000	150 000
3 years' ago	350 000	250 000
2 years' ago	300 000	200 000
Last year	450 000	300 000
This year	600 000	450 000

b   Total product sales (at home and abroad) of the six major items which the company produces, expressed as total unit sales provided to the nearest 5000 units:

Product	Total units	Export units
A	75 000	30 000
B	50 000	20 000
C	65 000	45 000
D	30 000	10 000
E	55 000	20 000
F	40 000	10 000

Note from Mary: I'm not sure whether these would be better presented as a composite bar or as two separate ones. Could you try both and we'll decide later? Thanks meantime.

c   The proportion of sales on different products this year:

Product	Proportion
A	3/8
B	1/16
C	1/4
D	1/8
E	1/16
F	1/8

6   Imagine that you work for a development corporation. In three month's time it is due to open its next major project – a shopping precinct designed to meet the needs of a recently occupied housing estate.

a   Your superior, the Project Manager, likes to plot progress towards such deadlines. Devise a suitable chart which will enable him to indicate the ideal schedule for the three final major activities involved, namely painting and decorating, shop fitting and car park layout.

The painting and decorating is scheduled for completion at the end of week 8; the shop fitting midway through week 10; and the car park midway through week 11 of the twelve-week period leading up to the official opening. Your chart should be easy to follow. You will need to use your imagination and creativity.

Once you have completed the initial task, assume that you have reached week 5 and for the purposes of comparison indicate *clearly* the actual progress made (once again, use your imagination!)

b In the countdown for the official opening you are likely to be involved in the preparation of other forms of diagrammatical/visual back-up material which will be used in the following forthcoming instances:

  i *General publicity material*

ii *Advance press coverage* There must be a press conference one week prior to opening. This will be attended by representatives of both local and national press. As well as having a conducted tour, they will be given the opportunity to return to the office block to ask questions of the architectural and planning team about the general design and layout.

iii *TV coverage*

iv *Magazine coverage* Following the opening there will be a full feature in the *Architects' Journal* tracing the development of the project and illustrating it appropriately.

Under each heading indicate the sort of materials you would expect to have to organise and/or assist to produce and prepare, giving reasons for your choice of aid(s) in each instance.

10

Examining office equipment

Aim of the unit

This unit provides detailed information on the sort of equipment which secretaries can expect to encounter in the performance of their work. It also highlights some of the technical developments within offices as they move nearer towards full office automation, while pointing out the principal advantages and disadvantages of such developments and considering the implications for office staff and, in particular, for secretarial work.

Specific objectives

At the end of this unit you should be able to:

1 Distinguish between different kinds of typewriter.
2 Identify typical features to be found in modern electronic typewriters.
3 Indicate the benefits of word processing.
4 Distinguish between dedicated and non-dedicated word processors.
5 Differentiate between mainframe, mini- and micro-computers.
6 Distinguish between different system configurations.
7 Identify a variety of input and output devices used in conjunction with computers.
8 Suggest typical business applications for PCs.
9 Describe different types of dictation/transcription equipment.
10 Provide guidance for inexperienced audio typists.
11 Identify the benefits to be gained from introducing an audio typing facility.
12 Explain the design features to be found in modern desk and pocket calculators.

13 Compare and contrast different types of calculator.
14 Describe different reprographic processes and associated equipment.
15 Distinguish between duplicating and photocopying.
16 Suggest criteria on which reprographic equipment might be selected.
17 State the advantages and disadvantages of duplicating and photocopying.
18 State the advantages of phototypesetting.
19 Describe other machinery used to support reprographics services.
20 Consider the implications for staff and work patterns of implementing office automation and suggest likely future developments.

Introduction

As a secretary you will need to be well versed in the office equipment and machinery you can expect to encounter in the course of your work. Obviously the depth of understanding required will depend on several factors including:

- the precise nature of the job
- the type of equipment that could be used for the job
- the level of technology associated with it
- the range of equipment at your disposal
- how much responsibility you have for using equipment
- the degree of centralisation of services in existence
- how much influence you may have in the selection of new equipment.

In this unit we shall concentrate on the main items of equipment which any secretary can reasonably expect either to use directly or come into contact with in the course of their work. We will turn our attention more to the whys, whens and wherefores than the hows: it is not the intention to provide operating instructions for any of the equipment discussed.

Typewriters

Typewriters have existed for over 100 years, but the developments in recent years have been considerable.

When we talk about typewriters now we are usually referring to the electronic variety but we must not lose sight of the fact that many offices still use the more traditional types of machine, ie those with a standard type basket and moving carriage. Typewriters come in all sizes – from portable to heavy duty with a long carriage for legal work – and may be electric or even manual (many offices still like to keep a few in case of power cuts!).

In terms of traditional machines the main point to remember is that their versatility is restricted. The fixed basket of keys means that only one type style and type size in possible, unlike the more modern golf ball or daisy wheel, single element machines which enable the character styles and print sizes (pitch) to be easily interchanged. Also traditional typewriters do not have built-in correction facilities which are vital components to modern machines.

The move towards electronic typewriters

Just as the calculator market has moved from manual through electrically powered to electronic, so too has the typewriter market. A wide range of electronic machines is now available, of varying sizes and degrees of sophistication (*see* Fig 76). The following is a list of possible features which can be found in such machines:

- multipitch selection, often including proportional spacing
- automatic paper insertion
- automatic tabulation setting
- a range of line spacing and pressure options
- a repeater key
- a fastback key to take you to the start of the line

Fig 76 Electronic typewriter

- a backspace correction key – with varying memory capacity
- automatic centring
- automatic carriage return
- automatic decimal tabulation
- right-hand margin justification
- emboldening facility
- automatic underscore
- automatic inset

In addition to the type of facilities listed above, the more expensive models may have certain memory capacity to store set pieces of text, eg salutations, complimentary closes, certain standard sentences and perhaps even paragraphs. Some machines also have a visual display strip which shows what has been typed prior to printing (on-line typing).

With the growing popularity of electronic typewriters with these extra capabilities, many manufacturers have now extended their ranges, even to the extent of upgrading existing machines with VDU screens, so converting the typewriters to dedicated, fully comprehensive word processing systems.

When does an electronic typewriter become a word processor?

Basically the difference between an electronic typewriter and a word processor depends upon the memory capacity. Any machine with less than 2K permanent memory is still considered to be a typewriter. Also, despite the fact that some electronic typewriters do have a single-line display, they do not have full display screens like modern word processors.

Word processors

Word processing is not a new idea. It has been around since the earliest attempts to capture words in a recorded form, but as we know it today it is a logical progression of the automatic typewriter which was first introduced in the USA in 1914. The actual phrase 'word processing' was first coined in Germany fifty years later by IBM. We now tend to consider word processing in terms of the equipment and its applications.

What does the equipment consist of?

The hardware

- visual display unit (VDU)
- central processing unit (CPU) and disk storage (hard and/or floppy disk)
- keyboard
- printer

The software

A program from which the various word processing functions and applications are run.

Dedicated versus non-dedicated

In the early days of word processing the tendency was to favour dedicated systems, ie those designed specifically for word processing, because they were easier to operate. They usually run on their own manufacturer-specific word processing software, which is often very powerful and capable of handling complex operations quickly and effortlessly. Also they have dedicated function keys such as COPY, MOVE and DELETE rather than the general function keys found on micros running WP software packages, so making them very 'user friendly'.

However dedicated systems were limited in that most other useful office applications, eg spreadsheet and database, could not be run via the system, or if they could they were restricted in terms of the selection available, as well as being very expensive.

As a result, word processing packages capable of running on micro computers, ie non-dedicated systems, have improved substantially and a vast range of software is now available. Such systems offer organisations great flexibility in that investment in a relatively inexpensive micro computer can provide the possibility of operating a range of applications packages, including word processing.

The uses and benefits of word processing

The uses to which word processors will be put vary depending on the nature of the work performed by the organisation, and can range from basic text editing to more sophisticated applications. The following is a selection of possible uses, together with the benefits to be gained.

Storage and revision

The basis of all word processors is that, once stored, material may be:

- kept indefinitely
- printed at will
- redisplayed
- updated
- corrected
- totally revised.

This can be done easily in that word processors, in addition to possessing many of the useful features of electronic typewriters as outlined above, eg emboldening, right hand margin justification and automatic centering, are able to incorporate such changes as:

- massive deletions
- insertions
- major text movement
- substitutions
- pagination and repagination
- columnar interchanges
- table updates
- global search and replacement
- headers and footers
- decimal alignment
- footnoting capabilities.

Note: Consult the glossary at the end of this unit for any terms with which you are unfamiliar.

Block-building unique documents

An obvious extension of basic storage and retrieval is the building of individual documents from recorded 'blocks' of text and standard paragraphs.

There are two methods of doing this:

1 Creating special documents which contain standard text. These documents are usually referred to as:

- library documents – fairly *long* standard paragraphs
- abbreviation documents – shorter, more frequently used pieces of text.

2 Using a 'get document' function. Here the operator is able to include an alternative document at a specified point in the current document.

Paragraph manuals

Some organisations produce a paragraph manual which is issued to all staff making use of word processing facilities. Familiarity with this manual, which will perhaps have numbered or coded paragraphs, will enable users to prepare a standard letter or even a complex document by building up from standard paragraphs.

It has the added advantage of ensuring standardised usage throughout an organisation. It can also be invaluable where organisations deal with foreign countries and where the intricacies of translation need to be observed in all written communication. Executives can simply leave instructions in the form of a series of numbers or codes and so ensure that a document is accurately built up in the accepted house style from text in existing storage.

Mailing lists

In some systems this is referred to as list processing, while in others it may be referred to as mail merging. Whatever the name, the principles remain the same. Where a sender wishes to process apparently individual letters to a list of different addresses at a variety of destinations, this facility would be used to ensure that each recipient receives a personalised letter. Three different files are essential to this task:

a the database file, containing the names and addresses of the recipients
b the specification file, containing the selection requirements

c the formatter file, which determines the final appearance of the letter.

In addition, many systems have file and sort capabilities, placing them in the realms of data processing. In such a system it is possible to create and update lists containing any type of information, eg names, addresses, telephone numbers, age, sex, employee number and current salary, and then print out according to any of the categories on the list. For example you could require the machine to print out only females, from a certain city, of a certain age, and earning a certain salary. Not only could you do this, but by employing the 'sort' capability you could rearrange the list in alphabetical order.

Factors to consider in making a selection of hardware

Visual display units

VDUs come in various forms, shapes, sizes and capacities, from a 'thin window' single-line display to a full A4 page display. The following points for consideration are in no particular order of priority:

- tilting screen
- display capability, ie what can be seen on the screen
- anti-glare screen
- flicker-free screen
- colour combination, eg green on black, black on white, white on black, blue on grey, etc
- adjustable contrast control
- true upper-case and lower-case ascenders (ie h and l) and descenders (ie g, p, y, q)
- the number of characters to the line
- scrolling capacity – both horizontal and vertical
- the cursor – flashing underscore or half-tone block
- reverse video effect
- highlighting capacity
- status information position on the screen, ie information to the operator on page width, length, margins, tabs
- accessibility of hardware switches

Keyboards

Keyboards may be an integral part of the VDU or may be separate. They will either be dedicated to word processing or used in different sequence for different software programs. However, basically they will consist of a standard QWERTY keyboard and a numeric pad at the right-hand side. The following points, in no order of priority, would be looked for in a word processor keyboard:

- standard QWERTY layout
- detachable from the main unit for user convenience
- well-positioned special function keys
- understandably labelled special function keys
- user-programmable special function keys
- matt finish keys to avoid reflective glare
- perhaps a noise control switch to alleviate the dead sound of the keys (some keyboards do have this facility and many users welcome it)

Factors to consider when specifying software requirements

Factors to consider would fall basically into three categories. Obviously these are not fully comprehensive lists, only some of the possible features an average user may seek.

General

- creating and editing
- tabulation and line spacing format controls
- movement of text
- search facilities
- hyphenation
- pagination
- printing
- copying

Special editing features

- highlighting text
- library and abbreviation document facilities
- viewing invisible characters
- column control
- special system status information

Special software features

- user-programmable function
- list processing
- automatic paragraph renumbering
- spelling error detection

- document security protection
- mathematics
- graphics

Printers

Printers for use with word processors, or for that matter with other business applications, may be impact or non-impact, and some are bilateral, ie capable of printing in both directions. Impact printers involve the print head coming into contact with the paper as in the manner of a conventional typewriter. Examples are daisy wheel or thimble and dot matrix. Non-impact printers place the ink image on the paper without any character actually coming into contact with the paper. They may be thermal, electrosensitive, ink jet or laser in technique. The most common printing techniques are enlarged upon below.

Dot matrix

These printers operate by means of a printhead comprising a set of needles (9, 18 or 24 in number) which punch onto an inked ribbon and so mark the paper. This results in an image made up of a set of dots produced as the printhead moves across the page. The number of needles in the printhead determine the quality of the print produced. The lower end, which are the least expensive and most popular are sufficient to produce readable copy, but for business purposes it is really only considered 'draft' quality. The 18 needle head is faster but it needs the 24 needle head to secure near letter quality (NLQ) output.

Ink jet

In this method, based on matrix technology, the printhead is pierced by tiny nozzles which squirt ink in thin jets onto the print surface, which can be other than paper, eg ink jet printing can be done directly onto glass. It offers the option of printing in draft or NLQ modes.

Advantages

- good quality for the price
- quiet
- good for graphics
- able to produce good colour

Disadvantages

- problems with ink drying and clogging of nozzles
- tendency for copies to smudge
- no good for multi-part forms
- not a very good track record in terms of general reliability
- costly in terms of consumables

Laser

Here the print image is created using photocopying technology whereby whole pages at a time are scanned by a computer-controlled laser beam. Areas exposed to the beam show up as white on the final hard copy while toner adheres to the unexposed areas. Laser printing for the production of LQP is very much the success story of recent years.

Advantages

- quality copy
- fast (6–12 A4 pages a minute)
- quiet
- simple to use
- good graphics capability

Disadvantages

- expensive
- restricted to one colour printing
- not good for multi-part forms, labels or invoices
- restricted to A4 size copies
- limited life span of the machine

Computers

Reference has been made throughout this book to computer power and computer applications, so it is important here to stress some fundamentals of computers. Basically computers are electronic devices capable of carrying out specific arithmetic, sort, selection and storage operations. While not necessarily complex in themselves, such operations are often time consuming and cumbersome to perform manually and the results may not always prove to be totally accurate. Yet with computer power they become quick and reliable and information can be produced which is particularly useful in a business environment. The components of a computer, together with examples are as indicated in Fig 77.

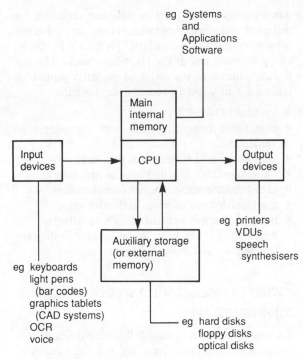

Fig 77 The components of a computer

Mainframes, minis and micros

Basically the distinction is one of size and scale of operation. Mainframes represent the large corporate installations used for processing round-the-clock workloads and hosting centralised information systems. Such installations represent a major capital investment and are housed in specially designed, controlled environments, managed by specialists.

Coming down a level, mini computers represent smaller scale systems serving fewer users and offering fewer applications, although recent developments have meant that mini systems rival the older mainframes in the variety of business applications they can support. They may be used to supplement larger computer installations, for example, by operating at departmental levels or on a stand alone basis to serve all of a smaller organisation's needs.

Lastly a microcomputer is the smallest of the three in terms of its processing capacity and is consequently less expensive. However, with rapid developments in networking (see LANs on page 75) and the movement towards IBM compatability standards, their potential both in terms of their versatility and their expansion capabilities via the provision of additional disk storage and extra terminals, has meant that they have become an increasingly attractive proposition.

Micros on the move

One particular development worthy of note is the increase in the number of portable systems on the market. These range from what are classified as 'transportables' and which are the oldest form of mobile computer, but which weigh from 9–14 kilograms, to the 'laptops' which weigh between 4 and 7 kilograms and either incorporate an integral carrying handle or are capable of fitting into a brief case. The main difference between these and the transportables, apart from the weight advantage, is that the laptops have 'flat' screens which are based on a different technology from standard desktop screens.

The main advantage with any portable item of equipment is the convenience factor of being able to use it virtually anywhere given that such computers are mostly either mains or battery operated. A principal use of portable computers is as a communication terminal whereby data can be transmitted from any remote location down the telephone line to a receiving computer. An example of a lap top computer is shown in Fig 78.

Fig 78 Desk-top portable computer; *Reproduced by kind permission of Toshiba Information System UK Limited*

System configurations

Whether referring to an installation made up primarily of word processors or of general computer terminals, a range of options is available in terms of how they might be set up. The four most common are as follows:

- stand alone
- shared logic
- distributed logic
- shared resource

Stand alone (see Fig 79)

This is a totally self-contained unit consisting of VDU, keyboard, processor and printer operated by one person at a time. It does not share the processing power of a central computer. The unit may be a dedicated one geared purely to word processing, or it may take the form of a microcomputer operating from one of the many software packages currently available.

A stand alone system has the advantage of being easily transported for use in other locations. Many stand alone systems now have additional optional facilities available to them. For example, it is possible to install communications links with other compatible equipment including distribution to/from central computing facilities and telex. Some also have optional peripherals, ie additional pieces of equipment which can be attached to the stand alone system. Examples would be a fast printer or optical character reader (OCR), or even a phototypesetter.

Shared logic (see Fig 80)

Here the configuration is such that the combination of equipment uses a common database. This means that each terminal (ie VDU and keyboard) shares the logic or intelligence of one computer (either mainframe or minicomputer). Here the terminals are 'dumb' if the central computer ceases to function. The number of terminals and peripherals (ie printers, OCRs etc) which can be handled by one computer will depend on the capacity of the computer. Where the capacity is 'stretched' there will be a delay factor in terms of terminal response time and also a danger of machine failure. One of the main advantages of a shared logic system is that several operators can be working on different parts of a complex piece of revision material at the same time, so enhancing productivity. Also it is cheaper to install and operate ten shared logic terminals

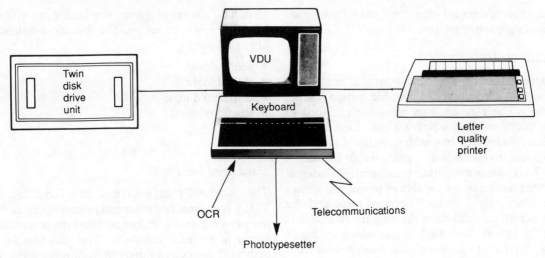

Fig 79 Stand alone system

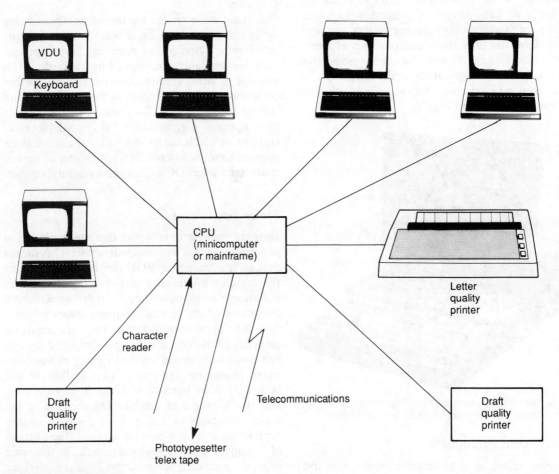

Fig 80 Shared logic system

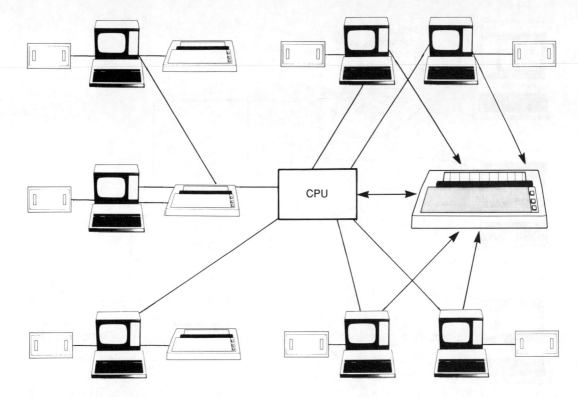

Fig 81 Distributed logic system

than it would be to use ten stand alone systems. The big disadvantage is that malfunction of the computer will stop work on all the terminals.

Distributed logic (see Fig 81)

The disadvantage of a shared logic system is reduced by opting for distributed logic. Here through the use of 'intelligent' or 'smart' terminals the operating intelligence is dispersed and no longer solely dependent on the one computer. Each terminal will, in addition to the CPU, have its own computing power which it can use to achieve individual control over its workload.

Shared resource (see Fig 82)

This is the term used to describe the situation where an 'intelligent' workstation is linked to another piece of equipment (eg hard disk storage, high-speed draft printer or OCR) so enhancing its processing power.

A word of caution about terminology

Considerable confusion can arise from the use or misuse of word/information processing terminology. Sometimes you may hear/read the term 'shared facility' used to describe what has just been described as shared resources. On the other hand, 'shared resources' can also be used to refer to shared logic or distributed logic. The main distinction, and the point to remember, is that *pure* 'shared logic' refers to the total dependence on one central processing unit for the intelligent operation of the terminals, which are 'dumb' without it.

Environmental aspects

When any sort of expensive equipment is to be installed, it is important that consideration is given to where the equipment will go and to any special conditions or facilities which will be required in that location. Whether one stand alone machine is

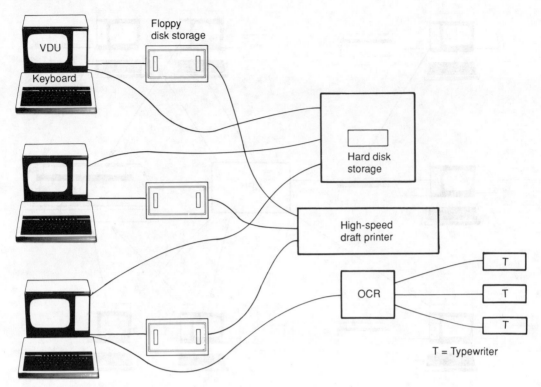

Fig 82 Shared resource system

being installed or a complete network, it will be essential to get the environment right.

The environment must be right for the equipment, but more importantly, now that equipment is less sensitive, it must be right for the people who will use it (*see* Unit 2).

Some hints on housekeeping

'Housekeeping' is the term used to cover the care and control of the equipment and the files created and maintained in a system. Obviously, as with any expensive equipment, it is important to look after it. This refers not only to general points like switching off when not in use, covering to minimise dust, cleaning the screens and changing ribbons on the printer, but also to the careful handling and storage of disks or diskettes (*see* Fig 83). Disks should be treated with care as they are susceptible to impurities from the atmosphere and also to the grease from our fingers. House-keeping will also refer to the logging of any system faults and to the updating, copying and deleting of files in a system (this is particularly vital in a shared system where valuable

disk space could be taken up with material that should have been deleted). In a large shared logic system, much of this may, in fact, be done by a Systems Manager who will handle all the disks, issue passwords to users, and may have the authority to restrict disk space and call upon users to update their files at given intervals.

Phototypesetting

In this unit and elsewhere in the book, reference has been made to phototypesetting. What exactly is it? In simple terms it is a method of setting type by photographic means. It enables text to be set out attractively on a page in any format desired.

Typesetting produces a very professional end product and is used in the preparation of many business forms, documents and such items as sales brochures and advertising literature. It can provide varied layouts including column work for easy quick reading, while offering a variety of type styles and sizes and enabling diagrams, drawings, photographs and the like to be incorporated within the text.

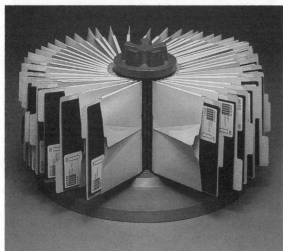

Fig 83 Floppy disk storage; *Reproduced by kind permission of Acco Europe Limited)*

Sometimes booklets may even be run off on glossy paper to give a more up-market finish.

Previously, all work of this type would have been sent to an outside agency as it was too specialised. However, the development of computer-based phototypesetting systems has provided organisations with the opportunity to produce their own in-house copy from which photographic plates can be prepared and prints produced. This photographic method greatly reduces the need to continually proofread and reset, so enabling last-minute changes or revisions to be made with ease in the minimum time and on less paper. Phototypesetting techniques enable considerable reductions to be made in the length of a document, eg a 100-page typewritten document could be reduced by as much as 50%.

The advantages of phototypesetting

1   It saves on printing and distribution costs.

2   An enhanced appearance and good visual impact is possible.
3   A wide range of print sizes and styles are available, including many special (eg scientific) characters.
4   There is flexibility in layout.
5   It permits an organisation to produce custom-designed formats in house.

Optical character recognition (OCR)

Another device which has been referred to, particularly in terms of interfacing with word processing configurations, has been the optical character reader. This is a scanning device which can read printed or typed characters and convert them into a digital signal for input into a data or word processing system.

One of the main areas for using OCR is where an organisation wishes to transfer from a paper based to an electronic system of filing. An OCR machine can scan pages of typed text directly onto a VDU which is far quicker than re-keying and eliminates the need to re-check. Some companies choose to rent OCR equipment purely for this purpose.

Advantages of OCR

1   It can extend the use of word processing in that any typist can prepare text on a standard typewriter and then input it into the word processor via the OCR machine, for editing, storage and later retrieval.
2   It helps maximise the use of word processing equipment within an organisation.
3   It causes less disruption of staff and necessitates less staff training. (The latter could be seen as a disadvantage!)
4   It greatly improves the handling of information.
5   It takes organisation one step nearer to the integrated office of the future.

Voice recognition

Despite advances in technology, full input into a computer via the voice is still a long way off. Two seconds of speech hold over 100,000 bits of data and human beings have the capacity to continually decode the spoken word regardless of volume, regional accents, imperfections due to colds and so on.

Nonetheless voice input remains an attractive proposition and much research is being done with various systems under development. There have been limited successes where machines do have the ability to recognise a limited number of words or commands. One area of success has been with car phones and the need to encourage 'hands free' operation.

The main problem is producing a system which is 'speaker independent' ie its use is not restricted to a recognised voice. One big advantage of voice recognition would be where computers could be used over a distance by either telephone or radio link. There would also be substantial benefits to the disabled who cannot use traditional input devices such as keyboards. However, until this method has been fully developed it is still faster and more flexible to key in unlimited amounts of text.

Dictation/transcription machines

Audiotyping has been with us for some time, and competence in audio work is an expected attribute for any practising secretary. Like typewriters, many different models of dictating machines are on the market operating on tapes, cassettes, disks and belts. The most popular now tend to favour the mini and/or micro cassette which is available in different recording lengths just like the standard cassettes, which are available as C60, C90 or C120. Equipment is available for different purposes, but the following three units are the most common:

- the dictation/transcription machine
- the transcription unit
- the portable dictation/playback machine

The dictation/transcription machine

As the name suggests the dictation transcription machine (*see* Fig 84) is capable of use both by the dictator to make the recording and later by the typist to transcribe. The dictator would simply need to use a hand microphone plugged into the unit, whereas for transcription purposes the typist would plug on a foot control pedal and a stethoscopic headset. Another facility which this sort of machine has is the ability to record telephone conversations

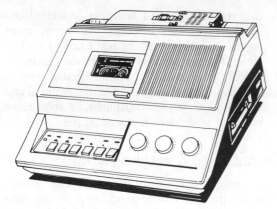

Fig 84 Dictation/transcription machine

by means of a simple attachment. This can be very useful where complex calls, perhaps from overseas, are expected.

Note: this attachment should not be confused with telephone answering machines.

The transcription unit

The transcription unit (*see* Fig 85) would simply be used by the audiotypist to transcribe the cassette prepared at some other location and on another machine (either desk-top or portable – but compatible). It has plug points for foot control and headsets and has both speed and volume controls as well as the normal fast forward and fast rewind buttons. Obviously this sort of unit will be less expensive than the dual function machine, and will be particularly useful where executives have frequent occasion to use portable machines and also the services of the same secretary or typist. In such a

situation it will be economically sensible to provide the simple transcription unit and accessories for the secretary and portable recording machines for each executive.

The portable recorder

Neat pocket-size portable recorders (*see* Fig 86) offer both convenience and flexibility. They can be used in virtually any location, in or out of doors, in this country or overseas, and cassettes can easily be posted back to the secretary for transcription if necessary.

What about centralised dictation units?

Many large organisations which use audio have established a centralised dictating system as part of their office services. Like a typing pool, audiotypists

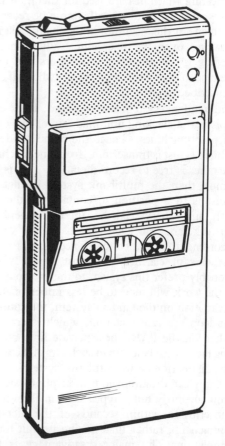

Fig 86 Portable dictating machine

Fig 85 Transcription machine

are placed under the general guidance and control of a supervisor whose duty it is to distribute the work amongst the audiotypists, check its accuracy and ensure that the work is turned over with the greatest possible efficiency. Basically a centralised dictating system can operate in one of four ways:

1 The executives have their own machines and simply take/send their cassettes to the 'pool for transcription.
2 A 'multibank' system may have been installed. This is a form of remote control dictation. A 'bank' of machines will be installed in the audiotyping centre and these will be wired up to the offices of the various personnel who may have occasion to use the facility. Members of staff wishing to make a recording will either use a special microphone wired to the system or the standard telephone instrument, which will be linked to the audiotyping centre. On dialling the appropriate code they will receive a signal indicating that lines are free for dictation purposes, and the material will simply be recorded on to one of the machines in the 'bank' just like speaking over the telephone. When the recording is complete the supervisors will hand the tape to one of the audiotypists who will then transcribe the material.
3 The 'tandem' system may be used. Here each typist has a stacking unit made up of two dual-purpose machines – hence the name 'tandem'. While a typist is transcribing from one machine, the other is free to record dictation. This is less remote than the multibank system in that the typist is in a position to contact the dictator with any query via the internal telephone network, and can even play back part of the recording to the dictator if necessary for the purposes of clarification. Most typists would probably prefer this system to the previous one as the work will tend to be less impersonal.
4 A variation on the tandem system, the continuous loop receives dictation, which is accessed either via the PABX or a private line, on one long tape which holds up to six hours of dictation. The distinction between the two systems is that not only can dication and transcription carry on simultaneously but a typist can, in fact, begin transcription within seconds of the dictation commencing rather than having to wait for its completion. The major disadvantage is that

material will, in most instances be transcribed in the order of its receipt. However, more sophisticated systems can be linked to a VDU which keeps a track of material and can locate specific passages as required. Similar systems can monitor the receipt of dictated material and enable work to be distributed in accordance with the proficiency levels of typists.

Essential of good dictation practice

Good quality equipment will obviously greatly enhance the effectiveness of any audiotyping system, but another factor which should not be overlooked is the quality of the dictation.

Preparing a good tape or cassette for transcription by an audiotypist is something of an art, and all practising secretaries will be able to relate stories of indecipherable tapes which they have been expected to transcribe!

The following is a list of points which any dictator (maybe even you, if you are in a position to delegate work!) should try to remember when preparing material for an audiotypist:

1 Begin by identifying yourself – your name, department and telephone extension.
2 Indicate what it is that you are going to dictate, with some sort of indication of the length if possible.
3 State whether it is intended as a draft or a final copy.
4 State how many copies you require.
5 Specify any special layout you wish to be adopted.
6 Provide any special instructions which may help the typist.
7 Try to give a clear distinction in your voice between instructions and actual material to be transcribed.
8 Speak clearly and at a steady pace, holding the microphone near to your mouth.
9 Avoid moving around while dictating.
10 Dictate such punctuation as will be helpful but resist the temptation to overdo it. This makes for a very tedious exercise on the part of a competent typist.
11 Spell any unusual words or names.
12 Be sure to cut the microphone when you are disturbed, eg by the telephone or by someone speaking to you.

13 Have any essential papers to which you wish to refer close to hand.
14 Clearly indicate the end of a piece of work.
15 Be sure to send the typist any enclosures you have referred to, together with the necessary supporting files.
16 Finally – if the material is to be prepared on a word processor, allocate a file name for the work and give some guidance regarding retention.

What are the advantages of dictating equipment?

Dictation machines and audio systems have the following advantages:

1 The dictation can be made at the convenience of the dictator and in a location other than the office.
2 The work produced by audiotypists can be measured, so increasing productivity and improving general efficiency.
3 Such systems enable management to make staff reductions.
4 Lengthy recordings can be sent through the post when the dictator is out of the office, so improving the communication link and avoiding a backlog on their return.
5 The secretary's time is not tied down to that required to take shorthand notes.
6 When a secretary is ill the work can more easily be transferred to someone else.
7 Dictation machines can be used as audio message systems, as well as for straightforward dictation (*see* later).

Are there any disadvantages?

Disadvantages as such are difficult to specify as they will be dependent largely on the users. Points which do need to be considered, however, are as follows:

1 The cost of equipment, accessories and possible installation charges.
2 Maintenance requirements.
3 The possibility of breakdown – including power failure.
4 The need for training of both dictators and typists.
5 The impersonality of the system compared with personal dictation – the consequent effect on morale and the quality of the working environment.

Other uses of dictation equipment

In addition to its primary purpose, a dictation machine can very conveniently be used by an executive and secretary for the purpose of leaving recorded messages for one another. Where this practice is adopted the sort of dictation/transcription machine featured in Fig 84 would be ideal. Such machines have a built-in microphone which enables recordings to be played out without the need for a microphone or headsets.

Any 'team' operating equipment in this way must check the machine automatically first thing every morning and possibly after lunch, just as one would check a diary and a telephone answering machine. Leaving recorded messages outside normal office hours or during a luncheon absence, for example, can be extremely convenient and will also enable extra – sometimes essential – detail to be included without the need to write lengthy messages.

Other occasions where machines can be successfully used are as follows:

- making notes 'on site' rather than using a notebook
- while performing some sort of check or stocktaking exercise
- to record important telephone conversations as referred to earlier
- to practise speeches.

The use of audio as an adjunct to word processing

Finally, it is worth noting the rise in the use of audio where used in conjunction with word processing. Recorded media are often used by word processing operators to prepare text.

Ultimately the intention is to bridge the gulf between dictation and transcription by enabling the machine to operate directly from voice recognition, but we are still some distance away from this, certainly in terms of commercial application.

Calculating machines

In addition to typewriters and dictating equipment,

all secretaries should be confident in the use of electronic calculators. It is neither fashionable nor acceptable for secretaries to profess ignorance when it comes to figures and to shirk the responsibility of getting down to some calculations – particularly with the wealth of calculators now available. Once again there is a wide selection to choose from in terms of size, capacity, ease of use and range of operations. When considering the selection of a suitable calculator you should first of all satisfy yourself of the answers to the following questions:

1   What do I want it to do?
2   How often will I use it?
3   How complicated is it to use?
4   How big is it?
5   Will I need to take it out of the office, eg to meetings?
6   Do I need a printout or will visual display suffice?
7   Does it need a memory?
8   How much money can I spend?
9   Does it have many facilities which I will never use?
10 Is it a well-tested make – one of the market leaders?

Once you have satisfactory answers to these questions you will be much better placed to make an appropriate selection. As far as the operation is concerned, all calculators come complete with comprehensive instructions and it is simply a matter of sitting down and working your way through them. All good instruction booklets give examples of different calculations which you can try for yourself. Illustrations of typical desk-size and pocket-size calculators are given in Fig 87 and 88.

Fig 87 Desk calculator

Fig 88 Pocket calculator

Reprographic equipment

Reprography covers a vast area from simple hand-driven duplicating machines to sophisticated copiers and facsimile transceivers. In its widest sense it could even include the use of carbon copies as a method of reproducing a copy.

For the purposes of this book I intend briefly to pass over traditional methods of duplication like spirit and ink and even offset lithography and concentrate on office copiers since they are more commonly used in normal secretarial work.

What is the difference between duplicating and copying?

One very important point to appreciate in relation to reprography is the distinction between duplicating and photocopying. Where a process of duplication is being used it is essential to prepare, first of all, an intermediary device, from which the copies are ultimately produced, whereas a photocopy is a facsimile reproduction taken directly from the original. This intermediary device in duplicating will normally take the form of a master (in spirit duplication),a stencil (in ink duplication), or a plate (in offset lithography). These masters, stencils and plates can be prepared in a variety of ways including the following:

- by hand
- by typewriter
- by thermal copier
- by electronic scanner
- by photographic or electrostatic processes.

Internal print departments

Where organisations still use duplicating processes, particularly offset lithography, it is likely that they will have set up a centralised print department which will produce all the necessary printing. Therefore secretaries are nowadays less likely to operate duplicating equipment, although they may be required to prepare stencils and plates. However, even that preparation is more likely to be performed as a centralised service in a typing pool.

Reasons for setting up an internal print department

1 Ability to train specialist operators.
2 Ability to centralise expensive equipment.
3 Ability to make maximum use of resources.
4 Eliminates waste of materials through the use of efficient staff.
5 Reduces machine breakdowns.
6 Economy – it can be cheaper to do printing internally where there is sufficient quantity rather than send it to an outside agency.

Such a department is often located near the mailing department for convenience in handling large mail shots; perhaps also close to the typing pool if many of the stencils and plates used are prepared by typists.

A word about lithography

Lithography is a method by which many copies can be obtained inexpensively from one plate. It is, in fact, a printing process which has its origins in Bavaria in the late eighteenth century. The finished product has an immaculate appearance in that ordinary typed reports appear as if professionally printed. The process relies on the fact that oil and water do not mix, so when the image (writing, typing, drawing or whatever) is prepared in a greasy medium and the remainder of the surface is covered

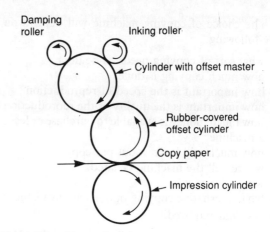

Fig 89 Offset lithography

with a film of water, the printer's ink from the roller will only adhere to the image. Lithography may be direct or indirect (offset); but the offset method is more popular (Fig 89).

Plates for use with an offset duplicator or printing machine (the former will be more likely to be found in an office and will be capable of producing large numbers of copies of highly professional work at a relatively low cost) can be of paper, prepared by hand, by typewriter or by electrostatic copier and used for between 10 and 1500 copies. Longer runs, eg blank forms and letterheads, may necessitate the preparation of plastic plates. Where a plate is used for very long runs (tens and hundreds of thousands of copies) of, for example photographic illustrations or quality colour work, and may be used again, metal plates can be prepared by photographic means and stored for reuse.

Office copiers

Copiers are machines which produce facsimile, ie exact, copies of original document. The great advantage of copiers as compared with duplicators is that you do not need to prepare any sort of master from the original document before you can produce copies. Like most modern office equipment the range, variety, capability and price of photocopying machines is immense, and it would be impossible to discuss them all here. What is important, however, is that you have an appreciation of their advantages and limitations.

The choice of copying machine will depend on the following:

- what sort of copying needs to be done
- how much copying is done
- how important is the speed of reproduction
- how important is the quality of the reproduction
- how much money is available to purchase or lease a machine
- how much will it work out per copy
- where will the machine be sited
- who will use it
- what alternative copying options are available
- is colour required?

The majority of copiers will now be of the plain paper variety, ie they do not need specially treated copy paper which is in itself expensive; many of the smaller less expensive copiers – suitable for occasional users – still require special paper. One of the other main options will be whether the machine is sheet fed (sometimes the sheets come in prepacked cartridges) or roller fed, where a guillotine attachment on the machine will cut the paper to the desired length. Another consideration will be likely to be whether or not the machine can copy from books and magazines, ie whether it is a flat bed copier (see Fig 90).

Many of the larger more sophisticated copier/duplicators, as they are termed, can produce thousands of copies at high speed, will turn the copies over and print on the other side, and finally collate the printed sheets for ultimate distribution. An example of a large photocopier/collator which can perform such functions, is shown in Fig 91.

Most electrostatic copiers also have the facility to prepare overhead projector transparencies and offset plates – useful features in any large organisation, particularly where there is an internal print department. Some also proportionally reduce material to a very high standard. A reduction facility can be a very useful inclusion in a machine, especially where, for example, handout material from newspapers and periodicals is being prepared in large numbers. Enlargement is also possible.

Machine operation is relatively straightforward, relying largely on pressing buttons, although a little more skill and some basic training is required with the more complex machines. Basically it is the ability to recognise a fault which is important. The maintenance of such equipment will have been a very important consideration at its installation stage, and most suppliers guarantee a 'same day' service for machine breakdown wherever possible. Where a machine has been purchased outright it is likely that the organisation will have taken out insurance and entered into a maintenance contract.

Colour copiers

Colour has been an option among the features of office copiers for some time but its expense has restricted its use largely to specialist bureaux. The introduction of colour cartridges has meant that a second colour could be introduced to black and white copies by feeding them through a second time with the colour cartridge in place. Alternatively, copies other than black and white, eg blue and white, could be achieved via the insertion of the appropriate toner cartridge the first time round.

It is important to note that the introduction of colour along with other special editing features increases not only machine cost but the intricacies of operation and so it is not recommended for the occasional user. Imagine the queues at the photocopier if it had such advanced facilities! Consequently it is desirable to have a more basic machine for everyday A4 copying and to restrict access to any machine designed for more creative applications such as zoom ratios and colour work.

The ultimate, of course, is a full colour copier but these are expensive and take much longer to produce a full colour copy and so would not be easy to justify in the average office.

What are 'intelligent' copiers?

If a machine is classed as an 'intelligent' copier, or 'smart' copier to use the American terminology, it simply means that the equipment is capable of making limited decisions on what to print. Such intelligent copiers are controlled by computer. The

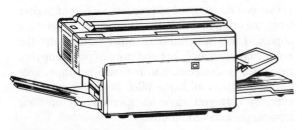

Fig 90 Flat bed photocopier

Fig 91 Photocopier/collator

computer guides the copier in the selection of print styles, paper sizes and so on.

The generation of material or text on to the paper will be from a digital source such as a computer or a word processor. Therefore, no longer will a hard copy original be required. All manner of material, data, text, charts and graphics, even signatures, can be stored electronically and recreated on demand thanks to laser technology. This dispenses with the need to store large quantities of printed forms and other documents. Also it guarantees that details are placed perfectly on the forms. The meagre carbon copy will become a thing of the past, as each document will now be an original. Via networking of machines there can be automatic distribution of information between copiers and workstations (the move towards fully electronic mail). Such network systems will have a buffer function which will queue jobs while the system is in operation and will enable the operator to decide on priority.

Selection criteria

This is obviously an area of great innovation and fast acceleration, and any organisation will be con-stantly reappraising its existing reprographics pro-vision. Careful thought should be given to the selection of new equipment and the method of reproduction to be used in completing any task.

The following are the sorts of questions which organisations need to ask themselves in relation to reprographic services:

1 What sort of reprographic work needs to be done?
2 How much is for internal circulation?
3 How much is for external publication?
4 What range of quality is required?
5 What length of print runs are envisaged?
6 How much of the work will be of a repetitive nature?
7 Will masters or plates need to be retained or preserved?
8 How important is speed of reproduction?
9 Who will have access to the equipment?
10 Do we need colour?
11 Do we need to print on both sides of the paper?
12 Do we need a reduction facility?
13 Must a machine be able to operate on different qualities of paper?

14 Do we need collation facilities as an integral part of the machine?
15 Where will the machine(s)be located? Might there be a need for several small copiers to be spread around offices, given that self-correcting typewriters frequently make use of photocopies rather than carbons, which are, strictly speaking, not feasible to use?
16 Do we have trained staff or are we prepared to train them?
17 How is our duplicating/copying dealt with at present?
18 Can we justify installing expensive equipment?
19 What will the overheads be?
20 Should we buy outright or might it be better to lease or rent?
21 What are the long-term developments envisaged in this area of work?

Machines used in the preparation and presentation of documents

Today considerable importance is placed on how things look. Most organisations take a pride in producing material which reflects their image and is favourably commented upon by others. This presentation will include their correspondence, their promotional materials and any reports they may produce.

In many organisations it is customary to present any document of more than a few pages in bound form with a descriptive cover, possibly including the organisation's logo. Where a company has its own print department or reprographics section, such work will normally be undertaken there.

The type of additional machinery which could be used might include:

● collating machines
● jogging machines
● punching/binding machines
● laminating machines
● lettering machines

Collating machines

Collating machines were referred to briefly in Unit 4 in relation to the processing of mail by a large organisation, but they may also be found in a reprographics section or print room. Frequently they are also found as an integral part of many modern photocopiers (*see* earlier in this unit). Where a document consists of several pages and where more than a few copies of the document are required, collating the pages can be a time-consuming, space-using and energy-sapping activity. Visualise collating 100 copies of a fifty-page document manually, and you will soon get the picture! However, with the help of a machine the task is soon completed with ease and in a limited area.

Jogging machines

Where lengthy documents are collated in preparation for binding, it is essential to get the pages even. By hand we would simply tap the pages on a flat surface, trying not to handle the copies too much in the process. However, with an electric jogger the relevant pages are placed in order on a page container (see Fig 92) and the machine vibrates gently, jogging the pages together exactly and without any damage to the edges.

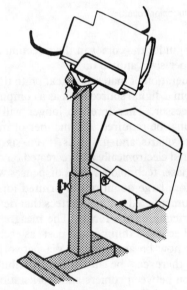

Fig 92 Jogger

Punching/binding machines

There are various different methods by which documents may be bound. In offices secretaries may frequently be called upon to present reports and other materials in bound form, particularly for use at board room level or where a professional pre-

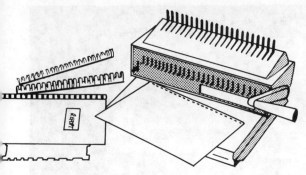

Fig 93 Spiral binding machine

sentation is desirable. Such presentation greatly enhances the appearance of typewritten material and will also prove more easy to handle and less likely to be lost. Where only a few pages are required to be placed together in the form of a booklet it may well be acceptable to use purchased file covers, which come in various designs and sizes and will have either some form of mechanism for attaching punched papers or a spine clip which is easily slid on to secure the papers tightly together.

Where an organisation prepares large amounts of material for distribution and submits a number of reports, it will probably invest in a binding machine. Many techniques are available but in the average office or print room examples of the most likely methods will be spiral binding (holes are punched first of all and then a plastic backing threaded through: available in various sizes, and manually or electrically operated) or thermal 'perfect' binding (papers are bonded together with an adhesive seal). An example of a spiral binding machine is shown in Fig 93.

Laminating machines

Laminating is the process of coating paper with a transparent plastic seal. This is useful where the document or article is to receive a lot of handling, and is now commonly found on things like identity cards and tags (often a photograph is included in these two examples), library cards, conversion tables, price lists, menus and other items.

Lettering machines

Any professionally prepared document or report will be enhanced by clear attractive lettering on the title page. It is, of course, possible to use stencil letters or the rub-on adhesive type, but machines are now available which simply and easily produce headings and titles in a matter of minutes. They are also useful for preparing presentation materials such as OHP transparencies.

Various types of machine are available. The less expensive ones operate on the principle of dialling the desired letters, numbers or symbols and the result is produced on a transparent strip of adhesive which may then be attached to the desired page at the desired position. This method is clean and simple to operate, and the machines offer a range of letter sizes and styles.

An advance on the dialled version is the desktop digital lettering system. This too produces adhesive backed ready-to-use tapes but the advanced micro-computer technology enables the user to create lettering in any size, style or colour combination to meet all manner of requirements. It also incorporates features like emboldening and underscoring. Operation is via a standard QWERTY keyboard with clearly labelled function keys. A line display enables the operator to see what is set up before actually printing out the tape. An example of a digital lettering machine is shown in Fig 94.

New developments

Sophisticated equipment designed to support all aspects of secretarial work is constantly flooding the market. Existing well-tested items are being continually up-dated and improved in the interests of what can best be termed 'The Three E's' – **e**fficiency, **e**ffectiveness and **e**conomy. They in turn will make for 'The Three P's' – **p**roductivity, **p**rofit and **p**rofessionalism.

In terms of offices the movement is still towards greater automation and streamlining with the consequent desire to remove the drudgery associated with the performance of many routine, time-consuming tasks.

What is office automation?

Office automation is the integration of a range of electronic devices into a total support system to serve the needs of the office. It covers the full range of office activities from text/data processing, through

Fig 94 Digital lettering machine; *Reproduced by kind permission of Kroy (Europe) Limited*

copying, transmission, distribution, storage and retrieval to its ultimate deletion or destruction. It addresses all the aspects which we have considered throughout this text, eg telecommunications, electronic mail, electronic filing, word processing, business applications packages and reprographics.

What are the implications?

Office automation is not something which can happen overnight. It takes time and requires due management consideration to be given to the principal issues involved in planning strategies and designing procedures which will ensure its successful implementation.

One very important aspect which needs to be addressed is that of the people involved in the introduction of any changes. Individuals, by their very nature, tend to prefer things as they are now and are suspicious of, and sometimes even frightened by, the prospect of change. Consequently change

needs to be handled with sensitivity and openness. It is important that staff are involved from the outset and that any decisions are communicated quickly and accurately to avoid unnecessary rumour and scare-mongering.

Training

Training will assume a high priority and training needs will have to be identified at the earliest opportunity to enable adequate and appropriate training to take place prior to the arrival of new equipment and systems. Different types and levels of training are essential within an organisation. For some staff, familiarisation training which provides an overview and general appreciation will be sufficient, while for others it will be necessary to provide full operator or supervisory training. Training can be a costly business but it is important that it is adequate and well-timed if a system is to be understood and used to its full potential by the maximum number of staff.

Health hazards

Another implication of installing technological support and moving towards office automation is that of health. In recent years health scares and concern over possible health hazards which might have been caused by using electronic equipment, and in particular VDUs, have grown and received an increasing amount of publicity. Concern arises in a number of different areas but the main ones are as follows:

- eye strain and eye problems generally
- epilepsy
- miscarriage due to using VDUs during pregnancy
- headaches
- nausea
- skin rashes
- postural problems
- increased stress levels
- possible exposure to low-level radiation.

Much research has been conducted into all of the above areas but no conclusive evidence has been found. However, organisations do tend to take such concerns seriously and while more research is undoubtedly needed in these areas, certain action can be taken to safeguard staff and reduce their levels of concern. The following are some of the steps which can be taken:

- introduce regular health checks including eye tests
- provide sufficient built-in breaks for those working with VDUs
- ensure that staff have ergonomically designed desks and chairs
- pay particular attention to environmental factors like lighting, ventilation and noise levels
- re-consider job descriptions
- provide a counselling service for staff
- follow the guidelines laid down by the Health and Safety Executive in 1983
- enter into discussions with interested groups such as trade union-sponsored working parties set up to investigate and advise
- keep up-to-date with current research projects.

Change

While major changes have affected office work since the days of the Industrial Revolution, Alvin Toffler's 'Third Wave' or Technological Revolution is currently challenging many of the traditionally accepted practices of office work. However, one point which must not be forgotten is that technology itself does not bring about change; it only creates the opportunities. Hence it is more positive to look upon developments as evolutionary rather than revolutionary.

Exploiting the opportunities

Both individuals and organisations are harnessing the opportunities. Middle and upper management are becoming increasingly involved once they realise and accept the potential to be exploited. Information is a valuable resource and needs to be maximised and handled efficiently and effectively if companies are to gain and keep the edge in a competitive business environment. Introducing a more automated office is just one way of moving forward.

Changing job descriptions

Such dramatic changes cannot be introduced without the resultant affect on jobs. Job contents have changed and will continue to change. New and different skills are required and priorities associated with traditional office and secretarial work, for example, are changing. So too, are skills sought in managers. New job titles are appearing and new career routes are becoming defined. Much office automation results in time-saving on routine, repetitive work, thereby freeing time for other activities requiring additional skills and competences, such as enhanced communication skills, improved numeracy, good organisational and administrative abilities, IT awareness, problem-solving, researching, and decision-making.

The greater the portfolio of skills, competences and abilities an individual has, the more attractive they are to an organisation. People need to be flexible and adaptable, willing to turn their hands to new things. We no longer live in an era of 'jobs for life'. Most people are likely to change career at least three times in their lives and in the future possibly even more.

The situation is changing rapidly and job descriptions need to be continually monitored and evaluated and, where necessary, changed to coincide with the new demands of jobs.

Changing work patterns

Not only are jobs themselves changing but so too are work patterns in order to adapt to new organisational and market demands. In the future workers will be more likely to negotiate their personal work patterns. Some may, for example, opt to work at least part of the working week from home. Such are the developments in communications and in multi-purpose workstations, that it becomes a viable alternative to spending hours in traffic jams travelling to and from the traditional office base.

Home networking

Home networking, or telecommuting as it is sometimes called, provides an added dimension to the whole concept of work. As far as the individual is concerned it provides a considerable amount of flexibility in terms of accommodating personal preferences and domestic arrangements and responsibilities, while providing employers with access to a previously untapped labour market in the form of those who could not consider a full-time 9 to 5 job but who can and do wish to provide a flexible part time service. Additionally, organisations can reduce their overheads in terms of expensive city accommodation, lighting, heating and so on, as well as reduce their overall staffing budgets by employing freelance and part time staff whose employment rights and benefits will also be less than the full time permanent staff equivalent.

Job sharing

Flexibility has become the key factor, whether from the perspective of the employer or the employee. An alternative to working from home is job sharing. Successful arrangements have taken place in a variety of organisations and their popularity is growing. Job sharing operates where two employees agree to share the work pay and perks associated with one full-time job. As far as the workers are concerned they will still have the challenge of the level of job they want but only for the agreed proportion of the working week.

From the employer's point of view, while not exactly employing 'two for the price of one', he is likely to have the added commitment of preparedness to cover for sickness or holidays while also enjoying the benefits of two fresh minds for the entire week! It must be noted, however, that not all jobs lend themselves to an easy or automatic division of responsibility and problems can arise where one party wishes to terminate the agreement.

Looking to the future

Any of us can crystal-ball gaze, but none of us can truly predict what the future holds in store with any degree of accuracy. We live in fast-moving, exciting times where change is the order of the day. We must do our utmost to be ready to meet the changes and challenges as they arise. We must be able to demonstrate that we possess the willingness, the understanding, the skills and the competences to take us forward with confidence into the next century.

In conclusion

Organisations must continually strive to meet these changing demands in an effort to maintain market position (in the case of manufacturing organisations) and community need (in the case of service organisations) by harnessing the technological power at their disposal. It must not be overlooked, however, that organisations are made up of people and without people none of this is possible. The application of modern business procedures is dependent upon the extent to which the education, training, knowledge, understanding, initiative, creative flair, skills and competence which individuals introduce to the working environment is utilised to effect. Clearly the role of a secretary is and must continue to be a key one.

Glossary of Office Automation Terms

Access time When the system is available for use, or the duration of time from signalling the computer to receiving information, or the time required to access the data and retrieve it from the disk.

Acoustics Ergonomic considerations in respect of sound levels.

Active files Those currently in use.

Administrative support Job functions of a non-typing nature which assist management.

Anthropometry The study of human body measurements to fit sizes, heights and shapes of individuals to furniture and equipment dimensions.

Applications software Software which instructs a computer to perform a specific function.

Archival storage The high volume, long term storage of information.

Archive To store information.

Artificial intelligence The field of study by which computer and other electronic equipment can modify and improve operations to more closely simulate the thought processes of humans.

Author The originator/creator (usually a manager or executive) of a document for preparation on a word processing machine.

Baud rate The rate of signalling speed in telecommunications expressed in approximately bits per second.

Bit The contraction of **binary** digit. A bit is the term given to each 1 or 0 in the string of 1s or 0s which comprise the binary or digital code.

Black box A translator or intermediate interpretation device used with equipment which has different protocols.

Bubble memory A form of magnetic memory with a very high storage capacity.

Bus network A network consisting of a length of coaxial cable along which individual devices tap into the communications cable. Signals move along the line in both directions to any station on the cable.

CAD/CAM Computer-aided design and computer-aided manufacture.

CAT Computer-aided transcription which is the capture of keystrokes onto a magnetic media which is then processed through a computer and printed out.

CBX Computerised Branch Exchange – an updated PBX.

Centralisation Location of one or more functions in one place with central support staff.

Closed user group Where only certain users have access certain frames of a viewdata system.

CIM Computer Input Microfilm. A microform-based information storage and retrieval system.

COM Computer Output Microfilm. Here production is direct onto microfilm or fiche without intermediate hard copy or filming stages.

Communications Transmission and reception of information.

Compatibility The ability of one system to handle something designed for another.

Computer graphics Graphical representations on screen, produced by computer.

Convergence The coming together of areas of common interest. Frequently associated with the merger of data and word processing.

CPU Central Processing Unit. The component which houses the logic and control circuits of a system.

CRT Cathode Ray Tube. Often used in American texts in place of VDU.

Database or data base The compilation and storage of pooled information for future access, retrieval and print-out by multiple users.

DBMS Database Management System. Computer software which handles storage and retrieval of records stored in direct-computer databases.

Decentralisation The location of mini computers and terminals with stand alone intelligence capability throughout various departments within an organisation.

Digital code Storage transmission and processing of information in digital code form is used and recognised by electronic office systems.

Distributed logic The term used where the intelligence of a computer has been dispersed to several peripherals of the system rather than concentrated in one CPU.

Downtime Time when equipment cannot be used due to malfunction.

EDP Electronic Data Processing. The manipulation of data by electronic computers.

Electronic filing The storing of information on machines for computerised access, rather than paper stored in conventional filing cabinets.

Electronic mail Communication between two or more parties using electronic technology to send computerised information, over satellites, cables or telephone wires. Information is visually displayed and need not be translated into hard copy.

Electronic mailbox A computer-based message system. Messages may be left at any time and remain there until the user makes an inquiry.

Ergonomics The science and study of human factors in system design with the intention of adapting machines and other elements of the working environment to the individuals performing the work.

Facsimile (Fax) The means of transmitting an exact copy of graphs, pictures, drawings and other data via telephone lines to a compatible receiver in another location.

Fibre optics Smooth, glass-like, hair-thin tubes which send out a light source generated from electric power and capable of carrying information at very high speed.

Full page display A screen capable of displaying at least 66 lines of 80 characters per line at one time.

Gateway An interfacing device by which information may be passed from one network to another.

Global network World-wide integration of many networks.

Hybrid system A mixture of centralised and decentralised word/information processing systems.

Inactive files Those unused but retained for statutory purposes or awaiting destruction according to a pre-determined retention policy.

Information processing The integration of data processing and word processing.

Information provider (IP) Any organisation which leases space within Prestel to set up databases and disseminate information from them to Prestel users.

Information retrieval The automatic searching and extracting of information from computer databases.

Integrated software Packages which combine functions such as WP, electronic spreadsheets and graphics into a single, easy-to-use programme.

Integrated workstations Sometimes called 'executive work stations', these provide both telephone and computer terminal capabilities within a single unit, thereby enabling both voice and data communicattion to take place.

Interactive The mode of operation by which a computer-based system can stop and start in reaction to each input from the user, eg interactive video.

Interface Used as a noun or a verb and referring to the connecting of devices.

IPSS British Telecom's International Packet-Switched Service for data transmission.

Keypad A compact keyboard of a few digits and control keys.

LAN Local Area Network. A means of linking electronic devices within a restricted area via a special cable.

Light pen A graphical input device used directly on the display screen to create or modify graphics.

Management workstation A work area designed to provide all-purpose facilities for the executive, eg a computer terminal with the text editing features, electronic mail, diary facility, personal files processing capability and other features.

Message switching The technique of receiving a message, but storing it until the appropriate circuit is available and then retransmitting it. Also referred to as 'store and forward'.

Mouse A small light-weight device used as a pointer and moved across a flat surface to control the movement of the cursor and select menu choices.

Network A series of points connected by communications channels.

OCR Optical Character Recognition (or Reader). This enables printed material to be electronically scanned for input into a word or data processing system.

Optical disk A disk which uses laser technology to provide high-density storage of information in either data or image form.

Optical wand A device held in the hand and used to read bar codes, eg in libraries.

Originator An individual who creates information or text.

Peripherals Pieces of equipment designed to work with, but not connected to, a word processor or computer, eg an OCR.

Phototypesetting The process by which camera-ready data can be reproduced via a sophisticated printing process which prints characters optically by photographing them at high speed.

Protocol The sequence of signals that controls the transmission between different devices; a standardised set of codes used to communicate in machine language.

PSTN Public Switched Telephone Network.

Records management The systematic handling of documents from creation through storage to retrieval or destruction.

Reduction rate The size ration between a film image and the original document.

Redundant data The same data stored on more than one file.

Replication The duplication of information in another form.

Reprographics A generic term to describe the various techniques used to reproduce information, eg duplicating, photocopying, phototypesetting, COM.

Retrieval The recall of stored information.

Ring network A network whereby devices are interconnected by a ring or continuous loop without a centralised host computer.

Satellite communications Electronic communications pass through a control machine which operates as a 'switcher' at the hub of a star-like configuration.

Star network A network whereby all communications pass through a control machine which operates as a 'switcher' at the hub of a star-like configuration.

Stylus A graphical input device used to enter commands which change or modify graphics on a VDU.

Systems software The programmes that run the computer ensure that it is operational and that it can perform a series of utility functions.

Telecommunications manager The individual with responsibility for the management of the personnel who plan, install, maintain and create networks of communication and monitor the transmission lines for the communications functions of the organisation.

Teleconferencing A system whereby the simultaneous

processing of data, messages and visual connections, sends pictures and voices through telephone wires to screens and speakers in other locations.

Thimble An alternative print element to a daisy wheel, used on high quality printers.

Topology The physical and logical configuration of networks, ie the way devices are linked together.

Total support system A planned structure integrating all services which were previously considered separate, into one centralised unit manned by support staff under the control of a supervisor.

Transitional approach A part way or short term approach to the introduction of office automation.

Utility functions Functions performed by the operating system, many of which pertain to file management.

VAN Value Added Network. This is the entrepreneurial leasing of communications links whereby cost savings are introduced via the use of a common carrier. It can also be used to link up services like electronic mail.

Video disk A television recording on magnetic disk.

Video tape A television recording on magnetic tape.

WAN Wide Area Network – the generic term for a public switched telephone network.

WIMPS The acronym for **w**indows, **i**cons, **m**ice and **p**ointers, this refers to support devices which facilitate the use of computerised applications packages and render them more 'user friendly'. (Icons are the graphical presentations which appear on screen as prompts, eg filing cabinets, boxes, disks, documents etc.)

WORM **W**rite **O**nce, **R**ead **M**any – refers to optical disks used particularly for archival storage purposes.

WYSIWYG **W**hat **Y**ou **S**ee **I**s **W**hat **Y**ou **G**et – refers to systems whereby the printed end product is exactly the same as what is represented on the VDU screen. In some systems this will even include italics and other type style changes and is particularly important in phototypesetting.

Self-test

1 List *six* special features you could expect to find on an electronic typewriter.
2 What distinguishes a typewriter from a word processor?
3 What does word processing hardware consist of?
4 Name *six* factors you would consider in selecting a VDU for word processing use.
5 Name *four* factors you would look for in a keyboard.
6 What is the difference between impact and non-impact printers?

7 Name a type of non-impact printer and state its advantages and disadvantages.
8 Name input and output devices which might constitute a computer installation other than keyboards and printers.
9 What is the main difference between mainframe, mini- and micro-computers?
10 What do you understand by the term 'shared resource'?
11 When might a portable dictating machine prove useful?
12 What is meant by a 'continuous loop' dictation system?
13 What advantages does audiotyping have over shorthand?
14 What would you look for in choosing a desktop calculator?
15 Briefly explain the principles of offset lithography.
16 What is OCR?
17 What is meant by an 'intelligent' copier?
18 Suggest *three* reasons why an organisation might set up an internal print department.
19 What are the advantages to be gained from phototypesetting?
20 Suggest ways in which the secretary's role is and will be affected by the increase in office automation.

Personal activities

1 Keep up to date by reading and absorbing literature on modern office equipment. It will be useful to build a portfolio of reference material.

2 Take any opportunity to visit equipment exhibitions and demonstrations.

3 Check the TV papers and try to watch relevant programmes. Additionally your library may hold some of the professionally produced videos which consider aspects of office automation and information technology. If so, make sure that you have viewed them, as a member of a group if possible, so that you can discuss what you have watched.

Group activities

The activities that can be undertaken as a group or part of a group will depend very much on your imagination and the facilities and time that you have at your disposal. If, for example, you do not have very much in the way of modern office machinery and equipment, you will need to try to compensate in as many ways as you possibly can. The following are some suggestions:

1 a Decide on all the items of equipment that you feel you would like information about.
   b Select a range of items and divide them among individuals or small groups.
   c Find the addresses of the manufacturers or suppliers.
   d Compose and type polite letters to each, requesting literature on the different items of equipment.
   e When the literature arrives, decide as a group how best to use it. You may, for example, wish to prepare wall collages/information sheets utilising the details and pictures received. Alternatively you may prefer to devise a machinery and equipment index on cards and file away all the literature. Or perhaps you could decide on a combination of these two ideas.

2 Enquire into the possibility of a local firm setting up a small demonstration/exhibition within your school or college. During a quiet time of the year, or where they may wish to practise the demonstration of new equipment to a less influential audience, they may be more willing to lay something on for you.

   You may be able to put forward a more attractive proposition to a supplier by inviting representatives from local firms and industry to attend the demonstration as well as students. In this way the equipment firm has an opportunity to make useful contacts, and even one positive contact could lead to a sale which would make the day or afternoon more than worth while for them.

   If you do decide to adopt this idea, be sure to plan it carefully and take the opportunity to incorporate all the organisational skills essential in making such an event a success. The following are a few points to remember:

   a selection of time and place
   b a format/programme for the day/afternoon – not just a haphazard 'happening'
   c sufficient advance notice to guests if any
   d appropriate invitations
   e formal introductions
   f refreshments
   g a timetable/rota where you intend opening the event to a number of classes (it is a disaster when everyone descends on the demonstration at the same time)
   h letters of thanks to all concerned

3 Organise a visit to modern local offices. This can be very interesting and worthwhile, as not only do you see a range of office equipment but you see it in practical operation, which enables you to analyse modern systems and procedures. Some suggestions for organising the visit are as follows:

   a Try to identify personal contacts which might exist within a group. For example, does anyone have a relative or friend who works somewhere which might be prepared to host such a visit? Alternatively your teacher/lecturer may have a contact.

   Note: It is important to remember that such an event is something of an imposition to a firm, and goodwill cannot be called upon too often.

   b Establish the maximum numbers that an organisation can accommodate at any one time.
   c Ask the organisation to select an appropriate time to fit in with their normal work pattern. This may mean rescheduling your own classes at school/college.
   d Transport problems – how will you get there?
   e Permissions – your teacher/lecturer will need to complete certain formalities in this respect.
   f Decide in advance what you hope to gain from the activity.
   g Have some questions ready to ask.
   h Someone should say a few words of thanks.

4 Try preparing a set of simple instructions for a piece of equipment in your practical area.

   This is never as easy as it sounds. It is easy to omit an essential step like where the on/off switch is located! As an exercise this is a very useful one and a good preparation for work as well. Often, when companies take delivery of new items of equipment they are given very minimal instructions and a brief demonstration in the use of the equipment, and left with a totally incomprehensible manual to fall back on. The outcome is often the preparation by staff of a simplified version for the use of staff generally. Practice in such preparations during your course will pay dividends.

   Work in pairs and see if you can come up with a completely logical set of instructions which *anyone* can easily follow. Where appropriate, incorporate a photograph or diagram, suitably labelled. This can greatly help to clarify the instructions. Finally, put your set of instructions to the test. Ask someone who has not used the equipment before to follow them through. Ask them to be critical so that you can evaluate what you have prepared.

1   You work as Secretary for the boss of a small private company and your work involves much complex typing requiring several carbon copies. Currently you use a standard electric typewriter which has seen better days and you would very much like to have a sophisticated electronic one such as the one you saw demonstrated at a local business efficiency exhibition last week.

Compose a memo for Mr Rogers, your boss, suggesting that he consider such an investment. You need to 'sell' the idea to him as he is not an easy man to persuade when it comes to parting with money, although he does set store on high quality work and is anxious to create a good image for his clients. Support your request with appropriate publicity material in the form of manufacturer's literature or newspaper advertisements.

2   Your office junior has arrived in your office having attended day release classes at the local college of further education yesterday afternoon. She is absolutely full of enthusiasm about a word processing system which she saw demonstrated there, but has a list of terminology which the salesman used during the demonstration and which she did not understand. Can you help her? Here are her problems:

a   He talked about 'booting' the system.
b   He referred to 'buffer storage'.
c   He talked about 'formatting'.
d   He referred to something called a 'modem'.
e   He mentioned something about 'reverse video'.
f   What did he mean by 'scrolling'?
g   What does it mean if a system is upgradable?
h   I can't remember what CPU stood for.
i   Would I be correct in thinking he talked about 'library documents'? If so, what are they?
j   Also there was something he referred to that sounded as if he was talking about football. Can you think what it might have been? If you can, will you explain it to me?

3   Imagine that you work as a Secretary for one of the following businesses or individuals:

a   a solicitor
b   an employment bureau
c   an estate agent
d   an author
e   a small theatre company

Prepare a well-considered case in support of the acquisition of a stand-alone word processor. Decide whether, given the opportunity of having one, you would opt for a dedicated system or a microcomputer with word processing software. Supply justifications for your decision.

4   Assume that you work for a local authority or your local council offices and that you are a member of a working party set up to investigate the possibility of gradually introducing word processing into your offices, beginning in six months' time. The working party has a remit which covers the following:

a   an investigation into the work of the offices
b   recommendations as to which areas of the work would be suited to word processing and the order in which the sections ought to make the transition
c   the selection of equipment
d   the siting of equipment and all environmental and health aspects associated with the installation
e   discussions with trade unions
f   the appointment of a Word Processing Supervisor
g   the selection and training of staff
h   the evaluation of the system after installation

Your tasks are as follows:

a   Describe, in detail, how your working party would go about investigating the content and nature of work in different departments, and highlight any problems you would expect to encounter.
b   What sort of work will tend to lend itself most readily to word processing, and why?
c   Prepare detailed specifications of the features you would look for:

  i in VDUs
  ii in keyboards
  iii in printers
  iv in software

d   Draw a room plan for the installation of *six* word processing workstations. Suggest a colour scheme and detail all additional equipment/supplies you would envisage being required. Also indicate any precautions you would take in connection with health aspects.
e   Outline the basis of your discussions with relevant trade unions and indicate any problems which you can anticipate in advance of such meetings.
f   Prepare an advertisement for a Word Processing Supervisor and draw up a job description for the post.

g Indicate in a memo to the Training Department the types of staff selection and training which will be required prior to and following the installation.

h Suggest ways in which the new system can be evaluated in the early months following its installation.

5 Your organisation has been using word processing systems for several years now, and you have been asked by your boss to represent the company at a local school where you have been asked to talk to a group of secretarial students on word processing. You have to assume that they can all type but that none of them knows anything at all about word processing, and they certainly have no WP equipment.

a Prepare notes for your talk.

b Draw up *three* simple diagrams which you will use to support your talk.

c Devise a brief handout (one side of A4 paper) giving some basic information which will substantiate what you have to say.

6 Your organisation has, for many years, favoured audiotyping services over shorthand writers, and it is at last being considered that such services be centralised to coincide with a move to new office accommodation. With this move and the introduction of a centralised system, many more staff will now make use of the facility.

a Explain in detail how you would organise the centralisation of the audiotyping services, indicating the type of system you would favour and giving reasons for your preference.

b Prepare a sheet of *clear* instructions on dictation techniques to be circulated among staff who will be using audio facilities for the first time.

7 You have just had a successful interview to join a new company of estate agents and valuers who are soon to open offices in your town. Part of your remit in this new post is to suggest the kind of machines and equipment you think will be required for the new offices. The staff is made up as follows:

2 Senior Partners with their own offices
2 Valuers who will share an office
You as Secretary/PA to the two partners with your own office

1 Clerk/Typist
1 Telephonist/Typist/Receptionist } all located in an open-plan front office
1 Office Junior/Person Friday

1 part-time Offset Litho Operator four half-days a week by arrangement) located in a small machine room.

The firm intends to produce all its own advertising materials, having gathered all its own information, including photographs, of properties handled.

With a view to the nature of the work, the staffing and the room allocation, prepare a comprehensive list of the kinds of machines and equipment you think will be required, giving reasons for your selections. Also comment on any additional items you think would be essential or would improve the working environment for the staff and enhance the appearance from the point of view of prospective clients and customers.

8 Your company is scrapping all its departmental copying and duplicating facilities in favour of a central Reprographics Department. Much doubt is being expressed throughout the offices as to the wisdom of such a decision, and many of your colleagues are decidedly against the whole idea.

You, however, feel it will be to the advantage of the office staff and that the service provided should be infinitely superior, given the range and quality of equipment scheduled for this new department. Also much of the work which previously had to be contracted outside the company can now be produced in house. Prepare a paper which you could be asked to put forward at a staff meeting explaining the advantages of such a department as you see it from the viewpoint of a member of staff, and stating the sort of work you think such a department should be able to undertake.

9 Imagine that you may select *all* new machinery and equipment for your new post as Secretary/PA to the Managing Director of an advertising agency, where your work will be very varied and where it will be expected that the standard of presentation is extremely high. Certain facilities will, of course, be on a shared basis with other secretaries, but you may assume that you have a major say as to what facilities you require, both personal and shared.

Provide details of the equipment and machinery you would like to have, justifying your selection.

10 As the General Manager's Secretary you have been using a word processor for several years now. However, the company is moving over to computer-based systems more and more as it progresses towards a totally integrated office. As part of an electronic office induction programme the Personnel Officer has asked you to speak on 'housekeeping'. You are asked to include the general care of hardware, reference to disk handling, labelling, copying and general storage and back-up. Prepare a brief talk and state how you would illustrate the talk and bring it to life for your audience.

Appendix 1
Studying effectively

People study to acquire knowledge and understanding of specialised information, sometimes theoretical or academic, sometimes practical and in other instances, as for example with secretarial studies, a mixture of both. The ultimate purpose of studying is to acquire qualifications which will indicate to prospective employers that you possess certain expertise and competence. Your success will help you secure a position in pursuit of your chosen career.

Study, if it is to be effective, is like working at a job and as such is dependent upon the skill with which you plan and prepare yourself. It differs from other jobs in that it does not appear on any curriculum and yet it is fundamental to everything you need to do in the learning process. It involves using some or even all of the skills illustrated in Fig 95 below.

Effective study is a matter of applying these skills and techniques to the subjects you wish to pursue. This in turn means recognising your strengths and weaknesses and acting upon them. We all have favourite subjects and even preferred topics within subjects and naturally we find it less demanding to devote our energies to these. Nonetheless it is important to give all aspects your attention and consequently, when you become better informed on a subject you are likely to find yourself enjoying it more.

None of us tends to feel comfortable in areas where we lack knowledge and understanding or display a poor level of competence, so it will be worthwhile to try to improve. However, it will be the areas you find less interesting or more difficult to master that will present you with most problems in terms of study and it will be here that you will need to develop efficient skills.

Studying is not a skill with which you are born and, like all other skills, is one you will need to work at if it is to be efficient and effective. It is a matter of how you organise yourself, manage your

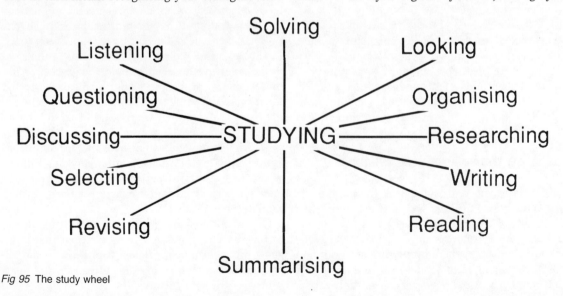

Fig 95 The study wheel

time and marshal all available resources at your disposal. There is no room for indifference when it comes to achieving mastery over any subject.

Avoid negative attitudes

Identifying your weaknesses is one thing but remedying them is another. Adopting negative attitudes is self-defeating: you need to do something positive to counteract them. Basically it will be a matter of asking yourself such questions as:

- What should I study?
- What techniques should I use?
- How much should I study?
- Where should I study?
- When should I study?
- What can I do to improve my notetaking ability?
- What can I do to improve my reading?
- What can I do to enhance my vocabulary?
- Why do I find it difficult to ask questions of the teacher?
- Why do I have difficulty in using the library?
- Why do I never seem to have time to study?

Honest answers to such questions will be the first steps in 'getting your act together' and being successful.

Know what is required of you

Whatever programme of study you are following it is vital that you know what is required of you. You must be totally clear about the format of your course, ie whether it all rests on a final examination, whether coursework is taken into consideration and if so to what extent, or whether it all depends on your performance in continuous assessment carried out over the year. The answer to this question should have a bearing on the way you work and plan your study.

Familiarise yourself with the syllabus

Always try to acquire the syllabus of the examining board whose qualification you are attempting to secure. Often your teacher or lecturer will ensure that you have the relevant information, but if you are in any doubt take the initiative and find out for yourself. It is simple to send for details from the appropriate board and vital that you know what

will be required of you, viz the format of the examination, its length, the subject areas covered, the element of choice (if there is one) and any special recommendations for study made by the board. Also, many boards produce reading lists and advice to candidates and you would do well to study these at the beginning of your course.

Devise your Personal Study Programme (PSP)

It is often a good idea to manage your study time on the basis of a carefully worked out personal timetable in order to establish a routine of study. Ensure that you are realistic when drawing up such a timetable. There is little point in producing a PSP which includes two hours or so on an evening when you like to watch a favourite television programme! The more genuine your PSP, the more likely you will be able to stick to it, thus giving your confidence a boost every time you complete a week according to plan.

Effective study requires you to use your time to the best advantage. Short, intensive study is a more efficient way of learning. You are less likely to become tired during your study sessions if you plan them on the basis of say, three one-hour sessions, with breaks for a rest in between rather than one session of three hours. Of course, how you organise your study time is a personal decision and depends largely upon your own preferences and circumstances.

When you study is also important and can be problematic when, for example, your best time might be considered anti-social in terms of the rest of the family or those with whom you share accommodation. Many people would advocate early in the morning as being the optimum time for achieving good results in that you should be fresh after a good night's sleep. However, others would argue that they are slow to 'come alive' and are infinitely better suited to 'burning the midnight oil'. Either way it is a matter of personal preference and the only thing to avoid is the danger of 'burning the candle at both ends'!

One important point to bear in mind is the need for leisure and relaxation: it is essential that you allow sufficient time for this in your PSP. In short, make sure that your programme is realistic and that it fits in with your life style.

Improve your reading skills

Most, if not all, of the information you need for written aspects of your course will be found in a variety of textbooks and associated literature. Effective reading includes recognition of alternative sources as well as getting the most out of your set textbook(s). If you have been asked to obtain a particular textbook be sure to do so at the beginning of your course. It is all very well to contemplate sharing with a friend or relying on obtaining a library copy but you owe it to yourself and your teacher/lecturer to get your own copy of the recommended text. Library books should be viewed as supplements to your own materials not as substitutes.

Many students make the mistake of attempting to read textbooks from cover to cover, thinking that they might miss something important or even feeling that they are cheating if they only read parts! A more realistic, if not honest, approach is needed. It is important to recognise the purpose of your reading: are you reading to gain information, to solve a problem, answer a question, or provide background and supplementary information? The reason for your reading will affect your technique, as will the familiarity and degree of difficulty you experience with the subject matter. Sometimes it will be sufficient to 'scan' read, while on other occasions it will be essential to recall in detail what you have read.

Effective reading will also be dependent upon basic factors such as your eyesight and the extent of your vocabulary. Where you experience any difficulties in reading you should ensure that you have your eyes tested regularly and if you feel that you frequently come across words you do not understand you must consult a good dictionary. Extending your vocabulary is an important aspect of successful study and something you should make a conscious effort to do. Also it is surprising, once you look up an unfamiliar word how quickly you will come across it again.

Be sure that your reading is active rather than passive. Active reading is really like being a detective – finding the clues, establishing the evidence and identifying the main issues involved. Active reading is about focus, being precise and solving problems. There seems little point in even picking up a textbook unless you want to know something or wish to substantiate a point or elaborate on some knowledge or idea you are in the process of exploring.

The practical, active approach to reading involves finding out answers to questions which are important, either in relation to coursework or examinations or simply because you want to know. Jot down your questions and carefully study your texts in search of the answers. Your strategy needs to be flexible. You will soon develop the skill of knowing when to skim and when to read closely and carefully.

SQ3R

The following is a well-tested technique which can be adapted to meet most reading needs. It is often referred to as SQ3R, which represents the initial letters of the **five** steps recommended in studying a book or chapter:

1 **Survey** to get the general idea of the text.
2 **Question** yourself on what you expect to get out of the reading on completion.
3 **Read** the text.
4 **Recall** (or try to recall) the main points.
5 **Review** again to check how well you have understood the main points.

The **survey of a book** should include:

- the title page
- the preface
- the contents
- the index (if there is one)
- a quick leaf through the book

the **survey of a chapter** should entail looking at:

- the first and last pages
- any summaries or checklists
- headings
- any photographs, figures or diagrams
- any specimen questions

Ten tips towards better reading

1 Always read with a sense of purpose – with questions to be answered.
2 When you read, do so initially to get a general impression and the main ideas. **Do not** make notes or underline things at this stage. This should come later when you review. Besides, your initial reactions may not be the right ones!
3 Identify the **important details;** sometimes this will require a second reading.

4 **Evaluate** what you are reading; be critical.
5 Try to develop a faster reading speed. Most people are capable of reading half as fast again while still having the same degree of understanding.
6 Try to increase your recognition span. Try to take in groups of words rather than reading word by word. A good way to test your ability to do this is to read newspapers. You should be able to read column widths without scanning across the columns. Your eyes should travel down the columns and not from left to right!
7 Try not to regress while you are reading, ie to go over pieces in a 'looping' fashion. Most of us are guilty of this, but it slows down our reading speed immensely and is something we should try to avoid.
8 How good is your eyesight? Might you need spectacles?
9 Do your lips move while you are reading? This is a bad habit and almost certainly means that you read slowly.
10 Build up your vocabulary. A wide vacabulary is essential both for understanding other people's ideas and better expressing your own.

Take good notes

Taking good notes is an important part of study skills and something which improves with practice. When you attend a lesson or lecture you should **always** be prepared to take **your own** notes, even if you know that a handout will be given out afterwards. Sometimes the task will be made easier for you if, at the beginning of the lesson or lecture, you are supplied with an incomplete handout. This is likely to take the form of headings with blank spaces after them, and perhaps a list of suggested headings at the end. What the lecturer is really trying to do is to channel your thinking and concentration along certain lines; the brief headings will be designed to follow the structure of the lesson/lecture and as such can be a useful aid to you in making good notes. In many instances, however, the responsibility is yours and you should not shirk the task. Making notes also has the benefit of acting as an aid to your concentration. If you decide to make notes you are, by the very nature of the activity, predisposed to listening to what is being said.

Listening

The key dimension to taking good notes is effective listening and sifting through the material to select the key points before summarising in your own words. Strange as it may seem, effective listening is something which needs to be cultivated as it is surprising how easy it is to **hear** without listening! Human beings have an in-built capacity to operate on several levels at once. We may think we are listening when in fact we are only hearing; we are really involved in our own thoughts which may have absolutely nothing to do with the matter in hand.

The three C's

Essentially effective note taking depends on clarity, conciseness and consistency – the three C's

Clarity

There is little point in making notes whether in longhand or shorthand if you cannot read them back later. Write clearly using a suitable pen or pencil and in a proper notebook rather than on loose scraps of paper which you are likely to lose. Re-read or transcribe your notes at the earliest opportunity. This way your recall will be sharper and you will be more likely to fill in gaps and elaborate on the detail.

Conciseness

Never attempt to take down everything – even where you use shorthand. Students with shorthand skills would seem to be at an advantage when it comes to taking notes but this is not necesarily the case and a verbatim account may be taken at the expense of comprehension. In such an instance lack of understanding can make accurate transcription extremely difficult, particularly where there may be a delay in writing back the notes.

Be selective: try to develop an ability to précis the main points. Sometimes, of course, it will be useful to write down verbatim the actual words of the speaker, eg when a definition is being given, or where there is a quote from a legal document. On other occasions it will be preferable for you to pause and listen carefully to what is being said and then jot down the main ideas expressed, using your own words.

Remember too, that everything you take down in the way of rough notes will need to be refined and transformed into logical notes to serve as useful revision at a later date.

Consistency

Consistency refers to the way in which you take notes in the first instance and how you transfer rough notes into a more structured, logical sequence, dating and titling all material, noting the lecturer's name, where appropriate, and adding any handouts or supplementary material collected. It involves things like your use of capital letters, underscoring, colour coding and highlighting – all of which facilitate revision at a later date.

Personal card index

Another useful point which you might like to consider is building up a personal card index to supplement your notes. This will help you to summarise your material onto suitably sized cards

and to identify the main points for revision purposes. Cards are both easy and convenient to use and simple to add to. You can use different coloured cards to divide your topics and include cross referencing to your own more detailed notes and to textbook references you have used.

These activities require the sort of discipline that is essential in anyone occupying a secretarial position and is part of your essential training.

Efficiency and effectiveness

There is obviously more to studying than meets the eye and it is your responsibility to ensure that you undertake the essential groundwork which will help you cope with the job. It is all a question of efficiency and effectiveness, of identifying your goals, of recognising your strengths and weaknesses and of managing your resources and the time at your disposal.

Efficiency is **doing the job right** while **effectiveness** is **doing the right job**. Remember that and you cannot go far wrong.

Appendix 2

Preparing for examinations

Preparation for examinations should be an ongoing activity from the time you embark upon your course of study. To achieve good results – and you should always aim to do more than scrape a pass – revision must form a regular part of your study routine from the very beginning. Where you adopt this sort of strategy there will never be any desperate need to try to cram all revision into the last minute. Research into memory indicates that early revision is important; it will make later material easier for you to learn, as there will be a better understanding of what has gone before.

Revision timetable

As examinations draw near you will need to adopt a more systematic approach to your revision. In the last five or six weeks you should prepare a special revision timetable, listing the topics you need to revise and the order in which you intend to tackle them. The same considerations as applied to your Personal Study Programme (PSP) referred to in Appendix 1 will also apply here. You will need to pace yourself and allow time for rest and recreation – especially during the last few days. You don't want to go into the examinations exhausted before you begin!

Study syndicates

Some students find it helpful to join with fellow students for revision. Obviously you will need to be able to work together as a group and be prepared to stick to your work schedule for such an arrangement to be successful. This requires immense discipline, but the benefits to be gained from the shared experience may make it worthwhile.

One point that perhaps needs to be stressed is that group working will only have maximum effect where the group is formed early in a course of study. Such groups operate to a large extent on a mutual self-help basis in that group members may use one another as 'sounding boards' for their ideas and problems.

An advantage of group study is that it may help you to be more objective about your course. When you work alone there will always be areas of study which you will tend to favour and perhaps devote more time to than is necessary. Where you are revising as part of a group, other people's preferences will differ from yours and consequently it is more likely that you will achieve better overall syllabus coverage.

Specific pointers to aid revision

One thing that is, I think, abundantly clear to all who prepare for examinations is the do-it-yourself nature of the activity. Ultimately, irrespective of how much tuition, advice and shared experience you have had during the year, it will be up to you and you alone when it comes to the examination. Nobody will be there to advise and assist you during the examination or to jog you along by offering words of consolation and encouragement. The experience – and for some students it can be a traumatic one – will be yours alone, and it will fall to you alone to do your best. This you can help ensure by being as well prepared as possible.

There are ways that will help you to maximise the time you spend revising (particularly when you have more than one subject) and to feel more confident about tackling the examination when the day arrives. The following are a few suggestions:

1 *Examination format* Be sure that you are fully conversant with the form that the examination will take (*see* later).

2 *Examination techniques* You need to master not only the factual information inherent in the study of the subject but also the techniques required to satisfy the examiner, ie how to tackle the paper.

3 *Answering practice* You need to practise writing answers for questions from past papers. Where the examination format is basically traditional (ie you are required to answer so many questions from a certain number in a given period) it is essential that you know how much you are physically capable of writing in the given time. And you need to practise!

4 *Materials* Practise using the same sort of materials as you are likely to get in the examination, ie use A4 broad lined paper with an inch margin on either side and write with a pen rather than a pencil. Whether you prefer to use a traditional pen with ink, a ballpoint or a fibre tip will be a matter for you to decide. However, it is worth while experimenting, from the point of view both of ease of writing and of the end product: which is the easiest and clearest to read?

5 *Time yourself* How much can you write in half an hour? As a benchmark, the average, mentally agile student of any subject, writing clearly in average-sized handwriting (about ten words per line) should be capable of filling approximately two sides of A4 paper in half an hour.

6 *Quantity or quality* It is important to appreciate that what you write must be what is required to answer the question. There is no point in being able to write two sides in half an hour if the content is irrelevant, incomprehensible and repetitive rubbish!

7 *Reading* Practise reading the questions and interpreting their requirements. The most common fault of all students at all levels and in all types of examination is *careless reading* resulting in *failure to answer the question*.

8 *What are the examiners looking for?* Time spent going through past papers will help considerably in establishing this (something you can usefully do in a group). There are only so many ways a topic can be viewed, and consequently only so many ways a question can be set – and therefore only so many answers! Every question will require some indication of factual subject knowledge in the answer. It is a question of identifying the appropriate slant and structuring your response in a logical, well-presented sequence.

9 *Making the most out of your notes* Good notes really come into their own during revision. Where they are detailed, you will be well advised to begin to condense them. The use of highlighting pens can be very useful as an aid to this activity.

10 *Revision cards* Eventually you should be in a position to reduce your notes on to manageable cards, containing the essential items of information. These may take the form of key words, dates, names – anything that will cue your recall of the more detailed material in the notes. Cards are useful in that they may be easily carried around and consulted at odd moments, eg on the bus or in the train. You should be able eventually to visualise the entire contents of a card in your mind's eye: think how useful that could be in the examination room!

11 *To select or not to select?* This is a question which you must consider carefully when it comes to deciding what exactly you are going to revise. Can you really afford to ignore a syllabus item in its entirety? This will depend to a large extent on the structure and format of the examination, ie how many questions you need to answer and how extensive is the choice.

12 *Using a cassette recorder* Sometimes it can be worthwhile reading your notes or extracts from your textbook on to cassette so that you can play it back later. This can help you consolidate, and does reduce the pressure of continually reading and rereading.

13 *Check the teacher/lecturer's written comments on assessed work* Teachers and lecturers often spend many hours reading through your work. Where they have offered comments you will be well advised to take heed of them, and they should certainly be useful for revision.

14 *Checking your own notes made during class revision* One particularly good time to make notes in class is during the run-up to an examination when you are probably going through past papers as a group. You should make notes (on the actual question papers if they are yours) while the questions are being discussed, and pay particular attention to any points which the teacher may add.

Past examination papers

Most teachers will spend at least some time with classes examining past papers and offering advice on how to tackle certain questions. You may even be set a past examination paper by way of a mock or dress rehearsal prior to your actual examination.

However, should time be very restricted on your course, or should your teacher have very limited access to past papers, it will be well worth your while to write off to the exam board yourself and secure some past copies. Most syllabuses from exam boards provide a list of the past papers available, together with the costs.

The study of a few previous papers will provide you with some indication of the overall syllabus coverage of the examination and will give you a 'feel' for the way questions tend to be set. Also, where you identify questions with which you would have experienced difficulty, you will know to which areas you need to devote more revision time! Where you have started to revise early enough you will be in a position to ask the advice of your teacher about a question that has caused you problems. Similarly, many teachers will ask students to suggest any topics they would like to revise in class time prior to the examination. The fact that suggestions are not usually particularly forthcoming is not in most instances an indication of supreme confidence on the part of the students! Rather it is a lack of awareness of the areas of difficulty.

Types of question and examination formats

I have already recommended the acquisition of official syllabuses. This is really essential to familiarise yourself with the requirements of the examination. Obviously different techniques require to be applied to different sorts of questions and to different sorts of examination, and it is important that you are well versed in the techniques of the examinations you are going to attempt.

Let me elaborate a little on what I mean by describing a few different question types and examining the format of different examinations.

Traditional examination paper

Here students are required to answer, for example, five out of eight or ten questions. Students are free to select any five questions of their own. Each question will carry equal marks, so it may be assumed that equal time should be allocated to each question – possibly half an hour per answer.

Sometimes there may be a compulsory question followed by perhaps any four others, while on other occasions the paper may be divided into sections with specific instructions as to the number of questions to be attempted from each section. In the latter it is important to be completely clear in your own mind of the options open to you.

In these sorts of examination the answers will basically be of an essay type, which means that they should be well structured with a good introduction, the development of the argument or theme, and a suitable conclusion. Incidentally, never waste valuable time rewriting the question. It is sufficient to number your answers clearly to correspond with the numbering of the question paper.

You will be well advised to undertake a brief essay plan before you commit pen to paper in the final format. Sequence is important and you want to try to present your points in a logical order. Also you want to include as many relevant points as you can to substantiate your answer. Advance planning will help you to achieve a good result.

Two-part examinations

Many examinations are structured so that students are required to attempt two quite separate parts. Part I may take the form of short answer questions or perhaps an objective test of some kind. The idea here is to provide you with a good opportunity to demonstrate your syllabus knowledge over a wide range of material, even though the treatment required is superficial. A time allocation is usually stipulated, eg 'You are advised to spend no longer than 40-minutes on this section.' Be sure that you follow the advice. If you really know your subject matter well you may find that you can actually complete this part in less than the 40 minutes and so gain some extra time to deal with Part II. This part will be in the form of full-blown questions along the traditional lines previously indicated.

Question types

Questions can be posed in a variety of different

ways, and it is vital that you assess them carefully to ascertain *precisely* what is required. A good way to do this is to look for the *key verb* in the sentence. This will help indicate the sort of answer you will be required to provide. Here are some common verbs used in examination questions:

describe	analyse
explain	indicate
define	criticise
compare	contrast
comment	discuss
justify	provide

Obviously if you are specifically asked to 'compare and contrast', and you simply write around the subject, little credit will be given for your answer. Similarly, if you 'describe' when you were asked to 'analyse', you have failed to answer the question.

Sometimes questions may be in two parts. In such instance be sure that you have tackled both parts. If there is an (a) and a (b) be sure that your answer is presented in such a way as to indicate clearly which part of your answer refers to (a) and which part to (b).

Where questions are broken down for mark allocation (eg the first part is for three marks, the second for five marks and the third for twelve marks), be sure that your answer is appropriately weighted towards these marks.

Follow any instructions implicitly. Where a question asks for something specific (eg 'give *three* examples . . .'), provide it (give *three* not four or five!) Where you are asked to write in so many words, do so. Do not write more or less. Where you are asked to write a report, write a report using the recognised conventions of report writing. Where you are asked to provide notes, provide notes – not an essay! These points may seem obvious, but it is amazing how many students fail to do what they are asked!

Situation-based questions

It is increasingly popular, particularly in secretarial examinations, for examiners to devise questions around situations. Here it is important that you answer the questions in a manner appropriate to the situations described. Sometimes the preamble to the question will be lengthy and even complex, and you may well need to read the question a few times to absorb the atmosphere and get the feel of

the situation. A highlighting pen is useful for this sort of question, as it will help focus your attention on any aspect of the situation which is particularly significant and relevant to the way in which you choose to tackle your answer.

Reading time

Many examinations provide reading time prior to the actual writing time allocated. In most instances this will be around ten minutes, and during that time you are usually allowed to make notes, although not actually to commence writing your answers. Reading time is extremely valuable and you should make the best use you can of it, making any notes, underlining or highlighting important points, perhaps determining which questions you will answer if you have a choice and in which order you will attempt them.

Advice for the day of the examination

1 Try to avoid 'previewing' on the way to the examination. What you haven't revised is not worth considering at this stage.
2 Try to avoid discussing the examination with other candidates. They are only likely to depress you by mentioning areas you have skimmed or omitted totally in your revision.
3 Arrive in the examination room in good time, preferably after a good night's sleep and something to eat. If it is important to you where you sit, and you think there may be a choice, be sure to arrive extra early!
4 If you are able to select your seat, choose a place where you will feel comfortable and where you will encounter the least distraction.
5 Try to relax.
6 When you get the paper *read* it through very carefully, making notes in the reading time if permitted to do so.
7 Do not be in a frantic rush to start – take your time and try to get the feel of the paper.
8 Be sure that you know how many questions you need to answer in the time allowed and allocate your time accordingly. Budget your time according to the number of questions and the marks awarded for them (if these are made known to you). Obviously this is more easily done where each question carries an equal

number of marks. It is useful to make a note of the times at which you expect to complete your different questions.

9　When reading the questions, make sure that you know what the examiner is asking for. Do not make the mistake of seeing a familiar phrase and leaping in and answering what you think the question may be about or what you wish it was about! Try to be objective and not to misread questions.

10　Be sure that you have understood the instructions. One of the most common errors made by candidates is failure to do what is asked.

11　When you have selected your questions, make some brief notes or a skeleton outline before you start writing your answer. Try to identify the main relevant points which you should include in your answer. Also allow for a bit of free association. Let your mind be open to any possible ideas which you think of, even though you may wish to discard some of them later. Jot down on paper everything that comes into mind, and then *plan* your answer from your notes. You want your answer to come out not like a rag-bag of thoughts and ideas, but to have an organised and logical structure; so it is necessary to plan.

12　Keep referring back to the question as you write to make sure that you are still answering it! If you feel that you are becoming bogged down, losing the thread or running out of inspiration, leave a big space and go to the next question. You may be able to return to it later.

13　Keep an eye on the time. Check periodically with your watch or the clock in the room.

14　Don't make the common mistake of spending too much time on your best question and consequently running short of time with the others.

15　Pay attention to spelling and grammar. Avoid misspelling words which appear on the question paper. This is inexcusable!

16　Try to be concise. There is nothing to be gained from excessive waffle.

17　Above all, write legibly.

18　If you manage to complete the paper before the time is up, do not rush out of the room. Read through your paper. You might spot an obvious error or omission or even have a last-minute flash of inspiration.

19　If you do find that you are running out of time, at least try to get the main points down on paper – without the detail.

20　Avoid post-mortems afterwards. They rarely help.

As I have stressed, when you come down to it examinations are very personal experiences – and experiences most of us would much rather do without! However, in today's competitive world they are a fact of life, and we owe it to ourselves to do everything we can to ease the process. Much of this depends on adequate and appropriate preparation, designed to suit our personal needs and circumstances. So take time and give the matter some extra thought. Careful planning and preparation usually pays dividends. Good luck!

Index